T0301542

Economic Socialization

Economic Socialization

The Economic Beliefs and Behaviours of Young People

Edited by

Peter Lunt

Lecturer in Psychology, University College London, UK

Adrian Furnham

Professor of Psychology, University College London, UK

Edward Elgar
Cheltenham, UK • Brookfield, US

Published by
Edward Elgar Publishing Limited
8 Lansdown Place
Cheltenham
Glos GL50 2HU
UK

Edward Elgar Publishing Company
Old Post Road
Brookfield
Vermont 05036
US

British Library Cataloguing in Publication Data
Economic socialization : the economic beliefs and
  behaviours of young people
  1. Young adults – Attitudes   2. Socialization – Economic
  aspects
  I. Lunt, Peter K. (Peter Kenneth), 1956–   II. Furnham, Adrian,
  1953–
  305.2'3

Library of Congress Cataloguing in Publication Data
Economic socialization : the economic beliefs and behaviours of young
  people / edited by Peter Lunt, Adrian Furnham.
    Includes index.
    1. Child consumers—Research.   2. Young consumers—Research.
  3. Consumer behavior—Research.   4. Economics—Psychological
  aspects—Research.   I. Lunt, Peter K. (Peter Kenneth), 1956–
  II. Furnham, Adrian.
  HF5415.32.E28   1996
  858.8'348—dc20   95–49730
                                                                  CIP

ISBN 1 85898 416 5

Contents

Tables

Contributors

Anna Silvia Bombi is Professor of Psychology of Development and Education at Rome University, 'La Sapienza'. Her main research interest is the development of social cognition, including children's ideas about macrosocial reality and children's conceptions of face-to-face relationships. She has published a book on the development of economic understanding (Berti and Bombi, 1988: *The child's construction of economics*, Cambridge: CUP).

Fiona Cram obtained her PhD, looking at children's understanding of ownership, from the University of Otago and is presently a Lecturer in Social Psychology at the University of Auckland. She has maintained her interest in children's economic development as well as developing an interest in health research, including the social construction of Maori health, and the effects of family violence on women and children. She has recently become the Director of the Discourse Research Unit, Psychology, at the University of Auckland.

Julie Dickinson is a Lecturer in the Department of Organizational Psychology at Birkbeck College, University of London. Her research interests include economic socialization, the development of beliefs about socio-economic inequality and explanations for pay differentials.

Helga Dittmar completed her DPhil on 'Material possessions and identity' in 1990 at the University of Sussex, Brighton, England where she currently teaches as a Lecturer in Psychology. Her current research focuses on the impact of the economy and mass consumer society on people's sense of self and identity, in particular shopping addiction, economic socialization in the UK and Russia, and cross-cultural and gender differences in the link between material possessions and identity.

Nicholas Emler is University Lecturer in Social Psychology at Oxford and Fellow of Wolfson College. His research interests include socio-moral development, political and economic socialization, and reputation management processes.

viii   *Economic socialization*

Adrian Furnham is currently Professor of Psychology in the University of London. He has wide ranging interests in applied psychology and is currently finishing a textbook in Organizational Psychology. He retains a long-standing interest in economic psychology.

Nileena Jhaveri received her undergraduate education in India and then completed her MA at the University of Otago, New Zealand. As part of her thesis, she carried out a cross-cultural study comparing Indian and New Zealand children's understanding of profit, private property and economic inequality. She also has a strong interest in the education of children who have learning disabilities.

Dominique Lassarre teaches social and economic psychology and leads a research group on economic socialization at the Laboratory of Applied Psychology, Stress and Society (University of Reims Champagne Ardenne, France). She chairs the board of MICROMEGAS, European network for research and exchange on children's and young people's way of life and consumption. Latest publication: *Psychologie sociale et economie* (1995), Paris: Armand Colin.

David Leiser is currently Associate Professor and Chairman in the Department of Behavioral Sciences, Ben Gurion University of the Negev, Israel. His research interests are naive theories, economic psychology, cognitive development, spatial cognition and vision. He organized, with Guje Sevon and Christine Roland-Levy, the international naive economics project, and is currently organizing a similar project involving adults and the relations of personality and demographic variables on economic models and values. He has many publications in economic psychology including one book (David Leiser and Christiane Gillieron: *Cognitive science and genetic epistemology*, Plenum, 1990).

Peter Lunt is Lecturer in Psychology at University College London. His research interests include economic psychology, the television audience and the relation between social psychology and social theory. His previous books (with S. Livingstone) are *Mass Consumption and Personal Identity*, 1992, Open University Press and *Talk on Television*, 1994, Routledge.

Sik Hung Ng was educated in Hong Kong and later in England where he obtained his PhD from Bristol University. A recipient of the 1986 Hunter Award for distinction in research, he was later elected Fellow of the New Zealand Psychological Society (1989) and Fellow of the British Psychological Society (1990). His main research interests are in social psychology, language and communication, and economic psychology. His publications include *The Social Psychology of Power, Nurses and Their Work* (with L. Jenkins, A. Dixon & F. Cram), and *Power in Language: Verbal Communication and Social Influence* (with J.J. Bradac). He is an Executive Member of the International Association of Applied Psychology and currently holds the Chair of Psychology at Victoria University of Wellington, New Zealand.

Patricia Pliner obtained her BSc at Purdue University in 1965 and her PhD from Columbia University in 1970. At present she is Professor of Psychology, Erindale College, University of Toronto. Her research interests are economic socialization of children, human food selection, development of food preferences and aversions.

William Walstad is Professor of Economics and Director of the National Center for Research in Economic Education at the University of Nebraska-Lincoln (US). He has published over 100 scholarly studies and is the editor of four books, the most recent being *An International Perspective on Economic Education* (Kluwer, 1994). Professor Walstad serves as Associate Editor of the *Journal of Economic Education* and has received several national awards for his research and teaching.

Paul Webley is a Reader in Economic Psychology and currently Head of Department of the Psychology department at Exeter University. His previous publications include *The Individual in the Economy* (co-authored with S.E.G. Lea and R.M. Tarpy, 1987), *Tax evasion: an experimental approach* (co-authored with H.S.J. Robben, H. Elffers and D.J. Hessing, 1991). *Children's saving* (co-authored with E.J.S. Sonuga-Barke, 1993) and *The New Economic Mind* (co-authored with A. Lewis and A. Furnham, 1995). His current research is concerned with personal money management (saving, debt, investment) and children's economic behaviour.

1. Introduction: social aspects of young people's understanding of the economy

Peter Lunt

INTRODUCTION

The citizen consumer of contemporary western societies, while often lacking formal training in economics, is a skilled user and interpreter of the economy. People not only manage their personal finances but have opinions about and attitudes towards the economy and its institutions. In most societies little formal education exists to aid the acquisition of the appropriate skills and knowledge to manage in the economy. Such skills are got informally in the home, among peers, and from the mass media.

Research into the way that children learn about and engage in the economy has, like research in economic psychology generally, a short history. Silvia Bombi suggests in Chapter 11 that the history of research in economic socialization can be understood in three phases or stages. First, there was a small amount of descriptive work which established that children had a developing understanding of economic life. Second, researchers attempted to map descriptions of children's comprehension of economic matters onto Piaget's theory of the stages of cognitive development. Third, an attempt is being made to introduce social factors into the explanation of the development of economic understanding. This 'third wave' is the subject of a recent review article by Webley and Lea (1993), who argue that there has been a burgeoning of research in economic socialization since the mid-1980s. However, they think that too much research has continued in the tradition of cognitive developmental studies and not enough attention has been paid to broader social and economic structures. The contributions in this volume represent a variety of ways in which social influences on the development of economic understanding are being conceived in the work of people active in the field. There is no overarching theory of the relation of social structure to economic structure which could be neatly applied to the domain of socialization. Therefore, what is needed, and what is represented in this volume, is an exploration of a variety of ways of theorizing and researching these issues.

1

The substantive contributions to this book are fronted by a review article by Furnham. His review supports Bombi's notion that there has been a recent change from the application of stage theory to research which examines the impact of social variables on development. Furnham also suggests that the concept of economic understanding that has been studied has been too narrow, particularly if we consider knowledge of the institutional aspects of the economy. Research has tended to concentrate on microeconomic issues related to personal and household finances. The contributions to this volume, therefore, represent an opening out of the concept of economic understanding to include various social and macroeconomic factors. There are thus two initial moves in the turn to the social in studies of the development of economic understanding: examining the social determinants of economic attitudes, beliefs and values and conceiving of economic understanding as going beyond personal finance to include broader economic issues.

The application of stage theory to economic socialization is represented by the work of Berti and Bombi (1988). This work is often the critical starting-point for the chapters in this volume. Although there have been various accounts of the stages a child goes through, there is broad agreement on the fundamentals as suggested by Lea *et al.* (1987):

> All authors find a first stage in which the child does not understand the role of money in transactions; the child knows that money must be used for the transaction to be possible, but sees this necessity simply as a rite or moral imperative, there is no concept of exchange. At an intermediate stage, the child understands immediate exchanges, but neither the network of exchanges which constitute the economic system nor the divisibility of money... The final stage, all authors agree, involves the understanding of all types of exchanges with money, including the concepts of profit, investments, and so on. (p. 326)

There has been a growing concern that a stage approach both underestimates the role and diversity of economic activity in children and reduces a process which includes the socialization of basic values to one of the development of cognitive ability. Dickinson and Emler argue that the cognitive–developmental approach implicitly treats the public as an undifferentiated mass and ignores social class as a determinant of economic knowledge. They argue that economic transactions take place between people in a variety of social roles. Economy and society are inextricably mixed and there is no clear and simple domain of economic knowledge separate from the broader social world into which the child is socialized. One aspect of the social differentiation of socialization is that different social groups possess different economic knowledge. Dickinson and Emler concentrate on knowledge about wealth and suggest that lags in development and context effects reflect the social distribution of economic knowledge rather than cognitive deficits. In a report of their own work on the developing knowledge of wage differentials, they suggest that there are systematic class differences such that working-class children emphasize personal effort as the basis of wage differentials whereas middle-class children recognize the importance of qualifications. In attributional terms the working class prefer effort attributions whereas the middle classes emphasize the external validation of qualifications. Dickinson and Emler argue that these differences in attribution bring about a self-serving bias which acts to justify inequalities and therefore reinforces the status quo of socially distributed economic resources.

A similar argument concerning the ideological dimensions of economic socialization emerges in the contribution of Leiser and Ganin, who begin their chapter with a reference to the changing historical context of children's involvement in the economy. In pre-modern times there was less separation between the domestic and commercial spheres. The development of modern capitalist economies led to an increasing separation between the home and the public world of economic activity. Children associated with the home were consequently distanced from economic activity. In both the home and the school, children were separated from the commercial by the oppositions of the system and lifeworld and public/private (Habermas, 1989). This separation leads to potential problems in the development of the citizen consumer because of the separation of the agencies of socialization and the economy.

Leiser and Ganin consider the domestic allocation of resources in terms of their potential for economic socialization. They suggest that the allowance system rather than forms of pocket money and payment for work in the home provides the best environment for the child to learn how to become a financially competent citizen. However, they also report that parents often have a preference for payment for work done.

Leiser and Ganin report a study of the social determinants of choice of allocative system and revealed a complex relation between demographic, social and psychological variables. Increased economic involvement was related to support for free enterprise. Middle-class adolescents supported a version of liberal capitalism, whereas the working classes were most concerned about inequality. These results point to a particular form of the social reproduction of the economy in Israel. Bourdieu's (1984) study of cultural reproduction of social and economic structures had pointed to a division in the middle classes between those oriented towards cultural capital and those oriented towards economic capital. In a similar way, Leiser and Ganin suggest that social conditions influence the system of financial allocation within the household, which then creates consumers with particular orientations towards the economy, which in turn reproduces the existing social organization of the economy.

Pliner *et al.* are also concerned with the allowance system of household allocation. They suggest that, although it is the preferred system in many western households, there is little research on what the underlying learning mechanisms are. They therefore conducted a number of experiments comparing children who received an allowance with those who did not. The children who received an allowance were found to be better able to make use of credit and to price goods. These skills also increase with age and therefore it appears that the allowance system brings forward the acquisition of consumer skills. Pliner *et al.* suggest that the allowance system works because it engenders a relationship of trust and expectation which requires the child to become financially 'literate'.

Dominique Lassarre's contribution has a similar set of concerns which are examined through an examination of consumer education in French families and schools. Lassarre reports an interview study which attempts to characterize the consumption behaviour of adolescents in a rural French town. Different estimates of the amount of spending money received by the children came from the parents as compared to those of their children. The differences reflect a difference in the definition of pocket money between adults and parents. In terms of family socialization Lassarre suggests that the best allocation strategy is the giving of allowances paired with discussions of the family budget. Lassarre argues that the mechanism that makes the allowance system so effective is the possibility it affords for discussions about financial matters within the family.

Lassarre suggests that the reasons why parents give allowances change as the child develops. The allowance is an attempt to control the increasing demands made by the child. Thus a straightforward pocket money system is often the first thing to be introduced, which then gradually evolves into a full allowance system which includes a variety of obligations on both parties. This kind of change requires a degree of flexibility in the parents. The role of parents in instructing children is also emphasized in an observation study of shopping. In a series of observation studies Lassarre observes that there are complex social roles in the shopping trip involving parents and children. Unlike the paradigm case in consumption studies of the same individual deciding what to buy, financing the purchase and making the purchase, these aspects are socially distributed across parents and children.

Lassarre also reviews French literature on consumer education in school. Although consumer education is not an official part of the French school curriculum, there is a good deal of informal instruction by teachers. Lassarre reports an interview study which highlights the various motives for and obstacles to such informal instruction. A national survey is also reported which indicates which topics are being introduced to which children. Lassarre discusses evidence that the basic aims of economic education do not differ for different social groups but that the content of the education did. Also teachers and educators were mindful that economic socialization had the potential to influence the reproduction of social class. Lassarre concludes that education in the domestic sphere is appropriately concerned with the development of autonomy in the child and that the school has an increasingly public responsibility in contemporary economies. This is a common theme in the contributions to this volume: there are growing opportunities and dangers for the consumer in contemporary western economies which require the socialization of more skilled, autonomous and informed individuals. These themes echo recent concern in social theory with reflexive society (Giddens, 1991) and postmodern conditions (Baudrillard, 1988; Harvey, 1989).

The studies of Dickinson and Emler, as well as Leiser and Gannin and Lassarre, reflect the relationship between social class factors and allocative strategy. There is a similar line of research into household allocative strategies amongst adults. This work has suggested the close link between different allocative systems in households and the particular economic context of the household, whether this be in terms of cultural variation (Miller, 1987) or of social class (Pahl, 1989). Under this reading the allocative systems of households are an important constituent of an economy. The same suggestion is implied in the work presented in this volume, for the choice of system for the allocation of money to children in the household plays an important role in the formation of citizen consumers. It can influence the consumer's approach to the economy on a number of levels: relation to enterprise; perception of the qualities required for economic success; acceptance of existing allocation of resources in society.

In Chapter 5, Dittmar is concerned with the development of the awareness that material possessions symbolize social status. This is a similar concern to that of Dickinson and Emler but, rather than studying knowledge of wealth, Dittmar conducts studies into the impressions people form on the basis of material possession. She argues that the process of immersion into material culture can be understood as part of the child's growing sense of identity formed through social interaction.

Dittmar then presents two studies of impression formation based on material possessions. Using a manipulated video presentation, she shows that there is a consensus about which personal qualities can be inferred from an impression based on material possession. Social class differences did not emerge in her study, in contrast to that of Dickinson and Emler, but rather the agreement suggests a strong stereotyping effect in impression formation.

Webley argues (in Chapter 9) that previous research has accepted the 'little adult' conception of the child and urges that the informal economic activities of children be studied. Drawing on Mauss, he suggests that the economic world of the child is more like a barter than a monetary exchange system.

However, many of the characteristics of monetary economies are present in a barter-type system and so children can learn about, for example, the relationship between price and scarcity, the distinction between capital and labour and competition. Consequently, Webley urges the use of ethnographic methods to uncover the economic world of childhood. His argument is that, if we were to examine the childhood economy on its own terms, we would understand the context in which transferable understanding occurs.

Webley's contribution suggests that there is a public process of exchange in the playground which is the locus of economic socialization. The distinction between public and private aspects of the economy is taken up by Lassarre, who contrasts home and school as agents of economic socialization.

Cram, Ng and Jhavari examine young people's understanding of public and private ownership. Cram *et al.* suggest that there are three dimensions to ownership: the right of use, control and transfer. Without broad social agreement and legal support for these rights, a capitalist society would be impossible. Psychologically possessions afford personal control and the expression of identity.

In relation to private ownership, Cram *et al.* argue that from infancy parents and siblings subtly signal which objects are the babies' by allowing/ disallowing touching and exploration of different objects. Early language and emotional development are also linked to possessions, but it is not until adolescence that a complex view of possessions emerges. This is illustrated by a stage-like development of the concept of 'stealing' which is not understood in relation to the economic system as a whole until the age of ten to twelve years. In terms of the rights of ownership, use and control are understood by five years, but transfer is not. This is partly attributed to the lack of resources that the young child has to engage in transfer. In a cross-cultural comparison, Indian children understood transferability earlier than New Zealand children. On the basis of these studies, Cram *et al.* suggest that there are a number of features which constitute an object as privately owned. The main features are the contractual, the physical and the egocentric.

Cram *et al.* also investigated children's understanding of public ownership. This requires an understanding of the public domain which is constituted by a more remote and complex set of institutions than the household. Previous work had concentrated on public utilities and looked at the stages of understanding through which children pass. Cram *et al.* conducted interview studies using a cognitive conflict paradigm. They found that talking to peers about a problem aided understanding. The resolution of conflicts in interaction provided a model for the resolution of problems within the individual. Having an environment which stimulates group resolution of problems through interaction provides a model for resolving complexes in understanding in economic socialization.

Incorporating social themes into economic psychology requires the exploration of new methods. The theme of new methods is directly taken up by Bombi in Chapter 11. She argues that studies of social context have tended to map correlations between concept use and interactional opportunities and hypothesize an underlying mechanism to explain the difference based on cognitive developmental theory. In contrast, studies of social class have emphasized subtle differences in the content of economic knowledge (see Dickinson and Emler in Chapter 4 of this volume). In her contribution, Bombi offers a new approach to the study of economic socialization: the study of children's drawings. She focuses on the pictorial representation of wealth and poverty, looking at gender and regional (north/south Italy) differences. Content coding of the pictures reveals a clear representation of the difference between rich and poor. There was greater complexity in the drawings made of the rich, particularly in those of the boys from the north of Italy. Social markers in the drawings also indicated a representation of the difference between rich and poor in terms of the presence or absence of goods and quality of goods. Different social roles were also used to represent the difference between rich and poor. Southern Italian girls most often used gender to discriminate rich and poor, this being an expression of their structural disadvantage in the economy.

In his review chapter, Furnham suggests that the dominant mode of data collection hitherto in economic socialization has been the interview. He argues that there needs to be an opening up of methods to provide competing findings in the area and to allow for the diversification of theories in the area. There is considerable diversity of approach represented in the present volume. There are a number of experimental studies (Dittmar; Pliner, Freedman, Abramavitch and Darke; Webley), public opinion surveys (Walstad), interviews (Lassarre), observation (Lassarre), questionnaires (Dickinson and Emler; Dittmar; Lassarre; Leiser and Ganin), the analysis of drawings (Bombi) and ethnography (Webley). This methodological diversity reflects the move away from the descriptive and stage approach to economic socialization. However, it is symptomatic of the present state of the field that such diversity in methods produces results that are difficult to compare.

A variety of themes criss-cross the different contributions to this volume. There is a concern that the social factors which influence economic socialization be articulated and empirically examined. The different factors which are examined here are social class in the contributions of Dittmar; Leiser and Gannin; Dickinson and Emler; and a regional variation by Bombi. Cross-cultural variations are considered by Cram *et al.* and Leiser and Ganin. Parental strategies are considered by Leiser and Ganin as well as Lassarre. The context of interpersonal communication amongst peers is considered by Webley. Institutional contexts such as school and college are considered by

Lassarre and Walstad. Although the results are equivocal in some cases and there is particularly disagreement over the role of social class even between those who propose it (Dittmar; Dickinson and Emler) across the contributions, it is clear that a variety of social factors are potentially implicated in economic socialization.

On a more abstract level there are a number of different approaches to incorporating the social into the study of economic socialization in the contributions to this volume. Leiser and Ganin attempt to model the relations between different social factors, treating them as factors in a causal model. Webley's approach suggests a study of the world of the child in its own terms with a careful analysis of the transferable skills and knowledge to the adult economy rather than seeing the child as a little adult. Lassarre's analysis of shopping raises the possibility of a symbolic interactionist approach where the traditional role of the rational decision maker is understood to be socially distributed in actual moments in the process of consumption. This could be understood as part of the discursive structuration of the family and the commercial sphere. Dittmar suggests that it is in the development of social judgements based on representations that the process of socialization is best seen. Dickinson and Emler argue that society can be understood in terms of differential access to knowledge about the economy. Walstad argues for process of public opinion formation and education. Cram *et al.* argue that the discursive quality of the child's environment is the key mediating social factor. Thus there is no agreement in the field about what the basic social factors and processes are which contribute to economic socialization. Indeed, each of these approaches has a different conception of the economy and the content and processes of economic beliefs and behaviour.

What advice could one extrapolate from the present research to parents and educators concerning possible positive influences on economic socialization and potential dangers? There is a growing consensus in the literature concerning the advantages of the allowance system which gives early experience of financial management (Leiser and Ganin; Pliner *et al.*) and involves the child in a trusting relationship with parents which subjects them to expectations and obligations. An issue that emerges out of Webley's work is that the child is gaining a rich understanding of economic matters in the world of play and therefore that formal education should carefully take into account the informal learning that children are accomplishing. A similar point is made by Lassarre concerning the vitally important role of the family in economic socialization. Walstad's work reminds us that attitudes towards economic matters are as important as knowledge and that attempts to introduce more positive consumers and economic managers will founder if negative attitudes towards the economy persist. Cram *et al.*, Leiser and Gamin, Pliner *et al.* and, to some extent, Bombi point out the potential importance of the quality of the interactional context which the child grows up in.

However, the greatest social concern across the present contributions is with the uneven distribution of economic knowledge within society. Economic socialization can appear to be one of the main agents of the reproduction of economic inequalities in society. Dickinson and Emler, Leiser and Ganin, Bombi and Lassarre are all concerned that basic motivations to become an active economic citizen are unevenly socially distributed.

CONCLUSIONS

The reviews and studies presented in this book are concerned with children and adolescents in modern western liberal or market economies (with the exception of the cross-cultural contrast in Cram *et al.*). The extension of consumer society to include children more and more in economic activity and the relative affluence of young people in contemporary industrial societies have produced children who are actively involved in the economy as they learn about it. Thus the immersion of the child in the economy becomes a potential 'social problem' and a number of issues can be seen to have driven research. Firstly, there was the growth of consumer culture in the postwar period which generally expanded the potential for psychological dimensions of materialism. Secondly, the invention of, first, the teenage and then the childhood market meant that children became a target for advertising and consumers in their own right. Also there has been an ideological shift towards individualism and the responsibilities of citizens, so that, for example, many of society's ills, including debt, are understood to result from failures in parental socialization of children to become competent and responsible citizens. Finally, there is the trend to complexity and expansion of consumer markets in western economies. The move from a cash to a credit economy, the increase in home ownership and other forms of complex economic activity by ordinary people mean that economic competence is growing in complexity and diversity.

The modern consumer is immersed in a complex economy and the demands made upon all of us in terms of economic understanding are constantly developing. Political debate in contemporary western societies is now mainly a question of different approaches to managing the economy, including the consumer economy. Thus, more and more, the classic division between the micro and the macro is being fudged by the expansion and elaboration of the consumer market. This is reflected in the studies presented here which are concerned with the development of the citizen consumer rather than people's more passive knowledge of the economy as something 'out there' (Leiser and Ganin).

Following up Leiser and Ganin's point about the historical and cultural relativity of the mode of involvement of children in the economy, we can suggest a current shift away from the modern detachment of the child from the public sphere of commerce and an increasing involvement and sophistication of the contemporary young consumer. So one of the key issues is the economic competence of citizens in an increasingly complex consumer society. Society needs people to be financially competent but also, because contemporary economies are partially demand-led, they require consumer commitment. Thus the issue of economic socialization goes beyond the issue of competence narrowly defined in terms of social skill to include orientation to consumer society. Consequently, as the contributions to this volume testify, issues of attitudes and values are part of the socialization of the modern consumer.

REFERENCES

Baudrillard, J. (1988), 'Consumer Society', in M. Poster (ed.), *Jean Baudrillard: selected writings*, Cambridge: Polity Press.
Berti, A.E. and Bombi, A.S. (1988), *The Child's Construction of Economics*, Cambridge: Cambridge University Press.
Bourdieu, P. (1984), *Distinction: A Social Critique of the Judgement of Taste*, London: Routledge and Kegan Paul.
Giddens, A. (1991), *Modernity and Self-Identity: Self and society in the late modern age*, Cambridge: Polity Press.
Habermas, J. (1989), *The Structural Transformation of the Public Sphere: an inquiry into a category of Bourgeois society*, trans. T. Burger with F. Lawrence, Cambridge, Mass.: MIT Press.
Harvey, D. (1989), *The Condition of Postmodernity*, Oxford: Blackwell.
Lea, S.E.G., Tarpy, R.M. and Webley, P. (1987), *The Individual in the Economy: A survey of economic psychology*, Cambridge: Cambridge University Press.
Miller, D. (1987), *Material Culture and Mass Consumption*, Oxford: Blackwell.
Pahl, J. (1989), *Money and Marriage*, London: Macmillan.
Webley, P. and Lea, S.E.G. (1993), 'Towards a more realistic psychology of economic socialization', *Journal of Economic Psychology*, **14**, 461–72.

2.   The economic socialization of children[1]

Adrian Furnham

INTRODUCTION

Socialization is generally defined as a process through which individuals learn to interact in society. It concerns learning social roles and acquiring the knowledge and skills related to them. So far comparatively little research has been done on economic socialization compared to other aspects of social development (for example, moral development). Still less had been done on *how* knowledge and beliefs are acquired as opposed to the *content* of the knowledge base (Berti and Bombi, 1988; Haste and Torney-Purta, 1992). Furthermore, it has not been until comparatively recently that researchers have looked at young people's reasoning about economic issues.

A detailed examination of the economic socialization of children and adolescents is of both academic and applied interest. In Great Britain in 1990, 14–16-year-olds had nearly £10 a week in disposable cash. West German 7–15-year-olds for instance received 7.5 billion DM of pocket money and monetary gifts in 1988 and the spending power of 12–21-year-olds amounted to 33 billion DM for that year. And, of course, in most western democratic countries, of 18-year-olds are allowed to hold bank accounts, make investments and accrue debts.

Many different aspects of young people's understanding and perception of the economy, their attitudes towards money and possessions, their spending and consumption habits are relevant to the teaching of economic principles in schools as well as to the research of psychologists, educationalists, marketing people and even to economists (Furnham and Stacey, 1991).

THE DEVELOPMENT OF ECONOMIC IDEAS IN THE CHILD

What do children know about the economy? How and at what age do they acquire their knowledge? To what extent are there differences of knowledge and belief due to gender, age, nationality, socioeconomic background and

11

experience with money? Strauss (1952) was among the first to examine the development of money-related concepts. In his 1952 study he interviewed 66 children of both sexes aged between $4^1/_2$ and $11^1/_2$ years and classified the answers into nine different developmental stages that reinforced the Piagetian idea of the child's advancement by stages rather than by continuum. According to Strauss, the content of the child's concepts undergoes systematic change as it moves from one level to the next, which depends on his having understood the respective prerequisite notions. Each level of conception, though, signifies not only a different degree of intellectual maturity but also a different level of experience, perception and values. Six years later, Danzinger (1958) asked 41 children aged between 5 and 8 years questions about money, the rich and the poor and the 'boss', to examine whether the development of social concepts in the child could be applied to Piaget's theoretical model of cognitive development. From the results he drew up four different stages in the development of economic concepts:

> (a) An initial pre-categorical stage occurs when the child lacks economic categories of thought altogether. There is no special realm of economic concepts differentiated from social concepts in general. (b) At the second, or categorical, stage the child's concepts appear to represent a reality in terms of isolated acts which are explained by a moral or voluntaristic imperative. (c) At the third stage the child becomes able to conceptualize relationships as such, by virtue of the fact that a reciprocity is established between previously isolated acts. But these relations are in their turn isolated and cannot be explained in terms of other relationships. (d) Finally, the isolated relationships become linked to each other so as to form a system of relations. We then have a conceptualization of a totality wherein each part derives its significance from its position in the whole. At this point a purely rational explanation becomes possible. (Danziger, 1958, pp. 239–40)

Danziger believed that first-hand experience enhances the advancement to the next level of conception. The children in his study appeared to be at a higher level in their understanding of economic exchange than in production and he attributed this to the fact that they had experience of buying, but none of work.

Sutton (1962) interviewed 85 children aged between 6 and 13 on money and the accumulation of capital. Irrespective of age, intelligence and socioeconomic background, the majority of replies were in the beginning stages of conceptualization, thus emphasizing the importance of first-hand experience in the development of economic concepts.

Jahoda (1979) conducted a role-play study in which 120 working-class Scottish children aged between 6 and 12 played the role of the shopkeeper and the interviewer that of customer and supplier. Children's responses were grouped according to whether the difference between buying and selling price had been realized. The results suggested that most children did not begin to understand the concept of profit until about the age of 11. The interview that followed showed that the development of the understanding of the concept of profit passed through three stages. In the first stage children were transforming an ignorance of profit into a conception of profit as observed ritual; in the second stage buying and selling understood as separate behavioural systems were gradually perceived to be connected, although with no price difference between the two activities; in the final stage an understanding of the difference between what the shopkeeper paid and charged was understood as a profit.

Burris (1983) found general compatibility with the Piagetian view that knowledge develops through a sequence of qualitative cognitive stages from the answers of 32 children at each distinct stage (pre-operational, concrete operations and formal operations). More recently Leiser (1983), Schug and Birkey (1985) and Sevon and Weckstrom (1989) supported these findings. Schug and Birkey, like Danziger, also stressed that children's economic understanding varies somewhat, depending upon their own economic experiences. Sevon and Weckstrom characterized younger children's perception of the economy as from the viewpoint of homo sociologicus (driven by moral and social norms) and the one of older children more as of homo economicus (striving for personal hedonic satisfaction). Of the three age groups 8, 11 and 14 the youngest group, when asked about the thinking and acting of economic agents, first felt the need to decide whether these agents would become happy or unhappy before thinking about why this was the case (for example, The shoe retailer would be happy about the reduction in shoe prices because 'people can save their money'). The answers of the younger children thus described *moral* or 'Christian' (concern for other people, other people's approval or disapproval of their own behaviour was important) rather than *economic* thinking (other people as means, constraints or obstacles to personal satisfaction). Some of the older children, however, saw the economy more as an instrument and the action of the individual as led by the search for opportunity to increase his own wealth.

Thus, although there have been a variety of studies which have claimed to support the Piagetian view about the development of economic concepts in the child, the studies have found different numbers of stages. This might be for several reasons: the age ranges of the subjects were different; the number of subjects in each study were different (sometime perhaps too small to be representative); and there were variations in precision in the definition of stage boundaries.

Table 2.1 shows that there is disagreement about the number of stages, points of transition and content of understanding at each stage. The trend among the more recent studies, though, seems to be that the number of (sub)-stages is summarized and three broad main phases are defined: (1) no under-

Table 2.1   Dates, samples and stages found in studies of the development of economic understanding

Researcher	Year	Subjects	Age range	Stages
Strauss	1952	66	4.8–11.6	9
Danziger	1958	41	5–8	4
Sutton	1962	85	grade 1–6	6
Jahoda	1979	120	6–12	3
Burris	1983	96	4/5, 7/8, 10/12	3
Leiser	1983	89	7–17	3

standing, (2) understanding of some isolated concepts, and (3) linking of isolated concepts to achieve full understanding. By no means do these stages suggest, however, that the child's understanding of different economic concepts always advances simultaneously. As Danziger (1958) stressed, a child's understanding of, for example, buying and selling may be more advanced than his understanding of work, as he might have had experience of the former but not of the latter. It would therefore be of great interest to further investigate whether and what other factors (such as parental practices and social class) actually tend to speed up or perhaps slow down the transition from one stage to the next. This is one of the questions addressed by contributions to the present volume.

In terms of methodology, nearly all the relevant research consists of self-report studies using interviews. Most Piagetian work is task-based (role play, games and so on) and it may well be that experimental studies on economic concepts would yield clearer, more interesting results. Again, the contributions in the present volume display a greater range of methods than self-report interviews.

All stage-wise theories appear to have a number of implicit assumptions. The sequence of development is fixed. There is an ideal end-of-state towards which the child and adolescent inevitably progress. Some behaviours are sufficiently different from previous abilities for us to be able to identify a child or adolescent as being in or out of a stage. In contrast, non-stage theories do not see people progressing inevitably to a single final stage since environmental forces are given more power to create a diversity of developmental responses. At the one end of the stage–non-stage continuum is the view that most of a young person's time is spent in one of several specific stages with short, relatively abrupt transitions between stages. As the length of time spent in a stage is perceived to be shortened and the time in transition is lengthened, one moves along the continuum until all the time is seen as spent in transition, and development is seen as continuous and non-stage. Since a non-stage theory does not necessarily dictate any specific end state or single developmental sequence, the study of individual differences assumes more importance.

Webley (1983 and Chapter 9 of the present volume) and others have criticized the application of the standard Piagetian approach and argued in favour of looking for what is distinct about economic concepts instead of treating economic cognition as just another area where general principles of cognitive development apply. Webley reproached researchers for their use of a static standard approach towards the investigation into children's development of economic thinking and regretted that no attempts have been made to 'produce a characterization of the environment which might allow variations in the development of economic thought apart from social class distinction'.

Furthermore, what is special about economic factors (such as property) is that they form the basis of power in society and interpersonal relations and the concepts/ideology a child develops are therefore of vital concern to the possessing. The need to relate to the economic structure of the society – an idea more radically expressed by Cummings and Taebel (1978) – and the importance of characterizing a child's environment (for example, exposure to own economic experience) are therefore aspects that might distinguish the development of economic concepts from others. In this sense the understanding of economics just as the understanding of history and politics is different from that of physics, chemistry and, say, meteorology. Social values and ideology are intricately bound up with the former and not the latter and can influence understanding profoundly. Again this critique forms the basis of a number of studies in the present volume.

RESEARCH ON THE DEVELOPMENT OF ECONOMIC THINKING

Although numerous studies of children's understanding of different aspects of the economic world have been carried out, it appears they have concentrated on some topics rather than others (Berti and Bombi, 1988). For example, relatively few studies exist on young people's knowledge of betting, taxes, interest rates, the up and down of the economy (boom, recession, depression, recovery and so on) or inflation. This might be because these concepts are considered to be too difficult for children to understand, although in a study in Yugoslavia by Zabukovec and Polic (1990) the children's answers clearly reflected aspects (such as inflation) of the then current economic situation, which shows that the 'difficulty' always depends on the circumstances (exposure to the economic world). There is, however, failed, detailed and replicated research on topics such as possession and ownership, wealth and poverty, entrepreneurship, prices, wages, money, buying and selling, profit and the bank. However, the common denominator to all economic interactions in the western world obviously is money and therefore its understanding is a prerequisite for all other concepts.

Money

As money is the basis of almost all economical actions today, its full understanding clearly is a prerequisite for other, more abstract concepts (such as credit or profit). Children's first contact with money happens at a quite early age (watching parents buying or selling things, receiving pocket money and so on) but research has shown that this does not necessarily mean that, although children use money themselves, they fully understand its meaning and significance. For very young children, giving money to a salesperson constitutes a mere ritual. They are not aware of the different values of coins and the purpose of change, let alone the origin of money. Children thus need to understand the nature and role of money before being able to master more abstract concepts.

To investigate children's ideas about the payment for work, Berti and Bombi (1979) interviewed 100 children aged from 3 to 8 years (20 from each age level) on where they thought that money came from. Four categories of response emerged. At *level 1*, children had no idea of its origin: the father takes the money from his pocket. At *level 2*, children saw the origin as independent of work: somebody/a bank gives it to everybody who asks for it. At *level 3*, the subjects named the change given by tradesmen when buying as the origin of money. Only at *level 4* did children name work as the reason. Most of the 4–5-year-olds' answers were in category 1, whereas most of the 6–7 and 7–8-year-olds were in category 4. The idea of payment for work (level 4) thus develops out of various spontaneous and erroneous beliefs in levels 2 and 3, where children have as yet no understanding of the concept of work, which is a prerequisite for understanding the origin of money. Although at that level they did notice occasionally that their parents take part in extra-domestic activities, children did not call them work or even see a need for them. Two years later, Berti and Bombi (1981) undertook another investigation (80 subjects aged between 3 and 8 years) into the concept of money and its value. Building on the work of Strauss (1952) and others, they singled out six stages: stage 1: no awareness of payment; stage 2: obligatory payment – no distinction between different kinds of money, and money can buy anything; stage 3: distinction between types of money – not all money is equivalent any more; stage 4: realization that money can be insufficient; stage 5: strict correspondence between money and objects – correct amount has to be given; stage 6: correct use of change. The first four stages clearly are to be found in the pre-operational period, whereas, in the last two, arithmetic operations are successfully applied. Strauss (1952) had found nine stages in the child's understanding about money, ranging from the first stage where the child believes that any coin can buy any object to the last where correct understanding is achieved.

Pollio and Gray (1973) conducted a more 'practical' study with 100 subjects, grouped at the ages of 7, 9, 11 and 13 and college students, on 'change-making strategies' and found that it was not until the age of 13 that an entire age group was able to give correct change. The younger subjects showed a preference for small-value coins (with which they were more familiar) when making change, whereas the older ones used all coins available. More recent studies have looked at such things as children's actual monetary behaviour. For instance, Abromovitch *et al.* (1991) found that 6–10-year-old Canadian children who received allowances seemed more sophisticated about money than those who did not. The developing understanding of money and its role in exchange is one of the themes examined in this volume.

Prices and Profit

Buying is one of the earliest economic activities a child can engage in. There are a number of prerequisites before a child is above to understand buying and selling, and therefore prices and profit: a child has to know about function and origin of money, change, ownership, payment of wages to employees, shop expenses and shopowner's need for income/private money, which, all together, prove the simple act of buying and selling to be rather complex. Furth (1980) pointed out four stages during the acquisition of this concept: (1) no understanding of payment; (2) understanding of payment of the customer but not of the shopkeeper; (3) understanding and relating payments made by both the customer and the shopkeeper; (4) understanding of all these things.

Jahoda (1979), using a role-play where the child had to buy goods from a supplier and sell to a customer, distinguished between three categories: (1) no understanding of profit – both prices were consistently identical; (2) transitional – mixture of responses; (3) understanding of profit – selling price consistently higher than buying price. Jahoda's study produced a stage less than Furth's that of understanding. However, this may be an artefact of the role play that concentrated on profit-seeking behaviour and did not require the child to produce an explanation that would indicate understanding. Furthermore, the child was already told to buy from a supplier, therefore he knew that he had to pay him in the first place (which in Furth's study was not the case).

Supporting the idea of gradually integrating sub-systems, Berti *et al.* (1986) pointed out that the concepts about shop and factory profit in 8-year-olds were not compatible. Despite improving their understanding of shop profit after receiving training, the children were not able to transfer their knowledge onto factory's profit, thinking that prices were set arbitrarily.

Berti *et al.* (1986) showed that children's understanding of profit could be enhanced by training. Both critical training sessions stimulating the child to puzzle out solutions to contradictions between their own forecasts and the actual outcomes and ordinary, tutorial training sessions (information given to children) that consisted in similar games of buying and selling proved to be effective. However, the results also showed that neither kind of experience was sufficient in itself to lead children to a correct notion of profit, partly owing to lack of arithmetical abilities. Nevertheless, the authors suggested that, although arithmetical abilities are essential, 'making children talk about economic topics they have not yet mastered, far from being an obstacle to learning may contribute to their progress, constituting in itself a kind of training, as Jahoda (1981) also found in different circumstances'.

In a recent study with 11–16-year-olds, Furnham and Cleare (1988) also found differences in understanding shop and factory profit: 'Of 11–12-year-olds, 7% understood profit in shops, yet 69% mentioned profit as a motive for starting a factory today, and 20% mentioned profit as an explanation for why factories had been started' (p. 475). The understanding of the abstract concept of profit, which depends on the previous understanding of the basic concept of buying and selling, grows through different phases. Young children (6–8 years) seem to have no grasp of any system and conceive of transactions as 'simply an observed ritual without further purpose' (Furth *et al.* 1976, p. 365). Older children (8–10 years) realize that the shopowner previously had to buy (pay for) the goods before he could sell them. Nevertheless, they do not always understand that the money for this comes from the customers and that buying prices have to be lower than selling prices. They thus perceive of buying and selling as two unconnected systems. Not until the age of 10 or 11 are children able to integrate these two systems and understand the difference between buying and selling prices. Of course, these age bands may vary slightly among children (or cultures) as experiential factors play a part in the understanding of economic concepts. Because of the obvious political implications of the ideas of profit and pricing it would be particularly interesting to see not only when (and how) young people come to understand the concepts but also how they reason with them.

Banking

Jahoda (1981) interviewed 32 subjects each of the ages 12, 14 and 16 about bank's profits. He asked whether one gets back more, less or the same as the original sum deposited and whether one has to pay back more, less or the same as the original sum borrowed. From this basis he drew up six categories:

1. No knowledge of interest (get/pay back same amount).
2. Interest on deposits only (get back more, pay back the same).
3. Interest on both, but more on deposit (deposit interest higher than loan interest).
4. Interest same on deposits and loans.
5. Interest higher for loans (no evidence of understanding).
6. Interest more for loans – correctly understood.

Although most of these children had fully understood the concept of shop profit, many did not perceive the bank as a profit-making enterprise (only a quarter of the 14- and 16-year-olds understood bank profit): 'They viewed the principles governing a bank as akin to those underlying the transactions between friends: if you borrow something, you return the same, no more and no less – anything else would be "unfair"' (p. 70).

Ng (1983) replicated the same study in Hong Kong and found the same developmental trend. The Chinese children, however, were more precocious, showing a full understanding of the bank's profit at the age of 10. From the same study he discovered two more stages (0 = funny idea stage; 2b = interest on loans only – unrelated to profit) in addition to Jahoda's original six. A study in New Zealand by the same author (Ng, 1985) confirmed these additional two stages and proved the New Zealand children to 'lag' behind Hong Kong by about two years. Ng attributes this to Hong Kong's 'high level of economic socialization and customer activity, and the business ethos of the society at large. ... Their maturity represents, in short, a case of socioeconomic reality shaping (partly at least) socioeconomic understanding' (pp. 220–21). This comparison demonstrates that developmental trends are not necessarily *always* similar throughout different countries, although they may prove to be so in many cases. A decisive factor seems to be the extent to which children are sheltered from, exposed to or in some cases even take part in economic activity.

POSSESSION AND OWNERSHIP

The topic of possession and ownership is clearly related both to politics and to economics but has been investigated mainly through the work of psychologists interested in economic understanding. Berti *et al.* (1982) conducted research into children's conceptions about means of production and their owners. They interviewed 120 children of ages 4–13 on three areas to find out children's knowledge about (1) ownership of means of production, (2) ownership of products (industrial and agricultural) and (3) ownership of product use. From the answers they were able to derive five levels:

1.   a. Owner of means of production is the person found in spatial contact with it (bus owned by passengers).
      b. Industrial and agricultural products not owned by anybody; anybody can make possession of them.
2.   a. Owner is the person who exercises an appropriate use of or direct control over the object (factory owned by workers).
      b. Owner is person closest to or using/constructing the object.
3.   a. Owner uses producing means and controls their use by others ('the boss').
      b. Product ownership is explained through ownership of producing means ('boss' must share produce with employees).
4.   a. Differentiation between owner (giving orders) and employers.
      b. Product belongs to 'boss'.
5.   a. Distinction between owner (top of hierarchy) and boss (between owner and worker).
      b. Products belong to owner of means of production, employees are compensated by salary.

Children's ideas about ownership of means of production develop through the same sequences but at different speeds. The notion of a 'boss–owner', for instance, seems to occur at 8–9 years for the factory, 10–11 years for the bus and 12–13 years for the countryside, perhaps owing to the fact that 85 per cent of the subjects in the study had had no direct experience of country life. Although very few had had direct experience of the father's working environment, they heard him talk a lot about his work and thus acquired their information. Cram and Ng (1989) in New Zealand examined (using 172 subjects of three different age groups: 5–6, 8–9, 11–12 years) children's understanding of private ownership by noting the attributes the subjects used to endorse ownership. Greater age was associated with an increase in the endorsement of higher-level (that is, contractual) attributes and in the rejection of lower-level (that is, physical) attributes, but there was only a tendency in the direction. Already 89 per cent of the youngest group rejected 'liking' as a reason for possessing, which increased to 98 per cent in the middle and oldest group, whereas the differences on the other two levels were more distinct. This indicates that, surprisingly, 5–6-year-olds are mainly aware of the distinction between personal desires and ownership. This does not necessarily contradict earlier work but makes it necessary to interview children younger than the ones in this study to find out whether, and at what age, egocentric ownership attributes are endorsed during earlier stages of development.

Furnham and Jones (1987) studied children's views regarding possessions and their theft. 102 subjects aged 7–8, 9–10, 12–13 and 16–17 filled out a questionnaire based on work by Furby (1980a, 1980b) and Irving and Siegal (1983). Results indicated that, as hypothesized, views about possessions become more sophisticated and 'realistic' with age. The type of favourite possessions proved to be age-dependent, varying from toys to sound and sports equipment, computers and clothes. The younger groups showed no preference for the means of acquisition of an object, whereas the older groups attached great importance to items they bought themselves and individually owned objects, motivated by a desire to affect and control their environment. As with increasing age the child's self-concept gradually depends more and more on his possessions, reactions towards theft become harsher and empathy with the victim increases, even under mitigating circumstances. Most of the younger subjects simply demanded a return of the stolen object, creating mitigating circumstances (poverty or unhappiness) even where there were none, whereas older subjects demanded conditional discharge or prison sentences of different durations as a punishment. Although the oldest group were relatively stringent in their actual demands for punishment, in moral terms they were rather lenient. This is understood as a pragmatic acceptance of the need for law and order to provide general safety.

For children of all ages the element of control over their environment seems to be the most important characteristic of possessions. For older children who are more active consumers themselves, possessions often imply power and status and an enhancement of personal freedom and security. This suggests that in societies or groups (like a kibbutz) where ownership is shared, young people acquire the understanding about possessing in a quite different way.

Concepts relating to means of production seem to develop similarly to those of buying and selling. They also advance through phases of no grasp of any system, to unconnected systems (knowledge that the owner of means of production sells products but no understanding of how he gets the money to pay his workers) and to integrated systems (linking workers' payment and sales proceeds), depending on the respective logic and arithmetical ability of the child. Although these concepts seem to follow the same developmental sequence, it cannot be said whether, to what extent and how the same factors (experimental, maturation, educational) contribute equally to the development of each concept. These issues are taken up by Cram *et al.* in Chapter 7 of the present volume.

POVERTY AND WEALTH

In 1975, Zinser *et al.* conducted a study to determine the importance of the affluence of the recipient to pre-school children's sharing behaviour. Most of the children favoured sharing with poor recipients rather than rich recipients. They were also more generous with low-value items than with high-value items towards both equally and these findings were consistent over all three (4–6) ages. There are two possible explanations for this behaviour: (1) societal values; for example, society already has communicated to these young children that poor people are more deserving as recipients of sharing than rich people; or (2) empathy; for example perceived need arouses affective reactions in the children that motivate sharing, which in turn reduces affective reactions.

Winocur and Siegal (1982) asked 96 adolescents (aged 12–13 and 16–18) to allocate rewards between male and female workers in four different cases of family constellations and the results indicated that concern for need decreased with age. Older subjects preferred to distribute rewards on an equal pay for equal work basis, whereas younger subjects supported the idea that family needs should be reflected in pay, but there were no sex differences in the perception of economic arrangements. This confirms Sevon and Weckstrom's (1989) suggestions that younger children judge from a homo sociologicus and older children from a homo economicus point of view.

Leahy (1981) asked 720 children and adolescents of four age groups (5–7, 9–11, 13–15, 16–18) and four social classes to describe rich and poor people and to point out the differences and similarities between them. The answers were grouped into different types of person descriptions: (1) peripheral (possessions, appearances, behaviour), (2) central (traits and thoughts) and (3) sociocentric (life chances and class consciousness) categories. The use of peripheral characteristics in descriptions decreased considerably with age and thus adolescents emphasized central and sociocentric categories, perceiving rich and poor as different kinds of people who not only differ in observable qualities but also in personality traits. Lower-class subjects tended to refer more to the thoughts and life chances of the poor, taking their perspective, and upper-middle-class subjects tended to describe the traits of the poor, perceiving them as 'others'. On the whole, there was rather uniformity across class and race in the descriptions and comparisons of the rich and the poor.

To explain these findings two theoretical models are conceivable: (1) a cognitive developmental model, suggesting that later adolescence is marked by an increased awareness of the nature of complex social systems, and (2) a general functionalist model, suggesting the socialization results in uniformity among classes and races as to the nature of the social class system and thus retains stability in social institutions. As there has been no research on that topic in other societies or historical periods, it is not possible to exclude the second model, although, from the way studies have been conducted and interpreted so far, results (understanding of all concepts reached through gradual advancement by stages) favour the cognitive–developmental model.

Stacey and Singer (1985) had 325 teenagers of 14¹/₂ and 17 years from a working-class background complete a questionnaire, probing their perceptions of the attributes and consequences of poverty and wealth. Regardless of age and sex, all respondent groups rated familial circumstances as most important and luck as least important in explaining poverty and wealth. With internal and external attributions for poverty and wealth being rated moderately important, these findings differ slightly from Leahy's (1981) results, as here adolescents clearly thought sociocentric categories to be more important than the other two. A reason for this might be that here all subjects were from a working-class background and, as Furnham (1982) found, subjects from a lower socioeconomic background tend to attach more importance to societal explanations than subjects from a higher socioeconomic background, who tend to offer more individualistic explanations (such as lack of thrift and proper money management) for poverty.

Most of the studies in this field have tried to describe the levels which children go through in their development of certain economic notions. The occasional disagreement as to the number of levels and points of transitions is probably mostly a matter of methodology; results have been interpreted within the Piagetian developmental idea – whether this is justified or not remains to be debated. Webley (1983, and Chapter 9 of the present volume) for instance, who questions whether the Piagetian approach is applicable for economic concepts, too, favours a social learning model. Furthermore, most of the researchers already agree that external stimuli (socioeconomic environment, personal experience with money, formal teaching, parental practices) have a great influence on the child's development of economic thinking and may contribute to premature knowledge. For instance, Wosinski and Pietras (1990) discovered in a study with 87 Polish subjects of ages 8, 11 and 14 that the youngest had in some aspects (such as the definition of salary, the possibility of getting the same salary for everybody, the possibility of starting a factory) better economic knowledge than the other groups. They attributed this to the fact that these children were born and had been living under conditions of an economic crisis in Poland. They had experienced conditions of shortage, increases in prices, inflation and had heard their family and television programmes discuss these matters. This, too, represents 'a case of socio-economic reality shaping (partly at least) socio-economic understanding' (Ng, 1983, pp. 220–21). It therefore seems to be that, to a certain extent, the development of economic notions can be accelerated through experimental and educational factors, which still merit further study.

CROSS-CULTURAL, SOCIAL AND GENDER DIFFERENCES

Various studies in different (mainly western) countries have been undertaken, but few that investigate specifically cross-cultural differences. Furby (1978, 1980a, 1980b) compared American and Israeli (kibbutz and city) children's attitudes towards possessions and found rather more differences between American and Israeli subjects than between kibbutz and all others.

The most comprehensive and extensive study in a recent cross-cultural project initiated by Leiser *et al.* (1990) was the 'Naive Economics Project'. It includes samples from ten countries, Algeria, Australia, Denmark, Finland, France, Israel (town and kibbutz), Norway, Poland, West Germany and Yugoslavia, and was administered to 900 children aged 8, 11 and 14. Topics covered were (1) *understanding*: who decides what, how and why (prices, salary, savings and investment, the mint); (2) *reasoning*: how well children appreciate the consequences of economic events of national dimensions; (3) *attitudes*: how they account for the economic fate of individuals. In accordance with previous investigations in various countries there was an obvious progression with age. However, there were some differences in answers between the participating countries. These could be due to the different political and economical systems and the prosperity of the whole country. The dominance of the government as a visible economic factor was reflected by the frequency with which it appeared in children's answers. The differences in each society's values and attitudes (such as more individualistic attitudes in western democracies, religion, the work ethic, different moral standards in Christian and in atheist or Moslem countries and so on) and slight differences in the conditions of the interview are all possible reasons for the disparity in country responses. Furthermore, the size of the sample (90 subjects from each country) may not have been large enough to provide for representative cross-cultural comparisons. The differences, however, show that the child's understanding of the way economic systems work is influenced by various factors in the child's environment, as suggested by the social learning model.

Class differences were very inconsistently reported by the various researchers. Although in some cases there was some indication of class differences, on the whole they were not as significant as the reported age differences were. There is a certain difficulty in finding comparable subjects in each country anyway ('middle-class' probably has a different meaning in Germany and in Algeria).

In a smaller study, Burgard *et al.* (1989) replicated a Scottish study by Emler and Dickinson (1985) in West Germany that asked 140 children of 8, 10 and 12 years from middle- and working-class backgrounds and 67 parents to estimate occupational incomes of a doctor, a teacher, a bus driver and a road sweeper and the cost of some consumer goods. Emler and Dickinson (1985) had found substantial social class differences but no age differences in their Scottish sample. In West Germany, however, there were significant age differences but virtually no social class differences found, among both parents and children. One explanation might be that socioeconomic differences in West German society are less pronounced than in the UK. Furthermore, there was no relationship between parents' and childrens' income estimates. This, according to Burgard *et al.* throws considerable doubt on 'Emler and Dickinson's (1985) contention that class-tied social representations outweigh developmental changes' (p. 285). These issues are taken up in Chapters 4 and 5.

Similarly, gender differences have been reported through several studies. While some authors have set out quite specifically to measure these phenomena, Kourilsky and Campbell (1984) set up a study, '(1) to measure sex differences in children's perceptions of entrepreneurship and occupational sex-stereotyping and (2) to assess differences in children's risk taking, persistence, and economic success' (p. 53). In all, 938 subjects aged 8–12 took part in an economics education instructional programme over ten weeks. Before the instructional programme, entrepreneurship was perceived as a predominantly male domain. After the instructional programme boys still possessed a stereotyped picture of the entrepreneur. This trend was also observable with occupational sex-stereotyping. In the Mini-Society, girls were more likely to increase the number of occupations they thought appropriate for women. As to ratings for success (profit made in a mini-business), persistence (sticking to a task until completed) and risk-taking (exposure to loss and disadvantages) boys and girls achieved similar results, girls even being slightly in the lead in the first two categories. Thus there are in this study at ages 8–12 no sex differences in the major characteristics that are associated with successful entrepreneurship. The fact that in reality there are few female entrepreneurs must therefore have different reasons (such as traditional sex socialization).

Gender differences most probably may be attributed to children's different upbringing and the role women play in society. If one parent stays at home or works only part-time, it is most often the mother. The father is seen as a source of money by young children ('brings it home from work'). All people that are thought of as important by the child are almost entirely men (presidents, 'bosses', headmasters, priests and so on). Children, therefore, already perceive men and women in different *roles* while growing up. This may again be more or less obvious in different countries. Wosinski and Pietras (1990), for instance, clearly attribute the gender differences they found in their study to traditional sex socialization, as in Poland economic problems are traditionally left to males rather than females.

As Kourilsky and Campbell's (1984) study showed, instruction can help change children's perceptions of 'realities' (such as gender roles) as well as increase their economic knowledge.

ECONOMIC VALUES

The determinants and structure of adolescents' beliefs about the economy were the subject of two studies by Furnham (1987). The first study examined the determinants of economic values in 86 adolescents aged 16–17 and the second looked at the economic preferences and knowledge of 150 subjects aged 18–19. Based on a questionnaire (Economics Values Inventory) by O'Brien and Ingels (1985), the determinants of economic values turned out to be most likely the subject's political belief rather than gender, religion or personal economic experience. O'Brien and Ingels (1987) had previously conducted the first study in the USA. Their findings, and that of Furnham, suggested socioeconomic status as the strongest predictor of economic values. Possible reasons for this could be, compared to the UK, the much weaker political interest in the USA (a far lower percentage of American citizens votes), different political traditions (strong trade unions in Britain) or less pronounced economical differences between socioeconomic status and political belief anyway (working class; 'left' middle class; 'conservative') and therefore, if examined, it might be the case that subjects who had a 'conservative' political opinion are predominantly from a middle-class background, which would then be in accordance with the American study again.

Furnham's studies showed a close affinity between political and economic beliefs and found that the latter are governed by the former. The way political parties publicly compare their agendas and families possibly discuss their present and future situation (jobs, education, health, finances and so on) at home may arouse political awareness. Being in favour of certain political ideas implies having economic priorities, as a lot of the differences between political parties are in their respective budgets. A possible reason for this may be that the economic topics covered were all macroeconomic topics of popular debate that were on the political parties' agenda, which suggests that there may also be 'less political' topics. As only beliefs (and not knowledge) were tested, the subjects only needed to 'have an opinion'. Opinions are shaped through debate, which again is a political process.

So far the majority of studies have concentrated on children's understanding of certain economic concepts, mainly in industrial societies. The reason for neglecting other concepts might be that children are not expected to understand them, perhaps even because not many adults are expected to understand them either (such concepts include exchange rates between currencies, macroeconomic situations as boom and recession and so on). Studies like Wosinski and Pietras (1990), Ng (1983) and Kourilsky (1984) have shown that children have sometimes been underestimated and that they were able to understand concepts that they were not expected to understand at their age, as the result of being exposed to certain external stimuli (such as instruction, experience and economic crisis) that helped speed up their understanding.

ECONOMIC EDUCATION

Formal instruction is one means by which young people acquire an understanding of the economic world. Whitehead (1986) investigated the eventual change in students' attitudes to economic issues as a result of exposure to a two-year 'A' level economic course. The 16–18-year-old subjects were divided into a test group of 523 and a control group of 483. The questionnaires did not test economic knowledge but economic attitudes (dis/agreement on, for example, private enterprise as the most efficient economic system; capitalism is immoral because it exploits the worker by failing to give him full value for his or her productive labour). In absolute terms, considerable correspondence existed between the responses of experimental and control groups with respect to those items where a large majority expressed either conservative or radical attitudes. On the whole, experimental and control group held completely differing views only on three items. However, for six out of the 18 items on the scale, students who had studied for 'A' level economics showed a significant shift in their economic attitudes.

In a similar study, O'Brien and Ingels (1987), who developed the economics values inventory (EVI), an instrument aimed at measuring young people's values and attitudes regarding economic matter, also confirmed their hypothesis that formal education in economics influences students' economic attitudes. The teaching of economics therefore not only increases children's understanding of certain economics contexts but also may help them review their values and attitudes which are mostly influenced by or even taken over from their parents. Understanding societal independencies better may help learning to question prejudices and therefore contribute to increased maturation.

Economics as a subject is most usually not taught in most countries before university or in some cases secondary school. The majority of adolescents who drop out of school after nine or ten years of education therefore never receive economics instruction. As macroeconomic knowledge obviously cannot be learned by observation (purchasing something or filling in a cheque might, but certainly not other fields of economic exchange such as the working of banks or even government borrowing and spending) there obviously is a need for the teaching of economics. Kourilsky (1977) proved, however, that even at the kindergarten it is not too soon to start educating economically literate citizens. In the 'Kinder Economy', an education programme, children became acquainted with the concepts of scarcity, decision making, production, specialization, consumption, distribution, demand/supply, business, money and barter. Kourilsky's study examining 96 subjects age 5 to 6 was designed to answer four questions:

1. Is the child's success in economic decision making and analysis related to instructional intervention or to increased maturity inherent in the passage of time?
2. To what extent and degree, through intervention, are children able to master concepts that, psychologically, they are considered too young to learn?
3. What type of school, home and personality variables are predictors of success in economic decision making and analysis?
4. What are the parents' attitudes towards the teaching of economic decision making and analytical principles as a part of early childhood education?

The examination of the first question showed a significant difference between the scores of the subjects in the Kinder Economy and in the control group, which proved that significant progress was induced by instruction. Four out of the nine topics covered yielded mastery levels of more than 70 per cent, the total average being 72.5 per cent. The mastery level was set at 70 per cent, as a previous testing of 40 elementary school teachers yielded an average of 68.5 per cent on the same test. This shows that children are in fact able to learn concepts which developmentally they are considered to be too young to learn. To answer the third question, six predictor variables were examined: parent report, verbal ability, maturation level, general ability, social ability and initiative. The first three proved to be the best predictors of success in economic decision making, the strongest, parent report, accounting for 62 per cent of the total variance.

Parents' attitudes towards the teaching of economics in kindergarten turned out to be rather positive: 96.7 per cent of the parents were in favour and 91.3 per cent thought that an economics programme should be continued throughout the rest of the grades. Some even mentioned that they were embarrassed to find out that their children knew more about economics than they did, encouraging them to increase their own knowledge. These findings and the general ignorance of children and adults concerning economic inter-dependencies and contexts seem to give clear evidence for the importance of economic education as early as possible.

Fox (1978), however, challenged the view that 'any topic can be taught effectively in some intellectually honest form at any stage of development'. She cited three things that children already possess (knapsack) when going to school: economic attitudes ('parent tapes' and proverbs), unprocessed direct experience (for example, shopping trips) and cognitive capacities (level of cognitive development). Fox saw difficulties in formal teaching of economic concepts to children who are, for instance, unable to understand the transaction of economic exchange in a shop. She warned that 'The fact that kindergarten children can learn economic terms is not compelling evidence that the concepts underlying those terms are in fact understood.' Instead, she pleaded for the use of direct experience as a basis for economic education in primary school and suggested that teachers use everyday situations of economic behaviour in the classroom to help children make sense of what they already know, always considering the level of the child's cognitive abilities. This contradicts Kourilsky's findings that children are to some extent able to master concepts that psychologically they are considered too young to learn. This contradiction might be an indication that Piaget's stages of general cognitive development, originally 'trying to explain the way that the individual represents physical reality', can simply be transferred into economics without any alteration.

Webley (1983) pointed out that, 'Since we learn about some aspects of the economic world mainly by actually engaging in the behaviour and not, as with the physical world, in two ways – both directly and didactically via the mediation of others – the nature of the construction may be different.'

In the *Journal of Economic Education*, solely dedicated to research into the teaching of economics, Davidson and Kilgore (1971) presented a model for evaluating the effectiveness of economic education in primary grades. 504 second grade pupils (6 to 7 years) in 24 classes from different socioeconomic backgrounds were subjects in one control and two different experimental groups. Pupils in the control group were taught their regular social studies curriculum, the first experimental group was taught with 'The Child's World of Choices' materials and the teachers in the second experimental group additionally received in-service training. Analysis showed that both experimental groups scored significantly higher results on the post Primary Test of Economic Understanding (PTEU) than the control group, but no experimental method proved to be superior. Pupils from a lower socioeconomic background (target schools) scored significantly lower on both PTEU pre and post tests than pupils from non-target schools. It could thus be concluded that elementary grade children can be taught basic economic concepts and growth in understanding them can be measured. Specially designed material prompted the pupils' growth in understanding but an additional full-scale programme in economic education for teachers did not have any significant effects on pupils' advancement.

As to the 'how' of teaching of economics concepts to children, Waite (1988) suggested that the child must be the centre of activity, as case studies have shown that the acceleration of children's conceptual understanding can be achieved using a number of different strategies. Since the child's economic awareness is acquired through information channels outside the classroom, case studies seem to be a good way of teaching children about the economy. Ramsett (1972) also suggested shying away from the traditional lecture approach and using daily life classroom events which are either directly or indirectly relevant to economics as a basis for further discussion and explanation. For example, if a pupil's family has to move away because his mother or father has accepted a new job, the teacher could take this opportunity to discuss employment, incomes, dependencies and so on.

More recently, Chizmar and Halinski (1983) described the impact of 'Trade-offs', a special series of television and film programmes designed to teach economics in elementary school, on the performance in the Basic Economic Test (BET). The results indicated that (1) as the number of weeks of instruction increased, the rate of increase in student score was significantly greater for students using 'Trade-offs'; (2) there were no sex differences in scores for students using 'Trade-offs', whereas for those being instructed traditionally gender was a statistically significant predictor of student score (girls outperforming boys). Furthermore, the grade level and teacher training (see also McKenzie, 1971; Walstad, 1979; Walstad and Watts, 1985) in economics were significant positive determinants of BET performance. These findings may indicate that gender differences here could possibly be attributed to the way instruction was given, as boys performed better under 'Trade-offs' than under traditional instruction. Under this premise it would be interesting to examine how sex differences found in other studies possibly could have been caused.

Hansen (1985), acknowledging that the teaching of economics to elementary school children has proved effective, demanded a firm installation of this subject in the curriculum of the primary grades. He briefly summarized the basic knowledge about children and economic education, which is as follows:

what happens in a child's early years – before the end of the primary years – has lasting effects into adulthood; children enter kindergarten possessing an experience-based economic literacy; children can acquire economic concepts and can do so earlier than previously thought; a variety of economic materials and teaching approaches are both available and effective; evaluation procedures are available, and new ones are being established even though they need continued refinement; economic education programmes show greater student gains where teachers are well versed in economics.

At present the apparent opportunity cost of economics (teaching and testing of reading and mathematics which still have top priority before any other subjects in today's primary schools) is still deemed too high to introduce economics into primary schools. If economics was not considered as a subject to be studied on its own, competing with other subjects in the curriculum, but rather being experienced in connection with already existing subjects such as mathematics (case studies), this problem could be avoided. These topics are examined in the present volume by Lassarre (France) and by Walstad (USA).

CONCLUSION

This review of literature on the economic socialization of children has tried to review research on the sociopolitical and economic thinking of children and adolescents. It appears that already at a pre-school age (before six years old) although most economic events are still simply observed and accepted as a mere ritual, through shopping trips with their parents, school games and television advertisements children begin to have a rudimentary economic understanding. With increasing age, growing experience of money, exposure to television and interaction with their peers, children gradually come to understand more of the economic life they encounter and start becoming consumers themselves.

Although researchers do not agree on the number of stages, points of transition and exact nature of the understanding at each stage, there seems to be basic agreement that children do advance through stages or phases in their understanding. However, there is also evidence that there are certain factors which have great influence on the speed with which the transition from one stage to the next takes place. These factors (such as experience in the use of money and exposure to the economic world in general, parental practice, social class and economics instruction in school) need further examination in order to find out – although the process of separation is difficult – which factor influences which concept, how and at what stage, so that it might be possible to discover how economic and political ideas and behaviours are established. Additionally, children's attitudes and understanding of yet more and other economic, political and historical concepts (such as debt, betting, exchange rates and interest rates) merit examination to gain a full understanding of the child's economic socialization.

NOTE

1. Parts of this chapter have appeared in Lewis, A., Webley, P. and Funham, A. (1995), *The New Economic Mind*, Hemel Hempstead: Harvester Wheatsheaf; and Carretero, M. and Voss, J. (eds) (1994), *Cognitive and Instructional Processes in History and the Social Science*, Hillsdale, New Jersey: LEA.

REFERENCES

Abromavitch, R., Freedman, J.L. and Pliner, P. (1991), Children and money: Getting an allowance, credit versus cash, and knowledge of pricing', *Journal of Economic Psychology*, **12**, 27–45.

Berti, A.E. and Bombi, A.S. (1979), 'Where does money come from?', *Archivio di Psicologia*, **40**, 53–77.

Berti, A.E. and Bombi, A.S. (1981), 'The development of the concept of money and its value: A longitudinal study', *Child Development*, **52**, 1179–82.

Berti, A.E. and Bombi, A.S. (1988), *The Child's Construction of Economics*, Cambridge: Cambridge University Press.

Berti, A.E., Bombi, A.S. and De Beni, R. (1986), 'Acquiring economic notions: Profit', *International Journal of Behavioural Development*, **9**, 15–29.

Berti, A.E, Bombi, A.S. and Lis, A. (1982), 'The child's conceptions about means of production and their owners', *European Journal of Social Psychology*, **12**, 221–39.

Burgard, P., Cheyne, W. and Jahoda, G. (1989), 'Children's representations of economic inequality: A replication', *British Journal of Developmental Psychology*, **7**, 275–87.

Burris, V. (1983), 'Stages in the Development of Economic Concepts', *Human Relations*, **36**, 791–812.

Chizmar, J. and Halinski, R. (1983), 'Performance in the Basic Economic Test (BET) and "Trade-offs"', *The Journal of Economic Education*, **14**, 18–29.

Cram, F. and Ng, S. (1989), 'Children's endorsement of ownership attributes', *Journal of Economic Psychology*, **10**, 63–75.

Cummings, S. and Taebel, D. (1978), 'The economic socialization of children: A neo-Marxist analysis', *Social Problems*, **26** (2), 198–210.

Danziger, K. (1958), 'Children's earliest conceptions of economic relationships', *The Journal of Social Psychology*, **47**, 231–40.

Davidson, D. and Kilgore, J. (1971). A model for evaluating the effectiveness of economic education in primary grades, *The Journal of Economic Education*, **3**, 17–25.

Emler, N. and Dickinson, J. (1985), 'Children's representations of economic inequalities: The effects of social class', *British Journal of Developmental Psychology*, **3**, 191–8.

Fox, K. (1978), 'What children bring to school: The beginnings of economic education', *Social Education*, **10**, 478–81.

Furby, L. (1978), 'Possessions in humans: An exploratory study of its meaning and innovation', *Social Behaviour and Personality*, **6**, 49–65.

Furby, L. (1980a), 'Collective possession and ownership: A study of its judged feasibility and desirability', *Social Behaviour and Personality*, **8**, 165–84.

Furby, L. (1980b), 'The origins and early development of possessive behaviour', *Political Psychology*, **2**, 30–42.

Furnham, A. (1982), 'The perception of poverty among adolescents', *Journal of Adolescence*, **5**, 135–47.

Furnham, A. (1987), 'The determinants and structure of adolescents' beliefs about the economy', *Journal of Adolescence*, **10**, 353–71.

Furnham, A. and Cleare, A. (1988), 'School children's conceptions of economics: prices, wages, investments and strikes', *Journal of Economic Psychology*, **9**, 467–79.

Furnham, A. and Jones, S. (1987), 'Children's views regarding possessions and their theft', *Journal of Moral Education*, **16**, 18–30.

Furnham, A. and Stacey, B. (1991), *Young People's Understanding of Society*, London: Routledge.

Furth, H. (1980), *The World of Grown-Ups*, New York: Elsevier.

Furth, H., Baur, M. and Smith, J. (1976), 'Children's conception of social institutions: a Piagetian framework', *Human Development*, **19**, 341–7.

Hansen, H. (1985), 'The economics of early childhood education in Minnesota', *The Journal of Economic Education*, **16**, 219–24.

Haste, H. and Torney-Purta, J. (1992), *The Development of Political Understanding*, San Francisco: Jossey-Bass.

Irving, K. and Siegal, M. (1983), 'Mitigating circumstances in children's perceptions of criminal justice', *British Journal of Developmental Psychology*, **1**, 179–88.

Jahoda, G. (1979), 'The construction of economic reality by some Glaswegian children', *European Journal of Social Psychology*, **9**, 115–27.

Jahoda, G. (1981), 'The development of thinking about economic institutions: The bank', *Cahiers de Psychologie Cognitive*, **1**, 55–73.

Kourilsky, M. (1977), 'The kinder-economy: a case study of kindergarten pupils' acquisition of economic concepts', *The Elementary School Journal*, **77**, 182–91.

Kourilsky, M. (1984), 'Sex differences in a simulated classroom economy: Children's beliefs about entrepreneurship', *Sex Roles*, **10**, 53–66.

Kourilsky, M. and Campbell, M. (1984), 'Sex differences in a simulated classroom economy: Children's beliefs about entrepreneurship', *Sex Roles*, **10**, 53–66.

Leahy, R. (1981), 'The development of the conception of economic inequality. I. Descriptions and comparisons of rich and poor people', *Child Development*, **52**, 523–32.

Leiser, D. (1983), 'Children's conceptions of economics – the constitution of the cognitive domain', *Journal of Economic Psychology*, **4**, 297–317.

Leiser, D., Sevon, G. and Levy, D. (1990), 'Children's economic socialization of ten countries', *Journal of Economic Psychology*, **11**, 591–614.

McKenzie, R. (1971), 'An exploratory study of the economic understanding of elementary school teachers', *The Journal of Economic Education*, **3**, 26–31.

Ng, S. (1983), 'Children's ideas about the bank and shop profit: development, stages and the influence of cognitive contrasts and conflicts', *Journal of Economic Psychology*, **4**, 209–21.

Ng, S. (1985), 'Children's ideas about the bank: a New Zealand replication', *European Journal of Social Psychology*, **15**, 121–3.

O'Brien, M. and Ingels, S. (1985), 'The effects of economics instruction in early adolescence', *Theory and Research in Social Education*, **4**, 279–94.

O'Brien, M. and Ingels, S. (1987), 'The economic values inventory', *Research in Economic Education*, **18**, 7–18.

Pollio, H. and Gray, R (1973), 'Change-making strategies in children and adults', *The Journal of Psychology*, **84**, 173–9.

Ramsett, D. (1972), 'Toward improving economic education in the elementary grades', *The Journal of Economic Education*, **4**, 30–35.

Schug, M. and Birkey, C. (1985), 'The development of children's economic reasoning', paper presented at the annual meeting of the American Educational Research Association, Chicago.

Sevon, G. and Weckstrom, S. (1989), 'The development of reasoning about economic events: A study of Finnish children', *Journal of Economic Psychology*, **10**, 495–514.

Stacey, B. and Singer, M. (1985), 'The perception of poverty and wealth among teenagers', *Journal of Adolescence*, **8**, 231–41.

Strauss, A. (1952), 'The development and transformation of monetary meaning in the child', *American Sociological Review*, **53**, 275–86.

Sutton, R. (1962), 'Behaviour in the attainment of economic concepts', *The Journal of Psychology*, **53**, 37–46.

Walstad, W. (1979), 'Effectiveness of a USMES in service economic education program for elementary school teachers', *The Journal of Economic Education*, **11**, 1–12.

Walstad, W. and Watts, M. (1985), 'Teaching economics in schools: A review of survey findings', *The Journal of Economic Education*, **16**, 135–46.

Webley, P. (1983), 'Growing up in the modern economy', paper presented at the 6th International Conference on Political Psychology.

Whitehead, D. (1986), 'Students' Attitudes to Economic Issues', *Economics*, Spring, 24–32.

Winocur, S. and Siegal, M. (1982), 'Adolescents' judgements of economic arrangements', *International Journal of Behavioural Development*, **5**, 357–65.

Wosinski, M. and Pietras, M. (1990), 'Economic socialization of Polish children in different macro-economic conditions', *Journal of Economic Psychology*, **11**, 515–29.

Zinser, O., Perry, S. and Edgar, R. (1975), 'Affluence of the recipient, value of donations, and sharing behaviour in preschool children', *The Journal of Psychology*, **89**, 301–5.

3. Children as consumers: in the laboratory and beyond

Patricia Pliner, Jonathan Freedman, Rona Abramovitch and Peter Darke

Fairly recently, Ward (1974) introduced the notion of consumer socialization, 'the process by which young people acquire skills, knowledge, and attitudes relevant to their effective functioning as consumers in the marketplace'. In this area, there has been a strong assumption that the family is instrumental in teaching children basic rational aspects of consumption (Parsons *et al.*, 1953; Riesman and Roseborough, 1955). Parents have general consumer goals for their children which include their learning to shop for quality products (Ward *et al.*, 1977), learning price–quality relationships (Moschis, 1987) and learning to save money for anticipatory consumption (Moore and Moschis, 1978). Studies examining consumer skills in adolescents have assessed knowledge of prices of selected products (Moore and Stephens, 1975), facility at money management and comparative shopping (Moschis, 1976, cited in Moschis, 1985), tendency to use price reduction (sales) as a criterion for choosing among brands (Moschis and Moore, 1980), proficiency at distinguishing facts from exaggerations in advertisements (Moschis, 1984, cited in Moschis, 1987) and ability to calculate risk associated with a specific consumer decision (Moschis and Moore, 1979, cited in Moschis, 1987).

Less attention has been paid to the consumer skills of younger children, although it is clear that they too have the opportunity to purchase. For example, a recent survey by McNeal (1987) revealed that, by age 7, 100 per cent of a sample of US children had made independent purchases while shopping with parents and 80 per cent had made independent shopping trips to stores. In an early study of consumer skills, Marshall and Magruder (1960) found children as young as 7 to be fairly accurate at pricing small dimestore objects and 12-year-olds to be almost perfectly accurate. Ward *et al.* (1977) examined the 'money use norms' of children ranging in age from 5 to 11, finding that about a third of the youngest and about two-thirds of the oldest endorsed long-term saving and similar proportions eschewed 'wasting' money.

Thus it is clear that even young children have acquired some of the consumer skills which their parents have as goals for them.

Although it seems obvious that the acquisition of such skills must be the result of socialization practices, the nature of the training which occurs is unclear. Several studies have shown that greater participation in economic activity is related to greater economic maturity (Jahoda, 1983; Marshall and Magruder, 1960; Ng, 1983). One means by which parents enable such participation is by the giving of pocket money or allowances. There has been considerable discussion in the literature of the consequences for economic socialization of the terms on which pocket money is given; that is, whether it is given as a non-contingent allowance or explicitly as payment for chores. Zelizer (1985) describes changes over time in attitudes towards the two practices. The early accepted view was that children's pocket money should be in the form of payment for chores, not as an allowance, which was denounced by one writer as 'one of the keys to that lack of adult responsibility about money which is widely deplored' (Furnham and Thomas, 1984a). However, by the 1950s, giving money to children was thought to have a much broader educational value, and the preferred way of providing children with spending money became an allowance that was not tied to work. Since then, many popular publications (for example, Briggs and Sullivan, 1955; Davis and Taylor, 1979; King, 1953) have advised parents to give children allowances to teach them about money. In the only empirical tests of the efficacy of allowance as a tutorial device, Marshall, (1964) Marshall and Magruder (1960) found few differences between those receiving an allowance and those not; however, among the youngest subjects, receiving an allowance was positively related to knowledge of prices.

Although there is little empirical confirmation of the more current recommendation, we believed that there might indeed be an advantage in giving an allowance rather than payment for chores. We reasoned that receiving an allowance implies a great deal of trust and gives children the implicit message that they must learn how to deal responsibly with money. Therefore children who receive allowances may feel more responsibility for the money they receive, may make greater efforts to deal with it, and may accordingly become more knowledgeable and sophisticated about money and its expenditure. In contrast, when children are given money for chores, the focus is on the work. Once they have done it, the money they receive is theirs to do with as they want. In a sense, it is given with fewer 'strings attached' than an allowance and may, as a result, occasion less learning on the part of the child. Thus we expected children who received an allowance to be more mature consumers than those who did not.

This chapter reports the results of some of our work on children's consumer behaviour. We will describe several studies in which children were able to display aspects of their consumer skills by reporting the prices of familiar objects, by choosing gifts varying in value, and by making hypothetical consumer decisions. These studies were conducted outside the laboratory in various local schools. We will also briefly report the results of two laboratory studies in which children received four dollars and were permitted to spend it (or not) in our experimental store. In all of the studies, we obtained information about parental practices related to the giving of pocket money.

SCHOOL STUDIES

We conducted a series of studies at grade schools in a socioeconomically diverse suburban area near Toronto, testing approximately equal numbers of boys and girls, ranging in age from 6 to 10. After obtaining the appropriate official approval to recruit subjects, we sent letters to parents, requesting permission for their children's participation. In addition, we asked consenting parents to fill out a brief questionnaire with items pertaining to whether the child received pocket money and, if so, on what terms it was given (for example, as an allowance, as payment for chores). In the questionnaire sent to parents we also asked for family income (as a marker for socioeconomic status – SES), since there is evidence that there are some differences in money use norms (Ward *et al.*, 1977), saving practices (Furnham and Thomas, 1984b) and amount of money available (Newson and Newson, 1976; Ward *et al.*, 1977) in children differing in social class.

The children, whose assent to participate was also obtained, were tested individually in their schools. The studies were conducted in several schools, with different grades, different numbers of subjects and different procedures in each. For simplicity, we will describe the findings along with the procedures.

Knowledge of Prices

We presented 250 8–10-year-old children with pictures of 16 common items, identified them (in case the children did not recognize them) and asked what they would cost in a store. The items ranged from inexpensive ones such as a pencil and a hamburger to much more expensive ones such as running shoes and a television set. Actual prices for the items were placed a priori into plausible categories ($0.01 to $1.00, $1.00 to $10.00, $10 to $100, and $100 to $1000) and responses were scored as correct if they fell into the appropriate category. Responses on the overlapping boundaries ($1.00, $10.00, $100.00) were counted as correct in either of the two adjacent categories.

Thus, for example, $1.00 was counted as correct for a pencil (an item we placed in the $.01 to $1.00 category) and for a hamburger (an item we placed in the $1.00 to $10.00 category). The children were quite knowledgeable, obtaining an average score of almost 11 correct out of 16. As expected, older children were more accurate (*Mean* (youngest) = 8.19, *Mean* (middle) = 11.19, *Mean* (oldest) = 12.26; $F(2, 248) = 61.40$, $p < 0.001$). However, no other variable was related to knowledge of pricing. Whether the children received allowances, were paid for chores, came from families with high or low incomes, or were male or female had no appreciable effects on their scores.

Price–Value Relationship

Given that the children were fairly good at pricing items, we wondered if they were aware of the general rule that items that cost more are of greater value in that they are more desirable or of higher quality. We know, of course, that this rule does not always hold in the world of commerce, but if one has nothing else to go on, it is probably a good rule of thumb. Moreover, it is one of the basic rules of exchange that are assumed by all economists and by those who study consumer behaviour. It seems fair to say that, to function effectively as a consumer, one must understand this relationship between price and value.

We assessed the children's understanding of this rule by offering them a gift for helping us. We showed them three small puzzles (the kind in which one must get small balls into the right holes by tilting a box). The puzzles were essentially identical, except that they were different colours and had slightly different formats. On each puzzle we marked its ostensible price – $1, $2 or $3 – counterbalancing both price and position of puzzles (for example, the blue puzzle was marked with each price and was in the left, right, and centre positions of the array an equal number of times). The children simply chose the puzzle they wanted as their gift. We assumed that in making their decisions the children would have little to go on except the price, since the puzzles were otherwise (in our view) basically identical. Thus, if they understood the economic 'price = value' rule, they should hold a preference for the more expensive and, therefore, presumably, higher quality puzzle. This procedure was conducted with only 64 children, and the numbers of choices were $1 – 15, $2 – 26, and $3 – 23, a distribution which does not differ from chance. There were no age, gender, SES, or allowance effects. On the basis of these results, we might argue that the children had no understanding of the price–value relationship since they did not choose the most expensive of the otherwise identical puzzles. However, closer examination of the data reveals that the children did not consider the puzzles to be identical;

rather, they had very specific preferences among the three different puzzles, choosing as follows: yellow – 9, blue – 24, red – 31, $X^2(2) = 11.84$, $p < 0.01$. Thus it is possible that differences in the perceived desirability of the particular puzzles overwhelmed any other differences in value signalled by the differing prices. In any event, whatever else they know about economics, the children do know that 'red is best'.

In order to pursue the price = value issue, we changed our strategy slightly, deciding not to rely on our judgement as to what objects would be 'essentially identical' in the children's view. We offered another group of children the opportunity to choose a present in return for their participation. They were shown three truly identical yellow boxes, each containing a gift and clearly marked with a \$1, \$2 or \$3 price tag. Prices were counterbalanced over positions in the array. The children varied widely in age, from 5 to 12. This time, the children indicated their clear understanding of the price = value rule. Of the 132 children, 83 (63 per cent) chose the most expensive box and only 13 (10 per cent) chose the cheapest one, $X^2(2) = 50.04$, $p < 0.0001$. When asked why they had made their particular choices, they verbalized the rule quite explicitly and succinctly, making such comments as 'When things are expensive, they're good', 'Expensive stuff is better than cheap stuff', 'The more expensive, the better they are', and 'If you pick the one that's more expensive, it's better quality than the cheaper ones.' When we divided the children into three age groups (5–7, 8–9, 10–12) and examined choices, we found a highly significant effect of age, $X^2(4) = 13.05$, $p < 0.01$. Surprisingly, although all three groups were more likely to pick the \$3 box than either of the other two, it was the intermediate group which showed this effect the most strongly, 76 per cent of the children doing so, as compared to 50 per cent and 61 per cent in the youngest and oldest groups, respectively. Examination of the children's comments revealed why this happened. Several in the oldest group, after choosing the \$2 box, made comments such as 'When you get a gift, you shouldn't take the most expensive one – just be happy with a gift' or 'It's not very nice to be greedy.' That such children clearly recognized the price = value rule comes across especially clearly in the comment of a 10-year-old, who chose the \$2 gift, saying, 'If I could be selfish, I would take the \$3 one because it is worth more.' Thus, interestingly, in the oldest group a social motive appeared to overpower the 'rule of greed' that predominates in traditional economic theories. There were no effects of allowance, chores, gender or family income on choices.

Spotting a Bargain

Our next study assessed the same children's ability to take advantage of a bargain in a simulated buying situation by telling them that they were going to go on a make-believe shopping trip. We gave them ten big cardboard 'dollars' and showed them an array of 12 attractive items (erasers, rubber balls, pencil sharpeners, slinkies, games and so on), each with a price ranging from $1 to $4. The prices were reasonable in the sense that the items that would ordinarily be more expensive had the higher prices. There was one twist. We carefully selected items that fell into six groups of two, with the members of a pair being quite similar (for example, a large colourful rubber ball and a small plastic 'superball'; a purple and a metal slinky). Within each pair, and within each price range, one item was assigned a low price and the other a high price (for example, one ball cost $1 and the other $2; one slinky cost $3 and the other $4). Which item was assigned which price was counter-balanced across children. Assuming that, within each pair, the items were equally attractive (and, this time, we had some pre-test data supporting our assumption), one was a bargain in comparison to the other. The children were told to pretend that they had the $10 to spend and to choose which items they would buy. They knew that they would not actually keep the items, but they seemed to take the task quite seriously.

We analysed their choices in terms of whether they chose the lower or higher priced item from a pair. In other words, their scores were based on how many $1 and $3 items they picked, compared to the number of $2 and $4 items. The results were impressive. They chose an average of 2.5 cheaper and 1.2 dearer items, $t(64) = 5.47$, $p < 0.001$. Somewhat surprisingly, there was no effect of age on these preferences, nor was there any effect of any of the other variables, including allowance, SES or gender.

Taken together, the results of these three studies indicate that children as young as five years of age have attained some level of consumer skill. They are reasonably knowledgeable about the prices of common objects, have some appreciation of price–value relationships and can identify a bargain. Although we obtained age effects on the pricing and gift choice tasks, we found no evidence for the effects of allowance, SES or gender in any of the studies.

EXPERIMENTAL STUDIES

The experimental studies were conducted in the context of a laboratory store designed to simulate a commercial toy store. The merchandise, displayed as in such an establishment, included toys, games, model cars, animals, dolls, erasers, books, stickers, and other typical items but excluded guns and food. The subjects were children ranging in age from six to ten, residing in the same suburban area as those in the school studies.

While the children were participating, we interviewed their mothers about their children's pocket money and other aspects of their own economic socialization practices. From these interviews we derived a set of variables, three of which were common to both studies: how much spending money the child had received that week from all sources; whether or not the child received a regular allowance; and whether or not the child was paid for doing chores. The last two were separate variables, since a child could be classified as 'yes' on either, both or neither. In the first experiment we also obtained a measure of the mother's maturity expectations for the child by averaging the minimum age at which she believed a child should be able to accomplish a number of activities alone (for example, crossing the street, caring for a younger child). In addition, in that study we also obtained from the child a measure of mathematics ability and information about knowledge of credit. In the second experiment we obtained from the mothers a measure of economic maturity expectations, similar to the measure described above but involving economic activities (for example, going to the store to purchase a small item and returning with the correct item and change). Factor analysing a set of items pertaining to the mothers' reports of their behaviour in consumer situations, we also derived a measure of gentle consumer guidance ('Talk to him/her about how to shop carefully', 'Suggest two or three products you think are all reasonably good and then let your child make the final decision' and so on) and heavy-handed consumer guidance (for example, 'Tell your child what to buy with his/her money', 'Complain to your child about something he/she has bought'). We examined the effects of these 'background' variables, as well as age, gender and our experimental manipulations (to be described below) on the children's behaviour in our laboratory store.

Experiment 1

In the first study, we assessed 6-, 8- and 10-year-old girls' and boys' spending in the laboratory store as a function of the form in which they were given the money to spend. The children could spend up to $4 but half were given cash and the remainder received an actual credit card with $4 of credit. All were told that any money or credit not spent in the store would be given to them in cash to take home. The results of this study revealed that, as predicted, children who received an allowance (as opposed to those who received no pocket money, were paid for chores or received their pocket money by some other means) showed a more sophisticated understanding of the essential similarity between paying for consumer goods with cash and with a credit card. That is, allowance children spent the same amount in the two conditions, while children who did not receive an allowance spent significantly more when they received their spending money in the form of credit (rather than cash) (interaction $p < 0.05$). In addition, girls spent more than boys ($p <$

0.01). When we examined the effects of other variables (age, how much money the child had available on a weekly basis, how much they knew about credit, their mothers' maturity expectations, and their mathematics scores, standardized within age), none produced a main effect or, more importantly, interacted with the cash–credit manipulation, to determine spending. Notably, there were no effects of the chores variable.

We also tested the children on the same pricing task that we used in the school studies. The results revealed significant effects of both age ($p < 0.001$) and allowance ($p < 0.01$); older children and those receiving an allowance were better at the pricing task. However, the variables also interacted significantly ($p < 0.02$), reflecting the fact that the allowance effect was largest in the youngest children and disappeared completely in the oldest. Of the other variables, only mathematics ability was related to knowledge of prices; children who scored higher on the maths test in comparison to other children of their age were more knowledgeable.

Experiment 2

In the second study we examined the effects of two experimental manipulations on the spending behaviour of 8-, 9- and 10-year-old girls and b₂ 's. First, we were interested in one of the consumer goals which parents have for their children: namely, learning to shop for quality products (Ward *et al.*, 1977). In our earlier research, one of the mothers' most common specific complaints about their children's consumer behaviour involved their 'inability' not to spend if they had money available even if there were nothing but 'junky' things available to buy. In this study, we manipulated the relative attractiveness of the items available for sale by creating two versions of the store, an attractive version and an unattractive version. To produce these versions, we examined our records to determine which items in the store had been most popular with children of comparable ages in two previous studies. These items, which included books, as well as several wind-up toys, hackey sacks, marbles, erasers, games and other objects, constituted the merchandise in the attractive store. The items which had been least popular in the previous studies were used to construct the unattractive store. We were careful to ensure that the distribution of prices was the same in the two stores, and we attempted to include equal numbers of male-oriented, female-oriented and gender-neutral items in the two stores.

The second manipulation was motivated by the seemingly common belief that 'money obtained by actually working for it is more highly prized by the child than is money simply given to him' (Sherman, 1986, p. 125). Accordingly, some subjects were offered $4 if they would clean up a 'mess made by some children who were here before', consisting of scraps of construction paper and coloured paper clips, thickly scattered over an area of four square metres. All did so and were then praised for the 'good job' and the large amount of work they had done. The remainder of the subjects were given $4 (explicitly) as a present with the explanation that 'We always give kids presents when they come here.'

We expected that children would spend less money in the unattractive store than in the attractive store, but that this would occur primarily when the money had been worked for (and was, presumably, highly prized) rather than when it had been essentially a windfall. We were also interested, as before, in the mediating effects of the economic socialization background variables described above.

Discussion

We found, first, a significant main effect of store condition: children spent more money in the attractive store than in the unattractive one ($p < 0.05$). In addition, as in the first study, whether or not the child received an allowance interacted with the manipulated variables to produce differences in spending behaviour. The results revealed that children who received an allowance and worked for their money in the laboratory spent much less in the unattractive (as opposed to the attractive) store ($p < 0.05$), while none of the other attractive–unattractive store comparisons was significant. Thus, as in the first study, children who receive an allowance appear to be more sophisticated about money (this time, more able to resist the lure of junk) than those who do not. There was also a sex effect similar to that in the first study, girls spending more than boys ($p < 0.01$).

In this study, unlike the first, several of the other economic socialization background variables also appeared to have an effect on the children's spending behaviour. Those who received gentle guidance and those whose mothers had high economic expectations for them (subjects were classified as above or below the median on these variables) behaved in the same way as children who received an allowance. That is, if they had worked for their money, they spent less in the unattractive (as opposed to the attractive) store (both $ps < 0.05$). Interestingly, the chores variable, in interaction with store attractiveness, also had an effect on spending ($p < 0.05$). Children who were paid at home for doing chores did *not* discriminate between the attractive and unattractive stores; those who were not paid for chores did do so.

Thus the two variables reflecting the means by which children most typically receive their pocket money show opposite results. Children who receive an allowance (at least when they have worked for their money in the immediate situation) are sensitive to the attractiveness manipulation – they appear to be wise consumers who do not 'throw away' their money on 'junky' things. In contrast, children who receive money at home for doing chores appear to be more susceptible than those who do not to the lure of junk. This would seem to indicate that receiving an allowance is related to 'good' consumer behaviour while being paid for doing chores is related to 'bad' consumer behaviour.

The results of these two studies are consistent with our initial theorizing about the effects of receiving an allowance and being paid for chores. We suggested that receiving an allowance implies a considerable trust and gives children the implicit message that they must learn how to deal with money. In both studies, children who received an allowance showed more mature or sophisticated behaviour. In the first, they correctly recognized the essential equivalence of cash and credit in the experimental situation and behaved accordingly. In the second, they responded appropriately to a situation in which the wise consumer decision was not to spend. In contrast, we argued that in giving money for chores the focus is on the work – the money is given with fewer 'strings attached' and with less communication of trust and expectations of responsibility than an allowance. And in the second experiment, children who were paid for chores at home actually showed less mature consumer behaviour than those who were not. Why the allowance and chores variables did not appear to affect children's behaviour in the school studies we do not know; however, we are inclined to take them less seriously than the laboratory studies, which were obviously much better controlled and examined behaviour in a much more realistic consumer situation.

It is perhaps worthy of note that in one of our two pricing studies (the one conducted in the schools) we found no effect of allowance, while in the other (conducted in the laboratory) we found an allowance by age interaction. However, in the former, the youngest group of children was 8 years old, and in the latter the allowance effect was most apparent in the 6-year-olds and was not significant for 8-year-olds. Marshall and Magruder (1960) found that 7-year-olds, but not older children, who received an allowance were more knowledgeable about prices than those who did not. Thus it may be that knowing prices is such a simple task that receiving an allowance confers an advantage only among very young children.

On the basis of the results of the second laboratory experiment, we would like to extend our line of argument regarding the importance of parental communication via economic socialization practices by suggesting that parents communicate trust and expectations of responsibility in other ways as well. Neither gentle guidance nor high economic expectations was related to the allowance variable. However, both were related to consumer behaviour in the same way as receiving an allowance, and both would also seem to be expressions of parental trust and expectations of responsibility. Indeed, the item which loaded most heavily on the gentle guidance factor ('Suggest two or three products you think are all reasonably good and then let your child make the final decision') almost epitomizes the notions of communication of trust and expectation of responsibility. Similarly, the belief that one's child should be able to conduct various economic transactions at a relatively early age implies trust and expectation of responsibility. Thus the means by which parents communicate these important ideas may vary from family to family, but their communication is related to mature consumer behaviour on the part of the children.

Our discussion so far has implied that it is the socialization practices of parents which produce the differences in consumer behaviour we have seen in the laboratory and that these differences are indicative of greater maturity or consumer ability on the part of some children. We do recognize, however, that it is not possible to be certain of the direction of causality. Another interpretation which is consistent with the data is that the parents of children who have displayed greater maturity or consumer ability use socialization techniques that accord with their observations of their children's behaviour. That is, parents who correctly perceive their children to be good consumers may give an allowance (with the trust and high expectations it implies), not pay their children for chores, use gentle guidance and have higher economic expectations than those who perceive their children to be bad consumers. However, we are inclined to favour our original interpretation. As we noted in our first study, 'When asked why they give allowances, most parents are quite clear on the reasons and they have little to do with the qualities of their own children' (Abramovitch *et al.*, 1991, p. 42). Clearly, only a study in which parental socialization practices were manipulated would be capable of resolving this issue.

NOTE

The research reported in this chapter was funded by grants from the Social Sciences and Humanities Research Council of Canada to the first three authors.

REFERENCES

Abramovitch, R., Freedman, J.L. and Pliner, P. (1991), 'Children and money: Getting an allowance, credit versus cash, and knowledge of pricing', *Journal of Economic Psychology*, **12**, 27–45.

Briggs, M. and Sullivan, C.M. (1955), 'Your child and his money', *Agriculture and Home Economic Circular No. 741*, University of Illinois.

Davis, K. and Taylor, T. (1979), *Kids and cash: Solving a parent's dilemma*, La Jolla, Cal.: Oak Tree.

Furnham, A. and Thomas, P. (1984a), 'Adults' perception of the economic socialization of children', *Journal of Adolescence*, **7**, 217–31.

Furnham, A. and Thomas, P. (1984b), 'Pocket money: A study of economic education', *British Journal of Developmental Psychology*, **2**, 205–12.

Jahoda, G. (1983), 'European "lag" in the development of an economic concept: A study in Zimbabwe', *British Journal of Developmental Psychology*, **2**, 110–20.

King, M.B. (1953). *Money Managements: Children's spending*, Chicago, Ill.: Household Finance Corp.

Marshall, H. (1964), 'The relations of giving children an allowance to children's money knowledge and responsibility and to other practices of parents', *The Journal of Genetic Psychology*, **104**, 35–51.

Marshall, H. and Magruder, L. (1960), 'Relations between parent money education practices and children's knowledge and use of money', *Child Development*, **31**, 253–84.

McNeal, J.U. (1987), *Children as Consumers: Issues and Implications*, Lexington, Mass.: Lexington Books.

Moore, R.L. and Moschis, G.P. (1978), 'Teenagers' reactions to advertising', *Journal of Advertising*, **7**, 24–30.

Moore, R.L. and Stephens, L.F. (1975), 'Some communication and demographic determinants of adolescent consumer learning', *Journal of Consumer Research*, **2**, 80–92.

Moschis, G.P. (1984), 'A longitudinal study of consumer socialization', in M. Ryan (ed.), *Proceedings of the American Marketing Association Theory Conference*, Chicago, Ill.: American Marketing Association.

Moschis, G.P. (1985), 'The role of family communication in consumer socialization of children and adolescents', *Journal of Consumer Research*, **11**, 898–913.

Moschis, G.P. (1987), *Consumer socialization: A life-cycle perspective*, Lexington, Mass.: Lexington Books.

Moschis, G.P. and Moore, R.L. (1979), 'Decision making among the young: A socialization perspective', *Journal of Consumer Research*, **6**, 101–12.

Moschis, G.P. and Moore, R.L. (1980), 'Purchasing behavior of adolescent consumers', in R.P. Bagozzi, K.L. Bernhardt, P.S. Busch, D.W. Cravens, J.F. Hair and C.A. Scott (eds), *1980 AMA Educators Conference Proceedings*, Chicago, Ill.: American Marketing Association.

Newson, J. and Newson, E. (1976), *Seven Year Olds in the Home Environment*, London: George Allen and Unwin.

Ng, L. (1983), 'Children's ideas about the bank and shop profit: Development stages and the influence of cognitive contrasts and conflict', *Journal of Economic Psychology*, **4**, 209–21.

Parsons, T., Bales, R.F. and Shils, E.A. (1953), *Working Papers in the Theory of Action*, Glencoe, Ill.: The Free Press.

Riesman, D. and Roseborough, H. (1955), 'Careers and consumer behavior', in L. Clark (ed.), *Consumer behavior. Vol. 2: The life cycle and consumer behavior*, New York, NY: New York University Press, pp. 1–18.

Sherman, M. (1986), 'Children's allowances', *Medical Aspects of Human Sexuality*, **20**, 121–8.

Ward, S. (1974), 'Consumer socialization', *Journal of Consumer Research*, **1**, 1–16.

Ward, S., Wackman, D.B. and Wartella, E. (1977), *How Children Learn to Buy: The development of consumer information processing skills*, Beverly Hills, Cal.: Sage.

Zelizer, V.A. (1985), *Pricing the Priceless Child: The changing social value of children*, New York, NY: Basic Books.

4. Developing ideas about distribution of wealth

Julie Dickinson and Nicholas Emler

INTRODUCTION

Learning to live in the economic world entails learning to participate in a number of economic relationships: buying goods or services, earning interest on savings, investing in stocks and shares, selling produce, swapping property, paying taxes, borrowing money and working for a wage are all examples of everyday economic transactions in which, sooner or later, most of us will play economic roles. Preparation for some economic roles starts in early childhood, as, for instance, when young children play at being shopkeepers, handing over toy commodities in exchange for imaginary money. Other roles, such as the role of investor, may not be learned until late adolescence or adulthood. Indeed, many adults have only a hazy notion of the activities and exchanges involved in stockbroking.

In learning economic roles children learn the appropriate behaviour for participants in the exchanges that characterize economic relationships: in playing 'shops' they learn that the shopkeeper must state the price of goods to be sold and that the customer must give the shopkeeper the correct amount of money to purchase the goods, and later, perhaps through their own experience of savings accounts, they learn that, when a customer deposits money in a bank, the bank will add interest to that money at regular intervals and according to published interest rates. Along with the behavioural roles, children learn the legal and moral rules that govern economic transactions – they know that taking goods without paying for them counts as theft and that in most western countries it is not the done thing to haggle over the price of goods in shops – and the situations, sequences of events and monetary processes that characterize economic transactions. All this takes time to learn and children can understand some aspects of economic relationships without understanding others. For instance, Berti and Bombi (1988) found that 6–7-year-old children recognized that workers in a factory received money from the 'boss' in exchange for their labour but did not understand how the 'boss' obtained the money. They were likely to think that the 'boss' was independently rich or was given money by the government. Not until 10 or 11 years of age did they begin to grasp the relationship between profit and income.

Described like this, economic socialization seems to be the gradual, cumulative acquisition of a number of skills – not so dissimilar from learning to drive a car or to cook. The cultural differences in the rules and patterns of behaviour in economic exchanges, like the set pricing of goods in shops versus haggling in the market-place, appear to be insignificant traditions adopted by different nations just as we in Britain drive on the left or cook roast lunch on Sundays. The economic activities, as described, require technical knowledge, they appear apolitical and asocial. To some extent this is true; much of the knowledge required to participate in economic exchanges is technical in terms of knowing how to carry out specific, semi-legal transactions like buying or selling goods or understanding the economic processes that underlie economic institutions like the creation of profit or the determination of interest rates, but we would argue that this in itself is not a sufficient preparation for participation in the economic world. It is not sufficient because much of the knowledge required for engaging in, interpreting and predicting economic activity is highly ideological and socially differentiated.

For instance, shopping is an activity which requires technical skills like numeracy, budgeting and a knowledge of the format of the interaction between shopkeeper and customer, but the character of the role of shopper, and the nature and goals of the transaction, are shaped by the social identity of the shopper as a consumer. As consumers our shopping patterns, in terms of what we buy, where we shop and how much we spend are determined by our values, our social and personal needs, our life styles and, above all, by how much we earn. Moreover, consumer behaviour is interpreted, not in terms of the exercise of technical skills and knowledge, though it is possible to be noted for expertise as a wise and cautious shopper or someone with an eye for bargains, but in terms of personality, attitudes, social status, social group membership and income. Making sense of economic behaviour and economic relationships demands an understanding of social structure and socio-economic relationships between groups and, in this sense, draws on political and social knowledge.

The political and social nature of such knowledge can be best illustrated by looking at the main focus of this chapter – ideas about the distribution of wealth. Wealth is perhaps the most fundamental factor affecting participation in all kinds of economic relationships. In the most obvious way it affects the degree to which we can participate in many economic exchanges, though many of the limits imposed by lack of money may not be recognized by children. To a small child consumer behaviour appears to reflect simply choice and need (Jahoda, 1959; Furby, 1980). Naivety about the buying power of money probably reflects young children's poor understanding of the value and purpose of money (cf. Strauss, 1952; Berti and Bombi, 1981) and the tendency to think jobs and possessions are primarily an outcome of personal choice (Furby, 1980). Children can make more sense of consumer behaviour when they grasp that wealth is unequally distributed in society. However, their perceptions of the extent to which wealth is unequally distributed appear to be related to the position of their families within the socioeconomic structure. The present authors (Emler and Dickinson, 1985) found that working-class children provided significantly smaller estimates of wage differentials than middle-class children. In this sense economic knowledge is socially differentiated. The social processes which create economic knowledge will be discussed later in this chapter.

How is economic knowledge political? There are two aspects of the understanding of distribution of wealth that can be considered political. Firstly, wealth carries power, not just buying power but power over others in economic relationships. The most obvious example is that employers by virtue of their ability to award or withhold wages have power over the labour of their employees. Wealth also aids access to certain services such as bank loans: banks are more willing to provide credit to people with evidence of some financial security such as a mortgage, a steady, permanent job and disposable income. Furby (1980) has argued that, from the age of 7 years, possessions are seen as a means of enabling the owner to enjoy or do something, that is a means of enhancing control. By 15 to 16 years notions of power and status are attached to possessions, and possessions are seen as important for both defining relationships between people and expressing one's individuality. In this way children come to understand wealth, as the wherewithal of possessions, as indicative of power, status and control. Secondly, the distribution of wealth is a political issue in that it can be regarded as good or evil, a source of conflict and the substance of political debate. A knowledge of the political arguments surrounding the distribution of wealth is as much part of economic understanding as knowledge of the extent of the differentials. Indeed, there is evidence that adults readily debate the fairness of wage differentials whilst possessing a fairly poor knowledge of the actual differentials (Dickinson, 1986a; 1992).

It is in this latter aspect of political understanding that the ideological nature of economic knowledge becomes apparent. Ideologies abound as to the function, necessity, cause and morality of inequality. We will argue that economic socialization, in so far as it entails the development of ideas about the distribution of wealth, and it is hard to envisage many areas of economic behaviour which are not affected by the distribution of wealth, is ideological in that explanations for inequality serve to present its existence as just or unjust, deserved or undeserved, useful or detrimental. For example, Dickinson

(1986a, 1990a) found that adolescents and adults explained wage differentials predominantly in terms of individual effort: how hard people worked, how much they had studied, how many qualifications they had obtained, how important they were to society. These types of arguments can be used to justify current wage differentials or criticize them; they do not in themselves form ideological support for inequality, but they do present wage differentials as the moral, earned and deserved outcome of individual behaviour and thus as a function of individual choice rather than economic systems. One outcome of this ideological device is that poverty can be blamed on the poor for their fecklessness and laziness and in this way it provides support for the 'fairness' of unequal systems of distribution.

We will argue in this chapter that the development of social, political and ideological understanding of economic roles is at least as important to economic socialization in childhood as understanding of the technical aspects. Our focus on developing ideas about the distribution of wealth is chosen not just because it exemplifies the social nature of economic knowledge but because inequality is a ubiquitous and pervasive feature of economic life. In Britain, even after tax and benefits have helped to even out the distribution of income, the mean income of the top fifth of household incomes is 4.3 times the mean income of the bottom fifth (Central Statistical Office, 1992). The minimum wage earned by the top 10 per cent of male employees is more than three times that of the maximum wage of the bottom 10 per cent of men (Government Statistical Office, 1991) and moreover the gap between the top 10 per cent of wage earners and the bottom 10 per cent has widened considerably in the last 10 years (Central Statistical Office, 1992). Distribution of wealth is a major focus for governmental debate about how society should be organized, ranging from the socialist argument that a fair system should have a more equal distribution of wealth to the capitalist insistence that large differentials are the natural outcome of market forces and serve as incentives for achievement. Differentials of wealth are also hotly debated in the media, most recently in the reports of steep pay rises for company executives. Inequality, then, is a fact of economic life, but to what extent is it perceived by children? What are the processes by which children and young people reach representations of the nature and causes of inequality in wealth? What are their feelings towards it? How does it affect their choice of careers and expectations of future salaries?

These are the questions we will address in this chapter. We will describe the development of children's knowledge of income inequality and examine the social and developmental processes which create this knowledge. In particular we will look at cognitive developmental accounts of the development of economic understanding and show how cognitive developmental theory underestimates the impact of social influence processes in the development of socioeconomic knowledge. Evidence for differential social influences on children's beliefs about inequality, especially their understanding of the rules that justify differentials in reward for work, will be discussed.

We will also look at the practical outcomes of learning about socioeconomic inequality in terms of the effects on job choice or preparation for employment, and the repercussions for continued inequality of wealth in society. Our starting-point will be a discussion of research on the development of conceptions of distributive justice.

DISTRIBUTIVE JUSTICE

What is distributive justice? Essentially, this is the name for the system of moral rules which govern the distribution of resources. Typically, when sweets or gifts are given to a group of children, they are shared equally amongst them – an equality rule is adopted. Alternatively, payment for work tends to follow an equity rule – that wages should be proportional to the effort expended, or value produced, by each individual worker. Another type of equity rule, where resources are allocated proportional to need, is used to determine welfare benefits. In each of these situations, participants will have an expectation of what the 'fair share' should be, governed by their understanding of distributive justice.

If there are rules for the distribution of resources, it seems likely that these need to be learned as part of the process of economic socialization. Distributive justice is also the focus for a body of research on the development of children's thinking about moral issues and the main arena for the explication of theoretical approaches to understanding the development of ideas about distribution. Piaget's early, seminal work on the development of moral judgement (Piaget, 1932) provided the first research on children's reasoning about distributive justice problems and the first attempt to explain the development of such reasoning. He found that the judgements children reached when required to allocate rewards and the explanations they provided appeared to fit a stage-like sequence of development. Children in the first stage, 'authority', believe that a fair allocation is whatever adults or those in authority determine the allocation should be. In the second stage, 'equality', which starts around 7–8 years, a fair outcome consists of equal shares for all involved. Around 11–12 years a further development of this stage takes place in which children start to take account of equitable solutions to problems of distribution; that is, they take into account relative contributions or needs when determining what would be a fair outcome. Piaget described this final step as a development of 'equality' in the direction of relativism; thus for him the main developmental step occurred in the transition from obeying authority to applying an equality rule. Although he believed that reasoning about distributive justice had its roots in individual cognitive development, so that the first stage, for instance, arose from the egocentrism of young children which makes them susceptible to every suggestion, he thought these roots were necessary but not sufficient conditions for development. Society provides the extra conditions for development both in terms of norms for distributive justice situations and the specific experience needed for development. Piaget argued, for instance, that 'equality' reasoning arises from the experience of cooperation with other children which demands mutual respect and an understanding of reciprocity.

Since the publication of *The Moral Judgement of the Child* there has been a great deal of debate about the existence of stages in the development of reasoning about distributive justice, the nature of these stages, their relationship to age and the cause of transition from one stage to the next. There are clearly repercussions for economic socialization if children must progress through sequential stages of reasoning about distribution and if progression through these stages is dependent on certain types of social experience. To illustrate we will examine some of the more recent theories of reasoning about distributive justice and their implications for the development of ideas about the distribution of wealth.

An extension and elaboration of Piaget's theory by Damon (1975) has been very influential. Damon believed there were a number of distinct phases in the development of reasoning about what he called 'positive justice' – justice which involves prosocial interaction such as sharing and helping, which includes distributive justice. In the earliest phase the child believes that rewards should be distributed to whoever wants them most. This gives way to a focus on non-relevant, external characteristics of participants in the allocation, such as age or size, so that the oldest or biggest one is given more than the others. The next phase emphasizes, somewhat rigidly, the equality rule in allocation but this forms the basis for a gradual recognition of reciprocity, multiple justifications and situational demands which lead to a belief in equity, first of all on the basis of merit – those who work harder should get more – and later on the basis of competing claims such as need as well as merit and the longer-term outcomes of a particular allocation situation.

Supporting evidence for Damon's stage model has been found in a number of papers (cf. Damon, 1980; Enright *et al.*, 1980; Enright *et al.*, 1984; Sigelman and Waitzman, 1991). Enright *et al.* (1984) argued that the development of distributive justice reasoning followed the development of logical reasoning: 'logical development tends for the most part to precede and set limits on reasoning in the distributive domain' (p. 1742) and thus was governed by Piagetian logical structures. This view is in keeping with Kohlberg's (1969) formulation of moral reasoning which argues for a universal structural sequence in moral development. There are important implications of this view. If decisions about distributive justice are, at least partly, dependent on logicomathematical cognitive development then some types of allocation must surely be superior to others and appreciation of their superiority must depend on intellectual maturity. Indeed, Enright *et al.* (1980) expressed concern that the lag they found in the development of distributive justice reasoning in lower-class children might lead to a persistent deficit in the understanding of the distributive norms of society and consequently some deficit in competent social behaviour. Damon takes a softer line on the relationship between cognitive development and reasoning about distributive justice in so far as he does not think that logical development is a necessary precursor of moral development but argues that 'logical and moral reasoning inform and support each other in the course of ontogenesis as a result of isomorphic structural features in the two domains' (Damon, 1975, p. 312).

The debate about the relationship between cognitive development and moral reasoning is inconclusive. Most theorists agree that cognitive development plays some role in moral reasoning, but that it might operate at a more general level than that implied in the contingency between stages in moral and cognitive development. For instance, Hook and Cook (1979) argued that a full understanding of equity requires an ability to compute ratios between work input and rewards, which is not usually learned before 13 years of age. However, they showed that children can understand ordinal equity from about 6 years.

Thus far we have only discussed theoretical approaches to explaining the development of thinking about distributive justice that are structural and thus essentially free of ideological and political influences. Cognitive developmental theorists would not discount the importance of social influences in moral development: cognitive developmental structure provides the necessary organization for moral development, but it is not sufficient without social experience which provides the stimulus for change from one level to another. However, most consideration of the nature of the social experience which brings about change has concentrated on social interaction, particularly with peers, in experimental allocation situations which may be relatively removed from normal social experience (cf. Damon and Killen, 1982; Keil, 1986). Other approaches, which pay more attention to the effect of social norms on development, do allow for more political and ideological influence. We turn to these now.

A number of studies have found that children's levels of distributive justice reasoning vary between allocation situations. These context effects have been explained by researchers in the cognitive developmental tradition as the effects of certain situations exerting a 'pull' on development because of the emphasis they place on more sophisticated criteria in allocation judgements

(Enright *et al.*, 1984). An alternative explanation places more emphasis on social psychological processes in terms of the effects of developing knowledge of the social norms of particular situations (Lerner, 1974; Sigelman and Waitzman, 1991). This does not necessarily mean that children simply observe and learn the custom and practice of distribution in particular situations or that they are indoctrinated with particular notions of legitimacy, although Sampson (1975) argued that the emphasis on equitable solutions to allocation in the western world reflected the capitalist values of individualism and competition. Children gradually reach a position where they can actively debate a number of alternative solutions to distribution problems in most situations, but the solutions are provided by society rather than derived from a logical analysis of the inputs, outcomes, needs and purposes in the allocation. If social influences are responsible for the development of distributive justice reasoning, then social and cultural differences in children's reasoning should be expected. Evidence for group differences is patchy but this may reflect greater or lesser cultural differences in the groups compared. For instance, Enright *et al.* (1984) found no differences in the sequence of development of reasoning about distributive justice between US and Swedish children, but Enright *et al.* (1980) found that, even controlling for vocabulary, working-class American children lagged behind middle-class children in the development of equity solutions to allocation problems. The working-class lag was explained in cognitive developmental terms and the similarity between the Swedish and American children was used as evidence for universal patterns of development, but it could be argued that the working-class lag reflected different class norms and the cross-national similarity reflected similar socialization influences in the USA and Sweden.

Stronger evidence for cultural influences has tended to be found in comparisons between more distinctively different groups. Nisan (1984) compared the judgements and reasoning of Israeli kibbutz and city children who were asked to allocate rewards for work between themselves and a partner. The kibbutz children were more likely than the city children to distribute equally than equitably, and less likely to judge the effort of the partner in terms of how much they produced. Nisan argued that the kibbutz children's decisions reflected the emphasis on equality as a norm in their socialization and community. This norm discouraged them from interpreting the partner's lower output in terms of bad intention. Nisan's analysis of the way in which these cultural differences arose is interesting because he did not see the kibbutz children's behaviour as simply conformity to the predominant social norm in their community – indeed, he showed that both the kibbutz and the city children believed that there should be a connection between effort and reward – rather he argued that the children interpreted contribution differently according to the social framework provided by their backgrounds. In this way, in terms of the development of different beliefs, perceptions and analyses of principles, it can be argued that there is a crucial ideological component to understanding distributive justice.

Few researchers interested in the development of reasoning about distributive justice have rejected the notion that there may be some structural parallelism between the development of logical reasoning and thinking about distribution, but an increasing number of studies have shown that allocation is determined by a complex set of factors including local and wider social norms (Nisan, 1984), different cultural emphases on the notion of contribution (Kashima *et al.*, 1988), group cohesiveness and relational aspects of the allocation situation (Chiu, 1991) and past histories of reciprocity with partners in the allocation situation (Keil, 1986). Given that most of these studies have been based on artificial allocation situations within the laboratory, the picture might be made even more complicated by social factors in the world outside the laboratory! Darley and Shultz (1990), in a review of the work on the development of moral judgement, question the continuing utility of the focus on structural aspects of reasoning about distributive justice and suggest, like Nisan (1984), that there is a need for greater understanding of the mental representations children have of particular domains and the way they employ these in making distribution decisions. We agree that mental representations are an important clue to understanding the development of distributive justice and in the next section will consider in more detail how such representations might develop and how social psychological processes might bring about understanding of allocation.

THE SOCIAL PSYCHOLOGY OF DEVELOPING IDEAS ABOUT DISTRIBUTION

Thinking about distributive justice appears to develop through a series of stages or different types of rationale, but what are the processes which bring about transition from one stage to the next? At the crux of the cognitive developmental theories of development is the concept of 'equilibration' as the motivating force which moves children into a more advanced stage of development. Piaget (1932) believed that conflict between representations of a domain or a phenomenon created pressure for some form of reconciliation between the representations. Take, for example, a child who holds an equality norm of distribution but also recognizes norms of reciprocity. When presented with a situation where a group of children work together to achieve some reward, he or she would judge that the reward should be equally distributed between the children. However, if the child is aware that one of the children has deliberately, knowingly contributed much less work than the others, he or she is likely to experience conflict between the norm of reciprocity and the norm of equality. The conflict can be resolved by shifting to an allocation decision based on equity. In Damon's (1975) terms, equity is a more balanced form of equality which allows for reciprocity between participants. This resolution of cognitive conflict is essentially the process of equilibration.

The conflict bringing about developmental change is, according to this model, entirely internal or based on the child's own observations and mental representations of the world. Some experiences can be assimilated to existing representations or cognitive constructs but others will create tension leading to an accommodating change in cognitive structure. Knowledge, then, is an individual creation which grows on the basis of drawing logical conclusions about experiences and observations. A crucial element of this argument is that true knowledge or understanding cannot be attained by the child taking over ideas or theories from other people, by social learning or imitation, because understanding is based on the development of new cognitive structures as a result of cognitive conflict. Socially transmitted information, or the information, accounts and explanations provided by other people, only has a role in development in terms of providing 'food for thought' (Jahoda, 1984).

We will argue that socially transmitted information is far more than food for thought. We are not suggesting that children learn rules for distribution or theories about economic relationships simply by imitating the rules and theories stated by adults, nor do we believe that they construct knowledge logically and entirely individually as posited by cognitive developmental theory. Instead we hold that the construction of knowledge is a joint activity, brought about through hearing others' views and theories of the social world and through conversation and discussion with both adults and children. In taking this view we are taking the theoretical position provided by genetic social psychology (cf. Moscovici, 1984; Doise and Mugny, 1984) which attributes a major role to social mechanisms in the generation of knowledge (cf. Emler *et al.*, 1990, for a more detailed exposition of our position). According to genetic social psychology the cultures and social groups to which children belong, help them to construct theories to explain their social world. Ready-made solutions to social problems, such as how to distribute rewards, are regularly presented to children through communications and instructions from sources such as parents, relatives, teachers, friends and the media. The solutions presented may vary from group to group – as we have seen, kibbutz children are presented with different solutions from Israeli city children (Nisan, 1984) – and they may conflict with other information received by the children, but it is very rare that children are left to find solutions to social problems on their own.

How can this process of social construction explain why children appear to prefer particular solutions at particular ages? What makes one explanation preferable to another? First of all, the child plays an active role in the construction of knowledge both in terms of actively communicating with others, asking questions, seeking clarification and trying out ideas, and also in terms of providing pre-established representations of the social world which provide the foundations for the joint construction of further knowledge. Unless information is tailored to existing levels of understanding it will go 'over the head' of the child. It takes time and a socially ordered sequence of information to build certain representations of the social world in children's heads. There is evidence for a socially ordered sequence in the construction of economic knowledge in Berti *et al.*'s (1982) finding that parents provide children with the information they think is relevant to their age. It appears that children are provided with accounts based on adult social representations of child development. These may, of course, vary from culture to culture.

Another important factor in the social construction of knowledge is that ready-made solutions are not 'value-free'; some accounts are more persuasive than others by virtue of their source, their construction or their mode of transmission. There is a wealth of literature on social influence processes suggesting that individuals are more susceptible to certain type of persuasion than to others (cf. Jaspars, 1978) and children are no exception to this rule. For instance, a source which is perceived as more expert, an adult or teacher compared with a child perhaps, is likely to be seen as having more correct information. More subtle than this, perhaps, is the gentle form of correction that occurs in interaction (see Dickinson, 1986b, for further information), where children's beliefs about the social world are accepted or rejected by others according to how much they conform to accepted reality. Furth (1976) cited the following excerpt from an interview as an example of how children gain spontaneous insight into the nature of economic transactions – in this case how bus drivers obtain money to buy petrol:

Interviewer: "Who buys the petrol?"
Child: "The bus driver."
Int: "Where does he get the money from? For the petrol?"
Ch: "The petrol man, he gives them petrol."
Int: "The petrol man?"
Ch: "Yes, the petrol man gives him some money, and the money ..."
Int: "Oh, why does the petrol man give him money?"
Ch: "Oh no, the man gives him money."
Int: "The driver gives the man money?"
Ch: "Oh, I get it – the driver – the people who go on the bus give the money to the people – the people who go on the bus give the money to the man, and then, the man can buy petrol."
Int: "That's right – that's right isn't it?" (pp. 356–7)

Furth interpreted the child's developmental step as the outcome of active logical thinking but the child is not making this logical step in a social vacuum. The interviewer keeps pushing him towards some kind of answer by repeated questions about who gives the driver money, until the child draws the connection between the passengers' fares and the money available for petrol, at which point the interviewer both accepts the explanation and clearly indicates that it is correct. If, instead of asking more questions, the interviewer had accepted the child's explanation that the petrol man gave the bus driver money – it is a common misconception amongst young children that people obtain money in the form of change from shopkeepers – the child probably would not have gone on to draw the more correct conclusion. Thus we can see how social influence can bring about knowledge development.

If the development of knowledge about the social and economic world is dependent, as we have argued, on social influence processes, then political and ideological influences on knowledge are inevitable. In the next section we will examine children's representations of the distribution of wealth in society – in the 'real' world – and the evidence for social influence processes.

CHILDREN'S CONCEPTIONS OF INEQUALITY OF WEALTH

Just as stages have been identified by Piaget, Damon and others in children's reasoning about distributive justice dilemmas, a number of researchers have found stages in children's understanding of the distribution of wealth in society (cf. Lauer, 1974; Connell, 1977; Stacey, 1987). There is evidence first of all for age-related differences in children's perceptions of inequalities of wealth and their explanations of the causes. Early research by Jahoda (1959) found awareness of social differences, in terms of housing, clothes and life style, in children as young as 6 years. The 6–7-year-olds tended to explain the social differences in terms of the type of jobs people did but made little mention of how much money they earned, whereas slightly older children, 8–9-year-olds, related the differences to earnings and wealth. It appears an awareness of the relationships between social differences, work and income is not reached until about 8 years of age. This contention is supported by Furby's (1980) finding of a similar pattern of development in children's beliefs about inequalities in property: 6-year-old American children attributed differences in possessions to some people having more money, earning more or having better jobs, but the relationship between jobs and money was seen as merely incidental, as a function of some people needing, wanting, or being given more money; 8-year-olds saw type of job and wages as more instrumental in gaining possessions and began to talk about jobs in terms of some being better or earning more than others.

A more elaborate stage model, concerning children's perceptions of inequality in terms of descriptions of rich and poor people and explanations and justifications for their wealth and poverty, was produced by Leahy (1981, 1983). He argued that there were three levels in the development of thinking about rich and poor people: the peripheral, central and sociocentric levels. At the peripheral level, children described wealth and poverty purely in terms of possessions and external attributes and tended to explain inequality by definition (for example, rich people are rich because they have money). This level characterized most of the responses from 6–11-year-olds but began to decline thereafter. The central level consisted of references to internal, psychological traits such as intelligence and ability and to explanations for wealth and poverty in terms of meritorious earning. Central-type responses increased with age, particularly between 6 and 11 years. Sociocentric responses were references to political power, social structure and life chances to describe and explain wealth and poverty. These also increased with age, but were rare even in late adolescence. Leahy regarded the levels as indicative of a developmental continuum which reflected cognitive development in so far as the central level reflected a decline in egocentrism and the sociocentric level required formal operational thought. In keeping with cognitive developmental accounts of reasoning about distributive justice, Leahy found parallels with Piaget's authority–equality–equity pattern of development in judgements of inequality.

Thus Leahy's and other researchers' stage models suggest that societal knowledge, in terms of beliefs about the nature, cause and legitimacy of inequalities of wealth, rests at least partially on cognitive structural development. Several other researchers have also explained stages in thinking about the inequality of wealth in society in terms of cognitive development (cf. Connell, 1977; Furby, 1980; Siegal, 1981). It seems unlikely, though, that cognitive development provides the whole story behind the development of beliefs about social inequality. Siegal (1981) noted that children who understood equity explanations of pay differed in their evaluation of the fairness of inequality for reasons that probably reflected ideological influences in their backgrounds. Lauer (1974) found that Canadian Catholic children were more likely than non-Catholics to explain occupational status in terms of the function or importance of the work and less likely to cite the prestige of various jobs. They were also less likely to legitimate status differentials in terms of the income earned by the jobs, although justifications in terms of income increased with age between 12 and 14 years. Lauer also thought that ideological influences in the form of Catholic religious teaching, which plays down the importance of material factors, might give rise to these differences.

Persuasive evidence for social influences on the development of conceptions of inequality can be found in the frequent reports of social class differences. Middle-class children tend to show greater class consciousness in
terms of being more aware of social differences (Tudor, 1971; Coles, 1977;
Connell, 1977; Stacey, 1978) and having more explanations for income differentials (Dickinson, 1990a; Emler and Dickinson, 1985). Types of explanations provided by children for income differentials have also been found to
vary according to social class background (Emler and Dickinson, 1985;
Dickinson, 1990a).

Could these differences reflect a working-class developmental lag, or are
they indicative of different social influences on class groups? Our research
supports the latter explanation in that we found class differences but not age
differences in children's perceptions of wage differentials (Emler and
Dickinson, 1985); middle-class children provided higher estimates of wages
for a number of jobs and perceived greater differentials between the jobs,
though they still greatly underestimated actual earnings. We found greater
support for income inequality amongst middle-class children at all ages from
7 to 16 years (Emler and Dickinson, 1985; Dickinson, 1990a) and class
differences in the types of explanations provided by all age groups. In particular, middle-class children and adolescents were more likely to explain and
justify wage differentials in terms of differences in the training or qualifications
required for different jobs (Emler and Dickinson, 1985; Dickinson, 1990a)
and middle-class adolescents were more likely to cite market forces to explain wage differentials (Dickinson, 1986a). Some of the class differences
reported in child and adolescent samples have also been found in adult
samples. Dornstein (1985) found that, compared with white-collar workers,
manual workers rated unpleasant working conditions, inconvenient working
hours and family needs more highly as ways of legitimating wage differentials. They rated indispensability and responsibility less highly

It is not clear how these social group differences are produced and in the
absence of a longitudinal study monitoring the effects of particular types of
social influence or information it is impossible to determine the effects of
social transmission versus other causes of knowledge development. Dornstein
(1985) believed that different occupational groups upheld different criteria
for wage differentials according to what best represented their own interests.
However, some criteria are supported in conflict with personal interests, as
evidenced by Dornstein in her finding that manual workers and white-collar
workers both consider education and qualifications to be important criteria.
Coles (1977) and Connell (1977) attributed greater support for social inequality amongst children from upper socioeconomic backgrounds to both
self-interest and inculcation of values and attitudes which support class div-
isions. The notion of deliberate inculcation of beliefs which legitimate in-

equality is extremely contentious but several writers have pointed out that children and adolescents do develop explanations for inequality which present the distribution of wealth in society as fair and meritorious (Lauer, 1974; Baldus and Tribe, 1978; Cummings and Taebel, 1978). People are seen as working for what they get. Does this mean that developing ideas about the distribution of wealth also means developing compliant citizens who collude with the maintenance of inequality in their society and accept as legitimate their own position within it? We will address the notion of compliant citizens and the function of representations of inequality in maintaining social inequality in the final section, but turn first to the effects of beliefs about inequality on occupational choice. As wages for employment form the main income for most people in western society, then occupation is the main determinant of socioeconomic position.

THE EFFECTS OF IDEAS ABOUT INEQUALITY ON OCCUPATIONAL CHOICE

One of the most stable findings about children's perceptions of social inequality is the accuracy with which they can rank order occupations in terms of both social status and income (Lauer, 1974; Siegal, 1981; Emler and Dickinson, 1985; Dickinson, 1990a). By the age of about 10 years, children can produce hierarchies of occupational status and income which do not differ significantly from those provided by adults. They are also able to provide explanations for the wage differentials they perceive. Children under 10 years tend to use fairly descriptive criteria based on the function of the job (for example, bus drivers are important because they take people to work) to explain the differentials, but with increasing age children acquire more explicitly equitable criteria such as the effort required to do the job, the difficulty of the job, the hours worked, qualifications needed, skills and responsibility (Furnham and Cleare, 1988; Lauer, 1974; Leahy, 1983; Dickinson, 1986a). Although the majority of children tend to support existing wage differentials as being fair (Emler and Dickinson, 1985; Dickinson, 1990a), they often use the criteria they have acquired to criticize some aspects of inequality. For instance, a child might argue that road sweepers deserve to be paid more money because they do an uncomfortable, dirty job in all weathers.

Despite this level of sophistication about relative wage differentials and their causes, children are very naive about the actual amounts that different occupations earn. They tend to underestimate both wages and wage differentials and working-class children underestimate more than middle-class children (Emler and Dickinson, 1985; Dickinson, 1990a; Furnham, 1982). While adults have a more realistic conception of wages than children and adolescents, they are sometimes still quite ignorant of the amounts earned (Dickinson, 1986a). For instance, in a recent study adult professionals provided estimates of the annual wage of a general medical practitioner ranging from £20 000 to £70 000 (Dickinson, 1992).

Thus, by early adolescence, children have a rich if patchy knowledge of the nature of wage differentials. How does this knowledge affect their choice of careers and how do they feel about their future likely positions in the occupational hierarchy? On the basis of the primacy given to the notion of effort – in acquiring qualifications, in working hard, in suffering long hours and risky work – in explaining wage differentials, it might be expected that young people see their occupational future as a function of their own application and toil: they will achieve the jobs they deserve. On the basis that they can debate the fairness of the occupational hierarchy, it might be expected that they will, to some degree, question the fairness of the rewards and the nature of occupational opportunity.

There is evidence that with increasing age children tailor their occupational aspirations to fit the qualifications they are likely to achieve (Gottfredson, 1981). It might be expected that young children aspire to those jobs which provide the greatest prestige and most affluent or glamorous life style and, indeed, many young children cite glamorous or romantic jobs, such as 'footballer' or 'astronaut', when asked what they want to do when they grow up, but by early adolescence aspirations tend to be approximately equal to opportunities and, as such, tend eventually to be achieved (Jencks, 1972). In this sense young people do choose their careers on the basis of a fairly realistic review of their achievements, although they tend to explain their choice almost entirely in terms of personal interest, either for the intrinsic interest of the job or for the associated life style (Dickinson, 1986a). These findings and the explanations for wage differentials presented above would suggest that occupational selection was an entirely meritocratic, morally acceptable process, were it not for the fact that academic achievements are not the only predictors of occupational achievement. Factors such as gender, socioeconomic status and race are strong predictors of occupational aspirations as well as academic achievement (Brook *et al.*, 1974; Gottfredson, 1981). Are such factors recognized by children and do they lead to some disenchantment with the system of occupational selection? Does successful occupational socialization rely, as Parsons (1977) argued it must, on a belief in equal opportunities?

Simmons and Rosenberg (1971), in an exploration of children's beliefs about the opportunity structure in the USA in general and their own personal opportunities, found that 70 per cent of the children in each age group between 9 and 18 years believed that not everyone had the same chances and cited socioeconomic, racial and ethnic factors as sources of disadvantage.

Further evidence for an awareness of disadvantage was found in a recent British study which examined children's appreciation of the effects of three factors on occupational attainment: socioeconomic background, academic success and personal interests. The younger children (8–10 years) tended to place more emphasis on people's personal interests in predicting their future jobs whilst older children (11–16 years) placed more emphasis on academic strength and socioeconomic background. The fact that a combination of academic success and high socioeconomic background was seen as more predictive of a high status occupation and high earnings than either factor separately suggests that adolescents are conscious of socioeconomic background as an important factor in occupational achievement.

Nevertheless, such awareness does not seem to lead to feelings of constraint on one's own occupational choices. Simmons and Rosenberg's mainly black and working-class subjects were optimistic about their own chances although there was a relationship between status consciousness and occupational aspirations. That is, the subjects who were aware that some occupations had poor prestige were more likely that those who were not to aspire to high status jobs. Dickinson (1986a, 1990a) also found that occupational aspirations were related to status consciousness in that middle-class children aspired to higher status jobs than working-class children and were more aware of the prestige and income differences between jobs. Given the findings reported above on children's naivety about the extent of wage differentials, it is possible that children who may be destined for quite lowly socioeconomic jobs are not too concerned because they do not perceive their relative loss of wages to be very large. A further effect of status consciousness is that most children and teenagers tend to see themselves as 'about average' in socioeconomic status (Dickinson, 1986a) and thus, perhaps, as neither particularly advantaged nor disadvantaged by their social position.

To summarize, the research evidence suggests that the development of ideas about inequality of wealth can lead to both justification of socioeconomic inequality in terms of individual merit and effort and criticism of inequality on the basis of these same criteria and the notion of equal opportunities. However, criticism of social inequality and concern about one's personal economic future in adolescence is tempered by a poor perception of the size of wage differentials. A more realistic representation of socioeconomic inequality may not develop until after entry into work and possibly until after events associated with young adulthood such as starting a family and buying or renting a home.

COMPLIANT CITIZENS?

Cummings and Taebel (1978) argued that economic socialization 'progressively orients children to a favorable view of capitalism and structured social inequality' (p. 198). Such a process is also regarded as necessary by sociologists who support the structural functionalist argument that shared beliefs about the legitimacy of inequality are necessary to stabilize and maintain a social and economic system (cf. Parsons, 1977). There would seem to be support for Cummings and Taebel's view in the evidence that children most commonly explain wealth differentials in terms of equity or rewards being appropriate to the work contribution or effort made by the individual. Furthermore, we have argued that this belief in equity derives less from an understanding of the relationship between work inputs and wages than from repeated and extensive exposure to 'equity-like' arguments used to defend wage differentials (see also Dickinson and Emler, 1992).

Does this mean, then, that society inculcates the kinds of beliefs that create satisfaction with, or at least acceptance of, social inequality? It would be premature to draw this conclusion without a longitudinal study which monitored both socially transmitted information about economic inequality and its effects on children's beliefs, and such a study has not been done. What we can say is that, while socialization produces tempered but widespread support amongst adolescents for the system of social inequality in western countries *as they perceive it* – and the predominant social representation or commonsense view of the distribution of wealth in western countries is that it is largely fair – it also produces the ability to criticize and argue against the status quo. Dickinson (1986a, 1990a) found that, while the majority of adolescents felt that most wage differentials in Britain were quite fair, they tended to argue that the lowest paid jobs should earn 'a little more', and to employ the same individualistic, equity-like criteria they had used to justify the differentials between the higher paid jobs to justify a wage increase for the lowest paid. Thus, while merit criteria such as qualifications, difficulty of the work, arduous conditions and dedication can be used to legitimate existing inequalities, they can also be used to criticize existing inequalities. For instance, a child might argue that teachers should be paid as much as doctors because they both make important contributions to society. The nature of thinking about inequality, as about other aspects of social structure, is essentially *dilemmatic* (see Billig *et al.*, 1988) in that people hold contradictory beliefs about the nature and cause of inequality and can employ these beliefs in a rhetorical fashion to argue for or against the status quo.

One problem for the analysis of economic socialization in the sense of understanding whether it produces compliant citizens is that little is known about the end product of socialization in terms of adult representations of social inequality. Darley and Shultz (1990) made the timely observation that the study of distributive justice in children suffers from the lack of a model of adult distributive justice practices, and the same observation can be made about the study of ideas about the distribution of wealth in society. There is evidence that adult thinking about inequality is more sophisticated in some respects. Dickinson (1990b, 1992) found that adults were more likely than adolescents to provide explanations for wage differentials in terms of economic and political criteria such as market forces, social values and trade union pressure, though such explanations are still less common in adulthood than individual equity-type explanations. Political and economic explanations for wage differentials do not present inequality as the moral outcome of individual endeavour. Indeed, they may present inequality as the result of group differences in power or the impersonal, amoral result of a free market system. It is perhaps no accident that Dickinson (1986a) found the greatest use of political and economic criteria in adolescence amongst middle-class, privately educated 15 and 16-year-olds, who, being already well prepared to achieve qualifications and prestigious jobs, could be safely exposed to ideas that contradict the moral basis for wage differentials.

The increase with age of the use of political and economic criteria to explain wage differentials parallels the increase observed by Leahy (1983) in political and economic explanations of wealth and poverty. Leahy attributed the change to cognitive development but Dickinson's (1992) finding that managers were more likely that non-managerial professionals to explain wage differentials in terms of market forces suggests that social influence processes are crucially important. An important clue to the nature of economic socialization from Leahy's work is that central-level explanations, or what we might call individual, equitable explanations, did not decrease as sociocentric explanations increased. The coexistence of such types of criteria in thinking about wealth and poverty or wage differentials suggests that people acquire various means of *accounting* for inequality and consequently the tools for the contention of inequality. If economic socialization produces compliant citizens we would argue that it is most likely to do so in so far as the differential social distribution of explanations or accounts of the cause of inequality may deny some groups the tools to criticize the distribution of wealth in society.

REFERENCES

Baldus, B. and Tribe, V. (1978), 'The development of perceptions and evaluations of social inequality among public school children', *Canadian Review of Sociology and Anthropology*, **15** (1), 50–60.

Berti, A.E. and Bombi, A.S. (1981), 'The development of the concept of money and its value: A longitudinal study', *Child Development*, **52**, 1179–82.

Berti, A.E. and Bombi, A.S. (1988), *The Child's Construction of Economics*, Cambridge: Cambridge University Press.

Berti, A.E., Bombi, A.S. and Lis, A. (1982), 'The child's conceptions about means of production and their owners', *European Journal of Social Psychology*, **12**, 221–39.

Billig, M., Condor, S., Edwards, D., Gane, M., Middleton, D. and Radley, A.R. (1988), *Ideological Dilemmas: A Social Psychology of Everyday Thinking*, London: Sage.

Brook, J.S., Whiteman, M., Peisach, E. and Deutsch, M. (1974), 'Aspiration levels of and for children: Age, sex, race and socioeconomic correlates', *The Journal of Genetic Psychology*, **124**, 3–16.

Central Statistical Office (1992), *Social Trends 22*, London: HMSO.

Coles, R. (1977), *Children of Crisis (Vol. 5)*, Boston: Little, Brown.

Connell, R.W. (1977), *Ruling Class, Ruling Culture*, Melbourne: Cambridge University Press.

Cummings, S. and Taebel, D. (1978), 'The Economic Socialization of Children: A neo-Marxist Analysis', *Social Problems*, **26** (2), 198–210.

Damon, W. (1975), 'Early conceptions of positive justice as related to the development of logical operations', *Child Development*, **46**, 301–12.

Damon, W. (1980), 'Patterns of change in children's social reasoning: A two-year longitudinal study', *Child Development*, **51**, 1010–17.

Damon, W. and Killen, M. (1982), 'Peer interaction and the process of change in children's moral reasoning', *Merrill-Palmer Quarterly*, **28** (3), 347–67.

Darley, J.M. and Shultz, T.R. (1990), 'Moral rules: Their content and acquisition', *Annual Review of Psychology*, **41**, 525–56.

Dickinson, J. (1986a), 'The development of representations of social inequality', unpublished PhD thesis, Dundee University.

Dickinson, J. (1986b), 'The role of social influence in the development of social knowledge', BPS Social Section Conference, Brighton.

Dickinson, J. (1990a), 'Adolescent representations of socio-economic status', *British Journal of Developmental Psychology*, **8** (4), 351–71.

Dickinson, J. (1990b), 'Business students and social science students' explanations for wage differentials: moral versus political and economic rhetoric', in S.E.G. Lea P. Webley and B.M. Young (eds), *Applied Economic Psychology in the 1990s* (Proceedings of the 15th Annual Colloquium of the International Association for Research in Economic Psychology), Exeter: Washington Singer Press.

Dickinson, J. (1992), 'Explanations for wage differentials: Managers' use of market forces', International Association of Research in Economic Psychology Conference, Frankfurt.

Dickinson, J. and Emler, N. (1992), 'Developing conceptions of work', in J. Hartley and G. Stephenson (eds), *Employment Relations*, Oxford: Blackwell.

Doise, W. and Mugny, G. (1984), *The Social Development of the Intellect*, Oxford: Pergamon.

Dorstein, M. (1985), 'Perceptions regarding standards for evaluating pay equity and their determinants', *Journal of Occupational Psychology*, **58** (4), 321–30.

Emler, N. and Dickinson, J. (1985), 'Children's representation of economic inequalities: the effects of social class', *British Journal of Developmental Psychology*, **3**, 191–8.

Emler, N., Ohana, J. and Dickinson, J. (1990), 'Children's representations of social relations', in B. Lloyd and G. Duveen (eds), *Social Representations and the Development of Knowledge*, Oxford: Blackwell.

Enright, R.D., Enright, W.F., Manheim, L.A. and Harris, B.E. (1980), 'Distributive justice development and social class', *Developmental Psychology*, 16 (6), 555–63.

Enright, R.D., Bjerstedt, A., Enright, W.F., Levy, Jr. V.M., Lapsley, D.K., Buss, R.R., Harwell, M. and Zindler, M. (1984), 'Distributive justice development: Cross-cultural, contextual, and longitudinal evaluations', *Child Development*, 55, 1737–51.

Furby, L. (1980), 'The origins and early development of possessive behaviour', *Political Psychology*, 2, 30–42.

Furnham, A. (1982), 'The perception of poverty amongst adolescents', *Journal of Adolescence*, 5, 135–47.

Furnham, A. and Cleare, A. (1988), 'School children's conceptions of economics: prices, wages, investments and strikes', *Journal of Economic Psychology*, 9, 467–79.

Furth, H., Bauer, M. and Smith, J. (1976), 'Children's conceptions of social institutions: a Piagetian framework', *Human Development*, 19, 351–74.

Gottfredson, L.S. (1981), 'Circumscription and compromise: A developmental theory of occupational aspiration, *Journal of Counseling Psychology*, 286, 545–79.

Government Statistical Office (1991), *New Earnings Survey*, London: Employment Department.

Hook, J.G. and Cook, T.D. (1979), 'Equity theory and the cognitive ability of children', *Psychological Bulletin*, 86 (3), 429–45.

Jahoda, G. (1959), 'Development of the perception of social differences in children from 6–10', *British Journal of Psychology*, 50, 159–75.

Jahoda, G. (1984), 'The development of thinking about socio-economic systems', in H. Tajfel (ed.), *The Social Dimension, vol. 1*, Cambridge: Cambridge University Press.

Jaspars, J.M.F. (1978), 'Determinants of attitudes and attitude change', in H. Tajfel and C. Frazer (eds), *Introducing Social Psychology*, Harmondsworth: Penguin.

Jencks, C. (1972), *Inequality*, Harmondsworth: Penguin.

Kashima, Y., Siegal, M., Tanaka, K. and Isaka, H. (1988), 'Universalism in lay conceptions of distributive justice: A cross-cultural examination', *International Journal of Psychology*, 23, 51–64.

Keil, L.J. (1986), 'Rules, reciprocity and rewards: A developmental study of resource allocation in social interaction', *Journal of Experimental Social Psychology*, 22, 419–35.

Kohlberg, L. (1969), 'Stage and sequence: The cognitive–developmental approach to socialization', in D. Goslin (ed.), *Handbook of Socialization Theory and Research*, Chicago: Rand McNally.

Lauer, R.H. (1974), 'Socialization into inequality: Children's perceptions of occupational status', *Sociology and Social Research*, 58, 176–83.

Leahy, R.L. (1981), 'The development of the conception of economic inequality. I. Descriptions and comparisons of rich and poor people', *Child Development*, 52, 523–32.

Leahy, R.L. (1983), 'Development of the conception of economic inequality: II. Explanations, justifications and concepts of social mobility and change', *Developmental Psychology*, 19, 111–25.

Lerner, M.J. (1974), 'The justice motive: "Equity" and "parity" among children', *Journal of Personality and Social Psychology*, 29 (4), 539–50.

Moscovici, S. (1984), 'The phenomenon of social representations', in R. Farr and S. Moscovici (eds), *Social Representations*, Cambridge: Cambridge University Press.

Nisan, M. (1984), 'Distributive justice and social norms', *Child Development*, **55**, 1020–29.

Parsons, T. (1977), *The Evolution of Societies*, Englewood Cliffs, N.J.: Prentice-Hall.

Piaget, J. (1932), *The Moral Judgement of the Child*, London: Routledge and Kegan Paul.

Siegal, M. (1981), 'Children's perceptions of adult economic needs', *Child Development*, **52**, 379–82.

Sigelman, C.K. and Waitzman, K.A. (1991), 'The development of distributive justice orientations: Contextual influences on children's resource allocations', *Child Development*, **62**, 1367–78.

Simmons, R.G. and Rosenberg, M . (1971), 'Functions of children's perceptions of the stratification system', *American Sociological Review*, **36**, 235–49.

Stacey, B.G. (1978), *Political Socialization in Western Society*, London: Edward Arnold.

Stacey, B.G. (1987), 'Economic socialization', in S. Long (ed.), *Annual Review of Political Science, vol. 2*, Norwood: Ablex Publishing.

Strauss, A. (1952), 'The development and transformation of monetary meanings in the child', *American Sociological Review*, **17**, 275–86.

Tudor, J. (1971), 'The development of class awareness in children', *Social Forces*, **49**, 470–76.

5.   Adolescents' economic beliefs and social class

Helga Dittmar

'TO HAVE IS TO BE': SOCIAL STRATIFICATION AND MATERIAL GOODS

The social inequalities which accompany stratification according to relative wealth and individual ownership of material possessions are fundamental features of contemporary western societies. Material goods clearly play an important role in our everyday social lives. They feature prominently, not only in advertisements and television programmes, but also in the ways in which we actually think and feel about ourselves and others. Material possessions, such as stereos or cars, involve much more than their self-evident functional or commercial purposes. They contrast with the view of classic utilitarian economics, because they also form an intricate system of social symbols, which communicate information about their owners (Douglas and Isherwood, 1979).

Possessions symbolize not only the personal qualities of individuals, but also the groups to which they belong and their general socioeconomic standing. Something as seemingly trivial as the choice of 'Reebok' brand trainers can convey the impression that a person is sporty and that they aspire to middle-class status. It has been found not only that people express their personal and social characteristics through their own material possessions, but also that they make inferences about the identity of others on the basis of *their* possessions (Dittmar, 1992a). Indeed, there is emerging evidence that our beliefs surrounding material goods have a significant bearing on the structure of our perception of other people and the social environment (for example, Burroughs *et al.*, 1991; Dittmar, 1992b). Part of our commonsense perspective on the economic world, then, consists of socially shared beliefs about material objects as symbolic manifestations of identity and status.

If material goods signify socioeconomic standing and social class, people's representations about possessions, consumer practices and life styles inevitably involve lay beliefs about stratification and social inequalities. Entering somebody's living-room not only tells us about their personal taste and values, but just as clearly informs us about their level of income and social class. This is true not only for adults, but also for adolescents and children. Children as young as 5 or 6 years old start to recognize the symbolic dimensions of consumer products and fully understand their social implications at 10 or 11 years of age (for example, Belk *et al.*, 1982; Driscoll *et al.*, 1985). Bourdieu (1984) goes further than the claim that representations about consumer goods and practices are linked to beliefs about social inequality. He postulates that social classes and power relations reproduce themselves ('cultural reproduction') through repetition of different consumption and life style practices, and through internalization of associated value systems and ways of categorizing the social world.

ECONOMIC SOCIALIZATION

In view of the central role of material goods it is surprising to note the neglect of research into pre-adult representations about material goods in the economic socialization literature. This neglect may arise from two prominent features of research on economic socialization. Firstly, Webley and Lea (1992) lament the formal and restricted approach to the definition of 'economic behaviour' which may, in part, be responsible for the lack of interest in consumption-related phenomena which extend beyond purchasing goods, and spending or saving money. Secondly, the economic socialization literature has been characterized, at least until fairly recently, by an emphasis on individual development. This individual-centred, developmental–cognitive approach tends to consider children and adolescents as 'solitary cognizers' and maps their growing understanding of micro- and macroeconomic processes in terms of their movement through a set of increasingly complex cognitive stages (cf. Stacey, 1982; Lea *et al.*, 1987). We know far less about young people as social beings embedded in a particular cultural and historical context and whose economic understanding is shaped by the commonsense, socially shared representations prevalent in their environment (for example, Emler and Dickinson, 1985). However, that part of the literature which has used a more sociological, social construction model conceptualizes economic socialization as progressive alignment with 'dominant ideology' and positive acceptance of social inequalities. It thus points to the conservative and status quo-maintaining influence of such socialization agents as the mass media or schooling on economic beliefs.

ADOLESCENTS' ECONOMIC BELIEFS, SOCIAL CLASS AND MATERIALISM

Within the economic socialization literature, children and adolescents have always been asked *directly*: What are wealthy and poor people like? Why are some people materially better off than others? The present chapter also deals with the question of what representations adolescents hold about people at different levels of the social–material hierarchy, but it employs a different perspective.

If a system of material symbols is part and parcel of the way we perceive our social environment, it follows that we use others' possessions to make inferences about their identities. Moreover, it appears that sets of material possessions are used initially to locate and place other people in a social–material hierarchy, which then leads to evaluations of their personal qualities (Dittmar, 1992b). In the research to be described, adolescents were not asked directly about their beliefs regarding what individuals from different wealth backgrounds are like. Instead they were shown the same person in either relatively wealthy or relatively poor material circumstances, in order to address the question of whether this material context gives rise to systematically different impressions and evaluations. In addition, two further questions are addressed in this chapter.

Firstly, it seems likely that a person's own material background would exert a profound effect on their economic outlook, and we would therefore expect that working-class adolescents would perceive a wealthy person (or a less affluent person) rather differently from middle-class adolescents. In fact, social identity theory (Tajfel, 1984) postulates directly that people are motivated to view members of their own and similar social categories in a positive light in order to bolster their self-esteem: thus perceptions of people belonging to one's own group are favourable and out-group members are discriminated against. However, if economic socialization is strongly bound up with internalizing dominant belief systems, which are ideologically loaded to favour the status quo, it could be argued that adolescents from different socioeconomic backgrounds may form essentially *similar* impressions by drawing on a societally shared frame of reference about what wealthy and less affluent people are like. If *both* groups of adolescents view the wealthy as intelligent, hard-working and skilful and the poor as lazy and lacking in skills and abilities – in contrast to the social identity model – their perceptions can be regarded as dominant representations in the sense that the status quo must be fair if wealth differentials are seen as the product of individual merit: the wealthy and the less affluent are different kinds of people.

The second question concerns materialism. One of the central arguments of this chapter, that first impressions formed about others are heavily influenced by the material objects they own, leads to the proposition that we place and evaluate others in a socioeconomic hierarchy. In fact, such an impact of material goods on first impressions could be seen as a facet of materialism, as our current predominant value system, at the level of social perception, or shared common sense. In contrast to such a social representations perspective, materialism has more often been conceptualized as a value orientation or a personality trait which characterizes individuals to different degrees (Belk, 1985; Richins and Dawson, 1992). From this perspective on materialism as an individual difference variable, we would expect that perception of others is more strongly influenced by their possessions for people high in materialism than for those low in materialism. But is it really the case that 'to have is to be' epitomizes our shared sociocultural system of perceptual 'drawers' into which we slot people at first sight?

CONSUMER PRODUCTS AND PERSONAL ATTRIBUTES

A whole host of consumer research studies gives interesting illustrations of the significance isolated material goods have for our perception of the buyer's identity. For instance, Wells *et al.* (1957) found that people hold different representations about the personal qualities of Ford, Buick and Chevrolet owners. One of the most typical methods employed in this kind of research is the 'shopping list' experiment. Respondents are shown a list of products allegedly bought by a particular person and asked to evaluate her or him in terms of personal attributes. Quite substantial differences in evaluations were demonstrated, for example, on the basis of such minor variations in consumer choice as that between real and instant coffee (Haire, 1950), different cat food brands (Reid and Buchanan, 1979) or different brands of beer (Woodside, 1972).

Clearly, then, material objects are used to make judgements about an individual's personal qualities and identity, but the focus of these consumer studies on specific objects or brands, and isolated personal attributes, cannot offer any systematic insights into the way material context influences person perception. Burroughs *et al.* (1991) took this kind of investigation several steps further in a social psychological direction by addressing two main questions. The first concerns the extent of agreement of such observer ratings with what owners think their possessions express about themselves, and the second deals with the relative usefulness of possession information for making personality inferences. They photographed American women students in their favourite clothes and in the part of their room they felt best reflected their personality, and asked them to provide lists of their most liked records and study programmes. Although students rated personal qualities on the basis of only one type of personal possession (clothes, room, records, study programmes), their judgements corresponded surprisingly well with the women's self-ratings. Moreover, a person's possessions were seen as more informative about their personality than their typical behaviours and social activities: not only did 84 per cent of observers prefer possessions over behavioural information when given a choice, but they also made more accurate personal inferences about the woman owner than those who had chosen other information. This would suggest, then, that people are not only able to make personal identity inferences from material possessions, but also that they frequently make use of objects as a particularly informative source for impressions.

MATERIAL GOODS AND SOCIOECONOMIC STANDING

When sets of material possessions are studied, rather than isolated items, it soon becomes clear that we also use them to draw inferences about the social groups people belong to, about their social status and about their socioeconomic position generally. Goods can symbolize social and political affiliations by serving, for example, as cultural signs for belonging to the counterculture of the late 1960s and early 1970s (Buckley and Roach, 1974) or endorsing radical feminism (for example, Cassell, 1974). But, mostly, judgements about social identity on the basis of material factors seem concerned with status, social position and class. For example, Douty (1963) demonstrated that particular sets of clothes led to similar judgements about the owner's socioeconomic status, regardless of the different people who wore them. People from different socioeconomic groups share stereotypes about the typical material possessions business managers (high socioeconomic status – SES) would treasure as compared to the unemployed (low SES) (Dittmar, 1991). A recent study by Cherulnik and Bayless (1986) asked respondents to rate photographs of adults who were depicted in either an upper-middle-class or a lower-middle-class residential setting. The person in the more affluent setting not only received higher occupational and socioeconomic ratings, but also consistently won more favourable judgements about their personal qualities.

This last study implies not only that people make status inferences on the basis of possessions, but also that status judgements are systematically linked to impressions of the owner's personal identity and characteristics – an argument put forward speculatively by Goffman (1951) over 40 years ago. One of the present author's studies, using an impression formation approach, started from the proposition that material possessions give rise to judgements about a person's relative wealth which, in turn, lead to evaluations of her or his personal qualities. Undergraduates were asked to read a one-page description of a person, allegedly extracted from a novel. The material possessions in the vignette were varied so that they portrayed the central character in either relatively wealthy or much less affluent material circumstances (living-room interior, transport and so on). Respondents agreed that one setting conveyed a much higher socioeconomic standing than the other, and their evaluations of the character's personal qualities differed strongly on that basis: the level of control people can exert over their lives and their assertiveness was thought to be greater with increasing wealth, in contrast to warmth and expressiveness, which were seen as diminishing with affluence (Dittmar *et al.*, 1989). These findings suggest that material possessions serve as symbolic manifestations of both socioeconomic standing and personal identity and that their meanings are therefore socially shared and constructed.

A SOCIAL CONSTRUCTIONIST PERSPECTIVE ON MATERIAL SYMBOLS

Material possessions cannot function as symbolic communicators between self and other unless people share a social understanding of their meaning. So, a Porsche cannot function as a symbol of virile, masculine identity unless the owner's reference group – at least – shares the belief that the car is indeed 'macho'. Evidence supporting this social symbolic view comes from disciplines as diverse as anthropology, sociology, gerontology, abnormal psychology and criminology (see Dittmar, 1992a). Material possessions can thus be viewed as symbols of identity on a social level: social class, gender, status or membership in social groups. They can also function as stereotypes. But they also symbolize more personal aspects of identity: individual qualities, values and attitudes, one's life history, or relationships with others.

The starting-point of a social constructionist perspective (for example, Gergen, 1985) is that we invariably perceive reality in terms of socially shared belief systems From this perspective, shared representations, including those about economic reality, are seen as forming a quasi-autonomous environment, which exists beyond individuals endorsing such representations and which thus forms part of the very structure of society itself (for example, Moscovici, 1988). With respect to material wealth and consumption, it is possible to extend Mead's (1934) symbolic interactionist approach to identity development in order to take account of material goods. The nub of Mead's position is that self-development requires an ability to take the 'perspective of the other' in order to gain a self-reflexive view of ourselves by drawing on shared symbol systems. Early on, a child can only interact with and adopt the perspective of one specific person at a time, and thus internalize the views that individual holds towards her. Subsequently, the child is able imaginatively to adopt the perspective of several people simultaneously, and thus comes to 'see' herself from the viewpoint of, say, her whole family or her group of playmates all at once. Finally, all encountered and imaginatively taken perspectives are generalized and integrated into an internalized set of representations – the 'generalized other' – which serve as a basis for organizing thought and action independently of the physical presence of others.

It is proposed that this process can equally be applied to the link between material possessions and identity. Initially, young children learn the range of symbolic meanings of material possessions through observing and imaginatively taking part in others' interactions with possessions, or through hearing comments about them. For one thing, they will experience that other people react to them in terms of the material possessions they have, such as their toys. In our culture, toys play a major part in the socialization and perpetuation of traditional gender roles: they embody role models (for example, Rochberg-Halton, 1984). For instance, a girl playing with her miniature dinner set may well hear approving comments from family or visitors about what a nice and generous young lady she is, serving (imaginary) cups of tea to everybody. More importantly for the present concerns, children also learn that material goods can tell us about who other people are. A mother may show her child a picture book and comment that the man who owns this beautiful, large house is very clever and successful. In this way, children are introduced to the idea that possessions can provide information about the characteristics of the owner. Belk *et al.* (1982) demonstrated that children and adolescents respond to photographs of cars and houses predominantly with status inferences (for example, has money), but also give consensually shared personal evaluations of the owner (mean, successful and so on). Driscoll *et al.* (1985) found in a comparable study that these 'stereotypical' impressions do not differ between children from different social classes.

It seems self-evident that the mass media must constitute one of the major socialization agents concerning material symbols, but research evidence is only sketchy. The fact that television plays a significant role in our construction of consumption-related social reality is documented by O'Guinn and Shrum (1991), albeit with respect to adults. Television life differs quite dramatically from reality because expensive possessions, costly consumer behaviours and wealth are heavily over-represented. Respondents were asked about their television viewing habits and estimated the percentages of adult Americans they thought (1) owned particular goods, (2) had extravagant incomes and (3) regularly engaged in certain consumption behaviours. The more television people watched, the more they tended to overestimate all the above percentages, such as the incidence of over-represented possessions like tennis courts, convertibles or car telephones. Moreover, media portrayals favour the rich. Belk's (1987) content analysis of wealth and poverty themes in American comics concludes that the wealthy, despite some ambiguous nuances, generally come across as hard-working, likeable and entitled to what they have, in contrast to the undeserving poor who are portrayed as lazy or unintelligent, thus lacking the internal motivation or ability to become wealthy. Taken in combination, the discussion so far leads to two main propositions which are examined in more detail in the remaining sections of this chapter. Proposition 1 is that the identity of others is visible in objectified form. In particular, because of our heavily stratified society, material possessions are used to locate and evaluate others in a social–material hierarchy. Proposition 2 is that meanings of material objects are established through social processes, at least to some extent. The socially constituted and socially shared meanings of possessions as symbols of identity reflect social power relationships.

ADULTS' EXPLANATIONS FOR SOCIAL INEQUALITY

If it is true that first impressions involve locating others in terms of their social standing, so that we can judge their personal qualities, then socially shared representations should exist about what people from different material backgrounds are like. Research which offers some insight into adults' beliefs about wealthy and poor people has mostly employed an attributional framework. Attribution theory is concerned with people's causal explanations for events and has customarily employed a central (though not unproblematic) distinction between causes internal or external to a person. The particular studies of interest here asked respondents to provide causal explanations for wealth, poverty and/or social inequality. These investigations demonstrate the importance of individualistic accounts – which explain why some people are rich and some are poor in terms of individual attributes – and often their predominance over external explanations in terms of socioeconomic structures or fate (for example, Feagin, 1972; Feather, 1974; Forgas *et al.*, 1982; Furnham and Lewis, 1986). Even among materially deprived people themselves, 30 per cent blamed individuals for their poverty, as compared to 25 per cent who blamed various aspects of the political system (Townsend, 1979). These attributional studies investigate beliefs about the personal qualities of the wealthy and the poor rather indirectly, but they suggest nevertheless that the wealthy are viewed as skilful, intelligent, hard-working and highly motivated, in contrast to poor people who are perceived as unmotivated and lacking in abilities, skills and proper money management.

However, would we not expect that these explanations for inequality differ according to the explainer's social and economic position? Nilson's (1981) analysis of the American National Election Survey failed to uncover differences in beliefs according to major social categories, such as class, income or occupation. But research findings have been mixed for the UK, which is more openly class-conscious. Some studies show differences between diverse social groups (for example, Furnham and Lewis, 1986), although individualistic explanations were always endorsed to a significant degree. Moreover, Forgas *et al.* (1982) stress the importance of sociocultural stereotypes shared throughout society about the wealthy and the poor, and Hewstone (1989) argues that explanations for social inequality may well reproduce 'collectively conditioned' beliefs rather than reflect individual attitudes and experiences. This suggestion that 'societal' forces inform people's representations is supported by cross-cultural research which documents systematic differences in social inequality explanations between different countries. It appears that 'explanatory strategies ... by and large reflect the dominant functional ideologies and values of the surrounding society' (Forgas *et al.*, 1988, p. 654). In conclusion, it appears that widely shared representations exist about the predominantly positive personal qualities of the wealthy and the negative attributes of the poor (see also Dittmar, 1996).

ECONOMIC SOCIALIZATION

Most studies concerned with the way in which children come to know about poverty and wealth, or ownership of material goods, describe in some detail the developmental sequences of children's ideas with a view to confirming or questioning Piaget's cognitive maturational approach to knowledge about the physical and social world. Essentially, this Piagetian cognitive–developmental perspective holds that each individual child passes through a quasi-universal set of qualitatively different stages of socioeconomic understanding, moving from simple–concrete to complex–abstract notions. For example, Furby (1980) outlines a general sequence in children's concepts of personal possessions. Initially, they view possessions in terms of physical proximity and custodianship of objects, and only later do they understand that somebody not present at the time may be the owner of an object, that possessions entail responsibility and care, and that property has complex legal underpinnings. Leahy (1990) studied the development of concepts about social inequality from a similar theoretical perspective. In the late 1970s, he carried out open-ended interviews with 720 American children and adolescents (aged 6, 11, 14 and 17) from different social class backgrounds about their perceptions of rich as compared to poor people, and their explanations for this marked social inequality. He interpreted his findings in terms of three main stages of development: peripheral, psychological and systemic. At 6–11 years of age children have peripheral conceptions of social inequality: they describe people at different levels in the social–economic hierarchy in terms of their material possessions (or lack of them), and by reference to appearance and behaviour. At 11–14 years of age, there is a pronounced shift to psychological, individualist conceptions of social inequality, where members of different socioeconomic classes are described in terms of their inferred psychological qualities, which are relatively stable. Inequalities are explained by differences in work, education, effort and intelligence. In other words, the 'rich' and the 'poor' are seen as different kinds of people. At ages 14–17, sociocentric conceptions start to emerge, such as differences in life chances. However, Leahy (1990) found that individualistic explanations continue to predominate in adolescence and moved away from a Piagetian approach in his conclusions: 'inequalities became increasingly legitimated by reference to individual differences rather than social–structural or political factors ... One might argue that the functionalist socialization to perceive inequality as legitimate is so strong as to override formal operational [Piagetian stage] thinking' (Leahy, 1990, pp. 115–16).

He thus establishes links with the social construction approach to economic socialization which tends to document the growing alignment of children's conceptualizations of political, economic and consumer aspects of material possessions with belief systems dominant in the society in question, which are transmitted through parents, schools, peers and the mass media (for example, Connell, 1977, 1983; Moschis and Smith, 1985). For example, Cummings and Taebel (1978) demonstrated that American schools progressively orient children towards a favourable view of private property, material inequalities and the capitalist system. Furnham and Stacey (1991) conclude in a recent review of this literature that the socialization process is intended to promote acceptance of the social order and that, as a consequence, 'Teenagers, like adults, show a strong tendency to hold the view that there is a need for a greatly unequal distribution of incomes and goods, and to be positively evaluative of people with riches' (p. 183).

The findings of a recent extensive cross-cultural study in 12 diverse countries (Leiser *et al.*, 1990; Leiser and Gannin in Chapter 6 of the present volume) can be used to assess speculatively the relative merits of the cognitive–developmental and the social construction perspectives on economic socialization. To aid comparability, a team of psychologists, economists and sociologists used exactly the same method and questions when interviewing children and adolescents of the same age groups (8, 11 and 14). Essentially, they found that the developing understanding of economic processes (such as banking or profit making) followed a general stage model, but that explanations for wealth and poverty were shaped by the culture in question and fairly stable across the age groups in the particular country. For instance, in (non-kibbutz) Israel, a highly individualistic society, 76 per cent of all responses referred to individual abilities (8 years: 74 per cent, 11 years: 72 per cent, 14 years: 81 per cent) and 3 per cent to systemic forces (8: 4 per cent, 11: 3 per cent, 14: 3 per cent). In contrast, in Yugoslavia, with a socialist heritage, 37 per cent of explanations were person-centred (20 per cent, 47 per cent, 43 per cent), whereas a full 49 per cent referred to social–structural factors (60 per cent, 47 per cent, 41 per cent).

The apparent opposition between the cognitive–developmental and the social construction model may therefore be reconcilable in part: cognitive and linguistic abilities clearly affect the complexity of information and processes children can comprehend and communicate, but the contents of their economic beliefs and values are shaped by the dominant, socially shared meaning systems in their culture.

ECONOMIC BELIEFS AND SOCIAL CLASS

Despite recent arguments that traditional social class boundaries are breaking down as a result of the widening 'purchasibility' of life styles (for example, Askegaard, 1991), a person's sociomaterial location still exerts a profound influence on both their spending power and their approach to material goods. In Britain, working-class people prefer instrumental and recreational possessions to ease everyday life and fill their leisure time, while middle-class people value possessions which serve symbolic needs in terms of status, personal history and self-expression (Dittmar, 1991). The explanations and justifications for income differences found by Emler and Dickinson (1985) showed that both middle-class and working-class Scottish children saw inequalities as fair, but that middle-class children had more spread-out (and realistic) income estimates of various occupations, and a greater arsenal of justifications and explanations than their working-class counterparts. It thus appears that, although working-class social representations of economic inequalities are less detailed, extensive and salient, they do not differ in kind from middle-class representations. Baldus and Tribe (1978) found virtually no social class differences in children's and adolescents' ideas about the favourable personal attributes of wealthy and negative qualities of poor people, with the exception of a negligible minority of adolescents who described the rich as bossy, ruthless or greedy.

The somewhat surprising lack of positive representations about the economically disadvantaged on the part of working-class young people is supplemented by research which shows that few adolescents seem to develop a firm sense of their own social class position or strong feelings of class allegiance. At least during the 1970s, working-class young people in the USA, Britain and Australia tended to place themselves in some vague 'middle class' bracket of neither rich nor poor, and either denied or lacked awareness of their material deprivation (cf. Furnham and Stacey, 1991). Thus we find some social class differences in the differentiation of knowledge about economic reality, but less in terms of major qualitative differences in representations and economic beliefs.

The research evidence discussed so far strongly suggests that a person's material context should have a discernible influence on the way we perceive her or his personal identity, but does not offer insight into the processes which may shape first impressions. Social psychology offers two possible theoretical frameworks which can be applied to this issue: social identity theory and dominant representations (cf. Dittmar, 1992b).

ADOLESCENTS' SOCIAL IDENTITY AND INTER-GROUP PERCEPTION

Specific material possessions seem to be less important for determining how other people are viewed than a general assessment of their relative socioeconomic standing (Dittmar, 1990), which constitutes one of the important social categories we use to carve up our social environment. Tajfel's (1982, 1984) social identity theory (SIT) is concerned with inter-group perceptions and makes two important assumptions. Firstly, Tajfel argues that social categorization is similar to physical categorization in the sense that inter-group differences and within-group similarities are exaggerated as a means for clearly distinguishing between category member and non-members. But such a perceptual focus on social categorization is insufficient in itself to explain in-group favouritism and out-group discrimination. Secondly, SIT's motivational hypothesis puts forward the further idea that people seek to maintain a positively valued identity by comparing in-groups favourably with out-groups. In terms of possessions and impressions, SIT would imply that we form more favourable impressions of a person from a similar social–material background to our own and less favourable ones of people in different material circumstances.

However, in-group favouritism seems rather limited within the unequal power and status relationships in the 'real' world, once one moves away from the equal groups artificially created in the laboratory. Members of low status groups are often in agreement with high status groups about their 'inferiority' on a variety of comparison dimensions (consensual evaluations). Van Knippenberg (1984) therefore proposes two motivations in addition to in-group favouritism in order to explain why descriptions for and by high and low status members contain many consensual, rather than competitive, evaluations. Firstly, low status individuals might well exaggerate their disadvantaged social standing vis-à-vis high status groups in order to draw attention to status differentials and, at least implicitly, to question their legitimacy (strategic comments). Secondly, he suggests that group comparisons can be seen as acts of mutual validation that essentially preserve existing status differences. For instance, high status groups may be quite happy to agree with low status groups that the latter are superior on status-unrelated, unthreatening qualities, such as 'friendly', or 'cooperative'. Van Knippenberg (1984) offers a more complex analysis of motivational processes underlying the perception of people in different social groups than SIT, but his model nevertheless still implies that impressions formed of a 'wealthy' or 'poor' person should differ, depending on whether perceivers come from an affluent or non-affluent material background themselves. Such an interaction effect may be smaller than that predicted by original SIT, but it still occurs because in-group favouritism should appear on at least one comparison dimension and because lower status individuals tend towards negative exaggeration on status-relevant dimensions (for example, low-status individuals may claim to be poorer than they actually are).

The expectations derived from SIT assume that people identify with their own social–material category to some extent. However, many young people seem to lack such a 'politicized' awareness of socioeconomic stratification, as we have seen. Therefore, the adolescents' impressions studied in the present author's research may not be influenced by social identity, category-defensive concerns, but may reflect in quite a passive way widely shared representations about the characteristics of the 'wealthy' and the 'poor'. Socioeconomic socialization research suggests that children and adolescents increasingly endorse the legitimacy of wealth differentials, viewed as the outcome of individual merit, and that they do so quite independently of their own relative socioeconomic background (for example, Baldus and Tribe, 1978; Connell, 1977; Leahy, 1990). Thus it seems that our symbolic environment contains, not simply socially shared beliefs, but dominant representations, which favour the wealthy and inadvertently reflect the distribution of power and status in society. Such dominant representations differ from social representations (cf. Moscovici, 1988) in two ways. They are probably not generated within specific social groups, but constitute 'information which is free-floating, available to all regardless of their position in a structure of social relationships' (Connell, 1977, p. 150). Moreover, they form a part of dominant ideology (Abercrombie *et al.*, 1984) in a broad sense because they play a role in the maintenance of the social composition of society. However, this need not necessarily imply some form of working-class 'false consciousness' (Marx and Engels, 1965) – with the 'powerful' directly imposing representations of the characteristics of the affluent and the poor which serve their interests –

which is conceptually difficult to pin down and virtually impossible to verify empirically. Rather, dominant representations might be viewed more fruitfully as an integral part of culture and common sense, comprising the lay ideas of ordinary women and men (Billig *et al.*, 1988). This need not deny, however, that such representations do reflect prevailing power relationships (Spears, 1989). With respect to consumption and stratification, this claim is supported by research (already discussed) which suggests that the affluent are perceived in an overwhelmingly positive light, in stark contrast to the disadvantaged. The dominant representations perspective sketched here leads to the expectation that people form essentially similar first impressions of others on the basis of their relative wealth, drawing on dominant representations, quite irrespective of their own material background: impressions should be shared across different social classes.

ECONOMIC BELIEFS OF ADOLESCENTS FROM DIFFERENT SOCIAL CLASS BACKGROUNDS

In order to investigate the question of whether impressions are shared across socioeconomic groups or whether they differ for perceivers from different backgrounds, it was decided to use short videos offering a rich and naturalistic depiction of a person as stimulus material. To assess possible gender difference in relations to consumption and material possessions (Dittmar, 1989; Lunt and Livingstone, 1992), both a woman and a man were filmed separately in different surroundings. The results were four videos: two young people (one female, one male) in either fairly wealthy or much less affluent circumstances.

Because the same person was filmed in both an affluent and a less affluent context, any tendency of differences in impressions formed about that person can be related unambiguously to differences in material circumstances. The videos did not portray extreme wealth or poverty, but the material possessions displayed corresponded either to a middle-class context or to a less affluent context with basic essentials. Over one hundred 16–18-year-old adolescents, half middle-class and half working-class, were shown one of the four videos in small groups. They first of all gave an open-ended description of the video character, then evaluated her or him in terms of preselected personal qualities and, finally, described in their own words how similar the video surroundings were to their parental homes in terms of material wealth. Social identity theory predicts an interaction effect: the two groups of adolescents should differ in the impressions they form of the affluent and less privileged video character, and these impressions should be influenced by the similarity in social–material background between perceiver and target. In contrast, the dominant representations approach suggests that the two groups of adolescents would form similar impressions, and that they would favour the affluent person.

As expected, the middle-class adolescents saw the wealthy video setting as more similar to their home (X = 5.2; 7-point scale) than the less affluent video (X = 2.1) in terms of material wealth, whereas the reverse effect emerged for the working-class adolescents (X = 3.6; X = 4.5). When the open-ended descriptions were analysed, it emerged that the middle-class and working-class adolescents did differ in the person description categories they used spontaneously, but – contrary to social identity theory – the two groups of adolescents did not respond differently to the 'rich' or 'poor' settings in the video.

The middle-class adolescents commented frequently on the video character's physical appearance, while the working-class adolescents referred more to personal qualities. Moreover, the finding that personal characteristics emerged as the most prominent category overall fits well with Leahy's (1990) conclusion that individual merit and effort representations about relative wealth dominate adolescent thinking.

Ratings of the video character's personal qualities were summarized into five dimensions, which fall into two broad categories. The first consists of dominance qualities and comprises control, forcefulness, and abilities and resources (for example, intelligent, successful, educated). The second broad category contains two affective–expressive qualities: perceived warmth and individuality. The main findings were that the working-class adolescents shared the middle-class adolescents' impressions, with impressions differing only on the basis of the material setting in which the video character appeared. Combining perceived identity dimensions, both groups of adolescents agreed that the video character had more dominance qualities when she or he appeared wealthy, particularly having more intelligence and more control of their life and environment. In contrast, the poorer person came across as warmer and more self-expressive. It thus appears that the first impressions adolescents form of others in different material circumstances are influenced strongly by representations which are clearly shared across different social class groups. This is not what we would expect according to social identity theory.

MATERIALISM, SOCIAL CLASS AND PERSON PERCEPTION

The finding that categorical judgements about others' relative material standing are tied up with personal evaluations of their qualities as individuals echoes recent conceptual analyses of materialism. These identified as a central theme people's tendency to evaluate success and well-being of self and others by the number and quality of material possessions owned (Fournier and Richins, 1991). The impact of material goods on first impressions could therefore be seen as a facet of materialism at the level of social perception: socially shared representations about wealth and identity profoundly influence our perception of others' social qualities and, in turn, their personal qualities. In contrast to this social representations perspective, materialism has been conceptualized as an individual difference variable (Belk, 1985; Richins and Dawson, 1992).

A materialistic person is somebody who thinks that acquiring material possessions is central to her or his life, and that they are the main standards by which happiness is achieved, and self and others are judged. For example, individuals who strongly endorse materialistic values hold more unrealistic expectations about the likely psychological and social benefits they hope to acquire from consumer goods, and they experience more negative emotions after purchasing them than people in whose lives possessions play a less central role (Richins, 1991; Richins and Dawson, 1992). If materialism is thought of as an individual attribute, then materialistic people ought to be more strongly influenced by possessions in their perception of others than those low in materialism. In other words, individually held materialistic values may moderate the link between possessions and impressions. Moreover, people from different social classes differ in self-concept, values and consumption goals (for example, Coleman, 1983) and they have different orientations to material possession. This may well suggest that endorsement of materialistic values is related systematically to a person's social class background, and possibly reflects differential concerns with material and psychological security.

Thus a study by Dittmar and Pepper (1994) addressed the question of whether materialism as an individual value orientation affects middle-class and working-class adolescents' perception of the identity of a person who is portrayed as either affluent or lacking in expensive possessions. At the same time, it may reveal differences in materialism between the two groups of adolescents. Over 150 14–16-year-old adolescents read one of four short descriptions of either a young woman or a young man, living in either a relatively wealthy or a less affluent setting (indicated by car, furniture, housing and so on). They then described and evaluated the person they had read about in terms of earnings, personal qualities and life style. Finally, they completed a measure of materialism as an individual value orientation (Richins, 1991).

The working-class adolescents endorsed materialistic values significantly more strongly (X = 79.17; range 18–126) than the middle-class adolescents

($X = 75.12$), particularly in terms of items like 'I would be happier if I owned nice things' or 'My life would be better if I owned certain things I don't have.'

Not surprisingly, when the person in the vignette was described as affluent, she or he was thought to earn significantly more (about £16–20 000 a year) than when less affluent (about £8–12 000 a year). However, the middle-class adolescents saw a much greater earnings differential between the two material settings (difference of about £10 000 a year) than the working-class adolescents (difference of only about £4000 a year). This finding corroborates earlier research (Emler and Dickinson, 1985) and probably arises from middle-class adolescents' greater familiarity with the price of material goods that are affordable in higher wage brackets.

Yet, notwithstanding the social class differences in materialism and perceived earnings, the working-class and middle-class adolescents agreed once more in their evaluations of the person described in the vignette (which again comprised the two dimensions of dominance and affective personal qualities). When affluent, she or he was seen as much more intelligent, successful and hard-working, enjoying the life style all adolescents aspired to. But, at the same time, she or he was seen as less caring, less happy and less attractive as a friend.

However, the main focus of this research is on the potential impact of materialistic values on impressions. Surprisingly, this impact is comparatively minor when contrasted with the effect of the relative wealth cues given in the vignettes. The pattern of impressions remains virtually unaltered even when the influence of materialistic values is filtered out by statistical means.[1] However, endorsing a materialistic outlook does influence impressions overall, and is related significantly to the perception of the dominance identity dimension (intelligent, successful, hard-working and so on).

The way in which materialistic values affect impressions becomes clearer when extreme samples are taken. We examined those middle- and working-class adolescents highest and lowest in materialism (about highest and lowest 20 per cent). The more materialistic an individual's outlook, the more they will perceive a link between a person's abilities and their relative wealth, particularly where affluence is concerned. The non-materialistic adolescents perceived a much smaller connection between wealth on the one hand and intelligence, success and hard work on the other than the highly materialistic adolescents. They did not see expensive possessions as strong evidence for these qualities; in fact, they saw them as hardly any evidence at all.

CONCLUSION: MATERIAL CONTEXT AND SOCIAL COGNITION

In the first proposition formulated from a social constructionist perspective on material symbols, this chapter has argued that we use others' possessions to locate them socially and to evaluate their personal identity. If we accept that the first impressions adolescents formed of one and the same person were dramatically affected by the material circumstances shown in a video, we cannot doubt the profound impact of material factors on our perception of other people. Admittedly, these first impressions were studied before any interaction or communication had taken place. But we should not underestimate the influence of material symbols on social cognition, and the potential consequences of that influence. Firstly, a growing number of superficial, impersonal contacts in diverse contexts has become a commonplace form of interaction, which characterizes the urban environment of 'modernity' (for example, Giddens, 1990) and secondly, such first stereotypic impressions may then influence and shape subsequent interactions, and thus become 'lasting' impressions. They can even make a person behave in accordance with the expectations we have of them, as shown by the social psychological work on stereotypes as self-fulfilling prophecies (for example, Snyder, 1984; Word *et al.*, 1974).

Moreover, even if children and adolescents from different social class backgrounds differ in certain aspects of economic understanding and sophistication, they nevertheless agree on and reproduce widely shared, stereotypical views about people high and low in the socioeconomic hierarchy. Both working- and middle-class adolescents thought that intelligence, success, motivation, control and forcefulness accompany wealth, even if warmth and expressiveness go by the wayside. This argument is strengthened further by the similarities in findings between the video and vignette studies. This is disturbing evidence that adolescents may not even be aware how heavily their impressions are shaped by material factors.

Young people deny the link between possessions and impressions: undergraduates ($n = 240$) maintained, when asked directly, that they themselves were hardly influenced in their impressions by material factors (Dittmar *et al.*, 1989). Moreover, all the personal qualities investigated in the research described are normally believed to be essential, intrinsic aspects of identity, when people are asked directly whether having the quality in question is in any way linked to what a person owns, how they dress, which car they drive, and so on (cf. Dittmar, 1992a). In fact, 'intelligent' was described as the most intrinsic personal quality, but was then perceived radically differently on the basis of a person's wealth and possessions. Not being aware of the impact of material context on our perception of others, or denying it because it makes us uncomfortable, fits well with the dominant western view of personhood as a set of fixed personality traits which are not influenced by the social and material environment.

Thus contradictory representations appear to exist about the link between 'what we have' and 'who we are': a cultural, 'idealist' conception of personhood as autonomous individuality versus a negatively loaded, 'materialist' recognition that possessions and wealth can regulate not only large-scale societal processes but also interpersonal relations and perceptions. The idea that such a materialism–idealism paradox may exist in individuals' ideas about others' identities becomes less strange when related to recent arguments that common sense is complex and frequently contains such 'ideological dilemmas'. But, as Spears (1989) points out, 'it could be argued that it is precisely when the contradictions relating to unequal power relations are not articulated in "ideological dilemmas" of people's everyday thinking, that "ideology" in its critical sense is most evident' (p. 284).

The extent to which working-class adolescents share positive views about the affluent and negative perceptions of the less well off with their middle-class counterparts is disturbing. By so doing, they implicitly cast a negative light on their own lives and identities. This finding provides support for the dominant representations approach against the class-based social identification we would expect from SIT. However, individually held materialistic values do appear to affect person perception in a material context, if only to a moderate extent. More specifically, materialism as a value orientation works as an amplifier: it leads individuals to draw more strongly on dominant representations, or relative wealth stereotypes, about the personal qualities of people on different rungs of the socioeconomic ladder. However, the generality of these findings needs to be assessed in Anglo-American cultures beyond Britain.

Moreover, these socially shared notions can be conceptualized as dominant representations, because they appear to have ideological components: they depict wealthier individuals in a more flattering and positive light – as more intelligent, assertive and in control. However, representations about the wealthy also contained ambivalent elements: impressions of interpersonal warmth and expressiveness favour less affluent individuals, but these can also be fitted into an ideological interpretation. The dominant western conception of personhood exemplifies the central importance that is accorded to autonomy, control and self-reliance (Lukes, 1979; Shweder and Miller, 1985). Such attributes as 'warm' and 'friendly' may well be seen as pleasant, but somehow less important aspects of identity. Having 'warm' and 'friendly' poorer people certainly does not threaten the privileged position and positive identity of the economically advantaged, and may make the unequal distribution of wealth appear less unpalatable. It is therefore not surprising that people from poorer social strata are seen as such, and this may well play a role in the maintenance and positive evaluation of wealth differentials. In fact, Henley (1977) argues that warmth and emotional expressiveness characterize the powerless, because they are the ones who smooth over tension, pander to the whims of, and disclose personal emotions to, the powerful in such a way that status relationships are maintained.

It can be concluded, albeit speculatively, that dominant, ideologically loaded representations about our unequal distribution of wealth constitute a societal, commonsense frame of reference which informs causal explanations for social inequality and social perception of people at different levels in the socioeconomic hierarchy. In their barest essence, these representations portray the wealthy and the poor as different types of people who have different personal qualities. To then view these different traits and qualities as the reason for material achievement (or lack of it), and to assert that social inequality must be fair since it is the outcome of individual effort and merit, are two easy steps to take, however erroneous. Dominant representations about the wealthy and the poor, and about material possessions, may therefore serve easily to legitimize the status quo and social inequality, and they inform children's and adolescents' thinking through various socialization agents: schooling, peers and the mass media in particular. This highly significant layer of economic socialization – the progressive alignment with dominant representations about relative wealth and identity – deserves extensive research efforts, not neglect, in order for us to understand the impact of our current materialistic orientation on social perception and economic beliefs.

NOTE

1. Factor scores on impression dimensions (estimated by regression) were analysed by a 2 (Material Setting) × 2 (Social Class) × 2 (Target Sex) × 2 (Respondent Sex) MANOVA with and without materialism (individual total score) as a covariate. The adjusted factor score means from the covariance analysis show the impact of material setting when the level of endorsement of materialistic values is held constant statistically across respondents.

REFERENCES

Abercrombie, N., Hill, S. and Turner, S.T. (1984), *Dictionary of Sociology*, Harmondsworth: Penguin.
Askegaard, S. (1991), 'How people change life styles', paper presented at the Joint Conference of the Society for the Advancement of Socio-Economics and the International Association for Research in Economic Psychology on 'Interdisciplinary Approaches to Economic Problems', 16–19 June, Stockholm, Sweden.
Baldus, B. and Tribe, V. (1978), 'The development of perceptions and evaluations of

social inequality among public school children', *Canadian Review of Sociology and Anthropology*, **15** (1), 50–60.

Belk, R.W. (1985), 'Materialism: Trait aspects of living in the material world', *Journal of Consumer Research*, **12** (3), 265–80.

Belk, R.W. (1987), 'Material values in the comics: A content analysis of comic books featuring themes of wealth', *Journal of Consumer Research*, **14** (1), 26–42.

Belk, R.W., Bahn, K.D. and Mayer, R.N. (1982), 'Developmental recognition of consumption symbolism', *Journal of Consumer Research*, **9**, 4–17.

Billig, M., Condor, S., Edwards, D., Gane, M., Middleton, D. and Radley, A.R. (1988), *Ideological Dilemmas: A Social Psychology of Everyday Thinking*, London: Sage.

Bourdieu, P. (1984), *Distinction: A Social Critique of the Judgement of Taste*, London: Routledge and Kegan Paul.

Buckley, H.M. and Roach, M.E. (1974), 'Clothing as a nonverbal communicator of social and political attitudes', *Home Economics Research Journal*, **3**, 98–102.

Burroughs, W.J., Drews, D.R. and Hallman, W.K. (1991), 'Predicting personality from personal possessions: A self-presentational analysis', in F.W. Rudmin (ed.), *To Have Possessions: A Handbook on Ownership and Property*, special issue of the *Journal of Social Behavior and Personality*, **6** (6), 147–64.

Cassell, J. (1974), 'Externalities of change: Deference and demeanor in contemporary feminism', *Human Organization*, **33**, 85–94.

Cherulnik, P.D. and Bayless, J.K. (1986), 'Person perception in environmental context: The influence of residential settings on impressions of their occupants', *Journal of Social Psychology*, **126** (5), 667–73.

Coleman, R.P. (1983), 'The continuing significance of social class to marketing', *Journal of Consumer Research*, **10**, 265–80.

Connell, R.W. (1977), *Ruling Class, Ruling Culture: Studies of Conflict, Power and Hegemony in Australian Life*, Melbourne: Cambridge University Press.

Connell, R.W. (1983), *Which Way is Up? Essays on Sex, Class and Culture*, Sidney: Allen and Unwin.

Cummings, S. and Taebel, D. (1978), 'The economic socialization of children: A neo-Marxist analysis', *Social Problems*, **26** (2), 198–210.

Dittmar, H. (1989), 'Gender identity-related meanings of personal possessions', *British Journal of Social Psychology*, **28**, 159–71.

Dittmar, H. (1990), 'Material wealth and perceived identity: Impressions of adolescents from different socio-economic backgrounds', in S.E.A. Lea, P. Webley and B. Young (eds), *Advances in Economic Psychology, Vol. 2*, Exeter: Washington Singer, pp. 805–12.

Dittmar, H. (1991), 'Meanings of material possessions as reflections of identity: Gender and social–material position in society', in F.W. Rudmin (ed.), *To Have Possessions: A Handbook on Ownership and Property*, special issue of *Journal of Social Behavior and Personality*, **6** (6), 165–86.

Dittmar, H. (1992a), *The Social Psychology of Material Possessions: To Have is To Be*, Hemel Hempstead: Harvester Wheatsheaf.

Dittmar, H. (1992b), 'Perceived material wealth and first impressions', *British Journal of Social Psychology*, **31** (4), 379–91.

Dittmar, H. (1996), 'The social psychology of economic and consumer behaviour', Chapter 6 in G.R. Semin and K. Fiedler (eds), *Applied Social Psychology*, London: Sage.

Dittmar, H. and Pepper, L. (1994), 'To have is to be: Materialism and person perception in working-class and middle-class British adolescents', *Journal of Economic Psychology*, **15** (2), 233–51.

Dittmar, H., Mannetti, L. and Semin, G. (1989), 'Fine feathers make fine birds: A comparative study of the impact of material wealth on perceived identities in England and Italy', *Social Behaviour*, **4** (3), 195–200.

Douglas, M. and Isherwood, B. (1979), *The World of Goods: Towards an Anthropology of Consumption*, London: Allen Lane.

Douty, H.I. (1963), 'Influence of clothing on perception of persons', *Journal of Home Economics*, **55** (3), 197–202.

Driscoll, A.M., Mayer, R.N. and Belk, R.W. (1985), 'The young child's recognition of consumption symbols and their social implications', *Child Study Journal*, **15** (2), 117–30.

Emler, N. and Dickinson, J. (1985), 'Children's representation of economic inequalities: The effects of social class', *British Journal of Developmental Psychology*, **3** (2), 191–8.

Feagin, J.R. (1972), 'Poverty: We still believe that God helps those who help themselves', *Psychology Today*, **6**, 101–29.

Feather, N.T. (1974), 'Explanations of poverty in Australian and American samples: The person, society or fate?', *Australian Journal of Psychology*, **26** (3), 199–216.

Forgas, J.P., Furnham, A. and Frey, D. (1988), 'Cross-national differences in attributions of wealth and economic success', *Journal of Social Psychology*, **129** (3), 643–57.

Forgas, J.P., Morris, S.L. and Furnham, A. (1982), 'Lay explanations of wealth: Attributions for economic success', *Journal of Applied Social Psychology*, **12** (5), 381–97.

Fournier, S. and Richins, M. (1991), 'Some theoretical and popular notions concerning materialism', in F.W. Rudmin (ed.), *To Have Possessions: A Handbook on Ownership and Property*, special issue of the *Journal of Social Behavior and Personality*, **6** (6), 403–14.

Furby, L. (1980), 'The origins and early development of possessive behaviour', *Political Economy*, **2** (1), 30–42.

Furnham, A. and Lewis, A. (1986), *The Economic Mind: The Social Psychology of Economic Behaviour*, Brighton: Wheatsheaf.

Furnham, A. and Stacey, B. (1991), *Young People's Understanding of Society*, London: Routledge and Kegan Paul.

Gergen, K.J. (1985), 'The social constructionist movement in modern psychology', *American Psychologist*, **40** (3), 266–75.

Giddens, A. (1990), *The Consequences of Modernity*, Cambridge: Polity Press.

Goffman, E. (1951), 'Symbols of class status', *British Journal of Sociology*, **2**, 294–304.

Haire, M. (1950), 'Projective techniques in marketing research', *Journal of Marketing*, **14** (5), 649–56.

Henley, N. (1977), *Body Politics: Power, Sex and Non-Verbal Communication*, New York: Prentice Hall.

Hewstone, M. (1989), *Causal Attribution: From Cognitive Processes to Collective Beliefs*, Oxford: Basil Blackwell.

Lea, S.E.G., Tarpy, R.M. and Webley, P. (1987), *The Individual in the Economy*, Cambridge: Cambridge University Press.

Leahy, R.L. (1990), 'The development of concepts of economic and social inequality', *New Directions for Child Psychology*, **46**, 107–20.

Leiser, D., Roland-Lévy, C. and Sevón, G. (1990) (eds), 'Economic Socialization', special issue of the *Journal of Economic Psychology*, **11** (4).
Lukes, S. (1979), *Individualism*, Oxford: Blackwell.
Lunt, P.K. and Livingstone, S.M. (1992), *Mass Consumption and Personal Identity*, Buckingham: Open University Press.
Marx, K. and Engels, F. (1965), *The German Ideology*, London: Lawrence and Wishart.
Mead, G.H. (1934), *Mind, Self and Society*, Chicago: University of Chicago Press.
Moschis, G.P. and Smith, R.B. (1985), 'Consumer socialization: Origins, trends and directions for future research', in C.T. Tan and J.N. Sheth (eds), *Historical Perspective in Consumer Research*, National University of Singapore: School of Management, pp. 275–81.
Moscovici, S. (1988), 'Notes towards a description of social representations', *European Journal of Social Psychology*, **18** (3), 211–50.
Nilson, L.B. (1981), 'Reconsidering ideological lines', *Sociological Quarterly*, **22**, 531–48.
O'Guinn, T.C. and Shrum, L.J. (1991), 'Mass-mediated social reality: The social cognition and ecology of economic norms', paper presented at the Joint Conference of the Society for the Advancement of Socio-Economics and the International Association for Research in Economic Psychology on 'Interdisciplinary Approaches to Economic Problems', 16–19 June, Stockholm, Sweden.
Reid, L.N. and Buchanan, L. (1979), 'A shopping list experiment of the impact of advertising on brand images', *Journal of Advertising*, **8**, 26–8.
Richins, M.L. (1991), 'Possessions in the lives of materialists: An analysis of consumption-related affect and expectations', paper presented at the Joint Conference of the Society for the Advancement of Socio-Economics and the International Association for Research in Economic Psychology on 'Interdisciplinary Approaches to Economic Problems', 16–19 June, Stockholm, Sweden.
Richins, M. and Dawson, S. (1992), 'Materialism as a consumer value: Measure development and validation', *Journal of Consumer Research*, **19**, 303–16.
Rochberg-Halton, E. (1984), 'Object relations, role models and cultivation of the self', *Environment and Behavior,* **16** (3), 335–68.
Shweder, R.A. and Miller, J.G. (1985), 'The social construction of the person: How is it possible?', in K.J. Gergen and K.E. Davis (eds), *The Social Construction of the Person*, New York: Springer, pp. 41–72.
Snyder, M. (1984), 'When belief creates reality', in L. Berkowitz (ed.), *Advances in Experimental Social Psychology*, Vol. 18, New York: Academic Press.
Spears, R. (1989), 'Book review: Ideological dilemmas', *British Journal of Social Psychology*, **28** (3), 283–8.
Stacey, B.G. (1982), 'Economic socialization in the pre-adult years', *British Journal of Social Psychology*, **21** (2), 159–73.
Tajfel, H. (ed.) (1982), *Social Identity and Intergroup Relations*, Cambridge: Cambridge University Press.
Tajfel, H. (ed.) (1984), *The Social Dimension Vols 1 and 2*, Cambridge: Cambridge University Press.
Townsend, P. (1979), *Poverty in the United Kingdom: A Survey of Household Resources and Standards of Living*, Harmondsworth: Penguin.
Van Knippenberg, A. (1984), 'Intergroup differences in group perceptions', in H. Tajfel (ed.), *The Social Dimension, Vol. 2*, Cambridge: Cambridge University Press, pp. 561–78.

Webley, P. and Lea, S.E.G. (1992), 'Towards a more realistic psychology of economic socialization', paper presented at the International Symposium of Economic Psychology, 27 March, Tilburg, Netherlands.

Wells, W.D., Andriuli, F.J., Goi, F.J. and Seader, S. (1957), 'An adjective check list for the study of "product personality"', *Journal of Applied Psychology*, **41**, 317–19.

Woodside, A.G. (1972), 'A shopping list experiment of beer brand images', *Journal of Applied Psychology*, **56** (6), 512–13.

Word, C.O., Zanna, M.P. and Cooper, J. (1974), 'The nonverbal mediation of self-fulfilling prophecies in interracial interaction', *Journal of Experimental Social Psychology*, **10**, 109–20.

6. Economic participation and economic socialization

David Leiser and Margalit Ganin

CHILDREN, LABOUR AND MONEY

In modern western culture, attitudes towards children's participation in the economic world are often marked by ambiguity. The two central aspects of this participation are labour and money. In earlier times child labour was useful and necessary. The contribution of children to the toil on the farm was important, their work was expected as a matter of course, little praise was needed, no payment was offered and the child was satisfied with his contribution (Straus, 1962). Over the years, as the dissociation of home and economic unit (farm) transformed the basis of family cohesion, the prevailing concept of children and their obligations to the family unit has changed. Zelizer (1985) traces the developmental changes in attitude to children, from useful to useless and somehow 'sacred' around the turn of the century in the USA. A similar sentimentalization of the child took place in other places and times (Aries, 1973; Shorter, 1976). Child labour came to be seen as exploitative and wrong and, while extensive abuses still exist (especially in Asia), child labour is illegal in western countries and largely unknown there.

In a similar spirit, many parents who like to see themselves as adequate providers wish to shield their children from economic worries. Their children are accordingly kept away from serious discussion of family finances and excluded from the deliberations preceding important purchases. When there are financial difficulties, they are not made aware of them, on the ground that they are only young once, and will have to face those worries in their own adults' lives. Economic matters are grown-up preoccupations.

These concerns conflict with educational considerations. Children must be trained for this future economic independence. They should learn how to function with money, budget what they have, learn to postpone immediate gratification and to save, and perhaps also learn the 'value of money' by exerting themselves to earn it. There are pragmatic aspects as well. Children do need the money. In the modern consumer economy many goods are directed at the young, whose disposable income is far from negligible and whose susceptibility to clever merchandising is a byword. Some way has to be found to solve the insolvency. Finally, parents may wish to be left alone: let the child manage a budget, and the parent will not be bothered by cease-less requests for money to cover its petty expenses.

The attitudes to household chores are similarly value-laden. Children are often made to participate in various house chores, even though the value of children's work to parents in labour terms often falls below the effort of supervision. This being so, why do parents want children to do household work? There are both pragmatic and ideological commitments (Straus, 1962) to this practice.

The two issues we raised, relation to money and to work, are mutually relevant: one solution in principle to the insolvency problem of children would be paid work around the house. Labour would not be excessive, but sufficient to teach children 'the value of money', payment could depend on exertion, and there are limits to how much may be earned. Another, competing approach is to give them money unconditionally. There are considerations that militate against the exchange of money for services: chores should be done voluntarily, as one aspect of participating in the household. And, by the same token, the child deserves part of the family income, by dint of being a member. Such an arrangement might be held to support family cohesiveness and reciprocal obli-gation. A modern advocate of this attitude argues as follows:

> Being given a non-contingent allowance implies or represents a greater degree of trust than having to work for the money. Parents who give allowances are commu-nicating to their children that they are full members of the household, deserve a portion of the family's income, and must behave accordingly. They may also be telling their children that they are supposed to learn how to deal with money since this is, in fact, why most parents decide to give allowances. Children who get allowances may feel more responsibility for the money they received, may make greater efforts to deal with it, and may accordingly become more knowledgeable and sophisticated about money. ... In giving money for chores the focus is on the work and the contract for doing that work ... Parents are less free to tell the child how to deal with money that the children have earned. (Abramovitch *et al.*, 1991)

There are four ways to let children have money, without contravening the prohibition against child labour: (1) giving money to the child on an 'as needed' basis; (2) an allowance or 'pocket money', a fixed sum given at set time intervals; (3) paid work within the house: since the well-meaning parent is the employer, this may be seen as a 'shift from instrumental to instruc-tional' (Zelizer, 1985), whereby the child learns to work for money; and (4) the child may also work outside the home, in a 'real' part-time job that is typically poorly paid, but which the child can leave at short notice, and constitutes a first step towards real economic autonomy.

White and Brinkerhoff (1981) studied empirically why children are made to work in the family or, more accurately, the reasons given by their parents. The population studied comprised 790 homes where there lived a child under the age of 18. The reasons offered were classified under four heads: (1) developmental – sharing in the house chores develops responsibility and builds character; (2) reciprocal – mutual obligation and working in the house promotes cohesiveness of the family; it makes children feel they have their duties and share in making it a home; (3) extrinsic – their contribution is actually useful and required; (4) task learning – they need to know how to do those tasks, as part of becoming autonomous; eventually they will have to manage them on their own.

The distribution of the reasons is telling. Most parents endorse the 'developmental' view. Three-quarters of the respondents stated that the child has to work for his or her own benefit. The frequency depends somewhat on the age of the child. For older children, the importance of learning the task and an acknowledgment of the usefulness of their work become more frequent. This is of course natural, since the balance of effort spent on supervision and effort saved by the child's work becomes more favourable as the child grows older. Similarly, families with a higher workload (such as single mothers) stress more the pragmatic aspect. In view of this, the effect of social class appears paradoxical. Higher status and better educated parents tend to stress reciprocal obligations more than others. Similarly, Newson and Newson (1976) found that parents further down the social class expect less help and responsibility of their children (especially boys) despite a presumably greater need. Part of the explanation for this paradox may be a more indulgent attitude to children and a less future-oriented view of the world.

Parents' hope notwithstanding, the effect of children's involvement in household tasks on dependability and responsibility outside the house was found 'negligible' by Elder (1974), as it had earlier in a large-scale study (Harris *et al.*, 1954). The latter study (which suffered from some methodological shortcomings) found no correlation between children's involvement in household tasks and teachers' ratings of children for responsibility shown at school in 3000 schoolchildren.

The notion that learning is best done by practice, rather than by observation, is not universal. Goodnow *et al.* (1984) noted marked differences between Australian-born and Lebanese-born groups in an Australian suburb: Australian-born parents wanted children to practise, and were also concerned about teaching 'too late', whereas Lebanon-born parents were content to let their charges observe, expressing no particular concern about lateness of the teaching experience.

In a recent study, Abramovitch *et al.* (1991) set out to study empirically the educational effect of receiving an allowance. Their population consisted of young children (aged 6–10) belonging to the upper middle class. They checked the effect of receiving money for work or as an allowance on the amount of money spent when made available either as cash or a credit, with what was left redeemable as cash. To this end, the children were brought into a make-believe but realistic store, and their behaviour in that store was studied. In addition, the subjects answered a short questionnaire. As it turned out, there was no difference in the amount of money available between those who received an allowance and those who received it unconditionally. The data show no effect of any of the background variables studied (allowance size, family's income, maths score). However, children who received an allowance turned out to be 'more sophisticated in spending'. Specifically, they ignored the spurious difference between cash and credit. As the authors noted, 'children may consider cash quite different from a credit card: bank notes and coins are a concrete reality'. Overall, children do spend more with credit cards. Those receiving a regular allowance were also more knowledgeable about pricing, but this relation held only for the youngest children. The finding also contradicts an earlier report by Marshall and Magruder (1960), who found no connection between the fact of receiving an allowance and knowledge of what items cost, but did find a positive relationship with the amount of experience in dealing with money – the latter including allowances, but also other sources. The (debatable) relative superiority of the allowance group is explained by Abramovitch *et al.* (1991) as an outgrowth of their parents' approach:

> We would argue that this communicates to the children that they must deal with the money responsibly, and that this causes the recipients of allowance to pay more attention to the economic system, including such aspects of it as the meaning of credit and what things cost. (p. 41)

We saw above that higher status and better educated parents tend to stress reciprocal obligations more than lower-class parents, in their demands for house work. One would expect a comparable effect in the reasons for giving an allowance. The few studies which address this point do not support this view. Studying 7–12-year-olds in Britain, Furnham and Thomas (1984) found surprisingly few class differences. The trend was of more linking of behaviour to money amongst middle-class parents, but the authors admit class classification was unreliable. In another study that relied on a better assessment of socioeconomic status (SES), Newson and Newson (1976) found no relation at all: in all five class groups, one half of the parents reported that their children could earn money by doing household work, while 30–40 per cent of the parents opposed this arrangement, branding it as 'bribery'. Goodnow (1988) accordingly summarizes: 'Clearly, parents vary considerably in both opinions and practice, but socioeconomic status does not emerge as making the contribution it was expected to make.' This statement, however, has to be set against Stacey's (1982): 'in the first decade of life, the economic socialization of children does not appear to be strongly influenced by their own social backgrounds [except for the extremes]. In the second decade of life, social differences in the development appear to be more pronounced.' Indeed, most of the findings concern the lower age range. The study of adolescents to be reported below documents considerable differences in attitudes across social class.

ATTITUDES AND VALUES

Leahy (1981) found that middle-class subjects tend to explain wealth and poverty by personal characteristics (they are better, work harder, are more intelligent, and so on), which Leahy describes as justifications. The 'Naive Economics Project', in the course of which middle-class children in a dozen countries were interviewed, confirms these findings (Leiser *et al.*, 1990). Averaging across countries, wealth differences are attributed mainly to personal factors at all ages. Middle-class children, who are relatively well off, tend to think that differences in wealth are not sheer injustice but the consequence of objective personal characteristics. As they grow older, children's orientation becomes increasingly favourable to capitalist values:

> The data suggests the progressive development, in individual consciousness, of political ideas endorsing and legitimating some of the more important features of capitalistic economic thinking: private ownership of the means of production, individual striving and meritocratic explanation of inequality, and limited state intrusion into business affairs. Conversely, children appear to develop explicitly anti-collective, anti-union and anti-socialist sentiments. (Cummings and Taefel, 1978, p. 209)

Neither Furnham (1982) nor Goldstein and Oldham (1977) observed a difference of social class in explanations of social differences (Furby, 1979; Emler, 1985).

In more recent articles, Sévon and Leiser oppose two conceptions of economics held by children (Leiser and Sevon, 1989; Leiser *et al.*, 1990). According to the happy family conception, economic actors care for one another, factories are created to fulfil existing needs for products and the government is responsible for making everything function smoothly, giving each its due, preventing various excesses and so on. The other conception describes the economy as instrumental. The individual endeavours to interact with the economy – conceived as a complex, objective mechanism – to his best advantage.

In his investigation of adults' naive theories of economics, Salter (1986, p. 183) drew a germane distinction. Cluster analyses of the main concepts appearing in adults' economic analyses led him to distinguish two basic types of tacit theories, which he labelled the supply and the demand view. In the supply view 'actions by individuals much like oneself drive important events. That is, the major causal forces in the economy are connected to the (aggregated) activities of individuals.' In the supply view, abstract forces, operating 'out there', are the major causal agents: the individual has a minor role while actions in an essentially isolated causal system affect the individual. Salter notes that the first view 'implies a stronger notion of personal responsibility than the second view'. Somewhat related views were propounded by Holmes (1976) and Elster (1985).

The effect of age is not the same on economic understanding and on economic attitudes. Understanding deepens and widens with age. Children in different countries exhibit a distinct but parallel development, whereas values appear to be fairly stable over age.

Understanding does constrain the set of possible attitudes. Specifically, the instrumental approach requires a more sophisticated understanding than the happy family conception. Young children tend to conceptualize the economy from the perspective of the happy family, whereas some older children view economic affairs from a more individual, private perspective: the economy is viewed as an instrument for one's pursuit of happiness, or at least personal success. Similarly, Jahoda (1983) found that young Zimbabwean children (age 9–11) whose parents were involved in retail trading were more advanced than European children (in Scotland: Jahoda, 1979; the Netherlands: Jahoda, 1983; England: Furth, 1980). This was true especially for those children who helped. In particular, the African sample understood the profit motive at an earlier age (from 9 rather than 11). Jahoda (1984) suggests that this is the consequence of their living in a social environment where buying and selling are important (Berti and Bombi, 1988, p. 188).

While a certain sophistication is required to hold the instrumental approach, individuals may continue to espouse the 'happy family' view at any age. This is apparent when the appropriate values are endorsed by their environment. A good illustration is the finding that the altruistic attitude in economic matters does not decrease with age in the kibbutz, with its strong emphasis on socialist values, whereas it does so among city children (Leiser and Zaltzman, 1991).

An extensive conceptual analysis of the manifold influences that affect individuals' values is presented in Maital and Maital (1994). This multi-level model attempts to describe how a child's own experience, the behaviour of its parents and the various cultural norms and ideologies to which it is exposed affect its eventual economic values and behaviour. Unfortunately, their model is too rich for us to do justice to it here.

A STUDY OF ADOLESCENTS' ECONOMIC VALUES

The remainder of this chapter will be devoted to the presentation of a study of economic socialization of adolescents in Israel. The objective of the work was to identify the relationships among four of its aspects: economic activity; demographic determinants (age, gender, SES and school section); economic behaviour (saving, work, consumption); economic values and attitudes.

One half of the students were lower-class, the other middle-class or higher. The students were interviewed in small groups, with the help of three structured questionnaires, on each of the following topics: their own economic activity, their economic values and their knowledge of economics.

We analysed the relationships between those variables by multiple regression. A subsequent path analysis enabled us to study also the indirect influence of some of the determinants on economic values. The experimental sample consisted of 171 boys and girls, pupils in the same comprehensive high school in Beer Sheva in grades 9 and 11, in the academic and technical sections. Only pupils who were reported as not having special learning or other difficulties were included in the sample. The distribution of the sample was as follows: Group A: 64 pupils in ninth grade (ages 14–15); Group B: 107 pupils in eleventh grade (ages 17–18). The groups were about evenly divided in the relevant dimensions: there were 94 boys and 72 girls; 89 lower-class and 82 middle-class pupils; 72 were students in the technical section and 99 in the academic section.

Subjects were given the *Economic Values Inventory*. This is a tool developed by O'Brien and Ingels (1981). It contains 44 items that group themselves into eight reliable scales. We translated the questionnaire and introduced the few necessary minor adaptations. The eight scales, with sample statements, are: (1) Support for the Free Enterprise System: Our society owes much to the contributions of business. If workers want higher wages, they must work harder and produce more. (2) Trust in Business: Most businesses won't sell products they think are unsafe. Most people like their jobs. (3) Economic Alienation and Powerlessness: Getting ahead is mostly a matter of luck. Being in business means taking unfair advantage of others. (4) Government is responsible for social welfare: It should be the duty of government to be sure that everyone has a secure job and a decent standard of living. The unemployed shouldn't blame themselves for their situation; it's the fault of the economic system (reversed item). (5) Against Government Role in Price Setting: Companies should only be allowed to charge a government-controlled price for their products. (6) Against Powerful Unions (or, in our version, the General Federation of Labor): Unions are too powerful. (7) Workers Receive Fair Treatment: The average worker today is getting his or her fair share. (8) Against the Economic Status Quo: We need a way to make incomes more equal in this country. There are few real opportunities for the average person to start a business in our country today.

We added a ninth scale, Failure to Express an Opinion, which does not appear in the original O'Brien and Ingels (1984) work, but captures an interesting aspect of the answers. It was subjected to the same analyses as the other scales.

The subjects expressed support for the free enterprise system, and trust in business. They tend to agree that the state has a welfare function to fulfil, do not support powerful trade unions and do not much like the present state of affairs. They think the government should not meddle with prices, tend to judge that workers are treated unfairly, and do not feel alienated from the economic world. This, then, is their general outlook, and it is important to keep it in mind when we concentrate on the differences between various groups and the causes of those differences.

Subjects completed two other questionnaires: the *Economic Knowledge Questionnaire* contains eight questions derived from subject matter covered by a standard college introductory economics textbook and another textbook in use in some high schools in Israel; the *Economic Activity Questionnaire* was based on the one composed by Furnham (1984), again with a few minor modifications taking local conditions into account. The Israeli version was fine-tuned in a pilot study involving 20 pupils. It is composed of 20 questions relating to allowances, wages and savings; four questions on the importance attributed to allowance by the teenager; and four questions on the perceived sources of their economic knowledge. The respondent had to tick their answer on a 5 point scale (1 = never to 5 = always). The answers were subjected to a factor analysis, which yielded two interpretable factors. We labelled factor 1 'Allowance'. It contained the following items: Do you receive an allowance? How much money do you receive each time? At what age did you begin receiving an allowance? If you run out of money before the next time you are due to receive it, will you get an extra sum? Do you receive an allowance regardless of your behaviour? We labelled factor 2 'Participation in economic life'. It contained the following items: Do you do any paid work? Do you do some of the family's shopping? Do you participate with your own money in some of your clothing expenses? Do you sometimes have to reduce your expenses because of the economic situation in your family? Do you take part in your parents' discussions about the purchase of expensive items for the household? Do your parents involve you in planning their expenses for the household?

The Cronbach Alpha for the two scales are 0.78 and 0.60, respectively, and their distribution is close to normal, while their intercorrelation is low (Pearson $r = 0.13$). As a first step (Table 6.1), we present the results of nine multiple regression analyses. Only statistically reliable effects are reported. The main findings of the multiple regression showed that, as predicted, the more a teenager knows about economics, the more he or she will support the *free enterprise* concept. Contrary to our expectations, we failed to establish that either age or increased participation in the economic world lead to increased support for the free enterprise system.

We expected that trust and support for the *business world* would be more marked among the lower-class respondents, and this was indeed confirmed. The same is true of those learning in a technical section in school. Those who do not participate in the economic life tend to be more *alienated* from the economic world, and the same holds of those in the technical section. Contrary to expectations, younger respondents and those with less economics knowledge were not especially alienated. Older respondents attribute a *welfare function* to the state. There was no effect of social class. Those with less knowledge, however, support this function more widely. Children who receive allowances tend to object to *governmental price controls*. The same is more true of boys than of girls. Other variables had no effect. Students in the academic section oppose a strong *trade union* organization, but there was no effect of social class. Those who do not participate in economic life at home support strong trade unions. Younger students and those in the academic section consider more than their counterparts that workers receive a fair treatment; no effect of class was found. Students in the technical section oppose the *status quo*. Girls also tend to oppose the status quo that perpetuates the present state of inequality. As expected, failure to express an opinion is especially prevalent amongst girls, and amongst those without an allowance. There was no effect of knowledge level.

These are the initial results. To understand more fully how the variables are related, it is necessary to continue the analysis, since many of the independent variables are correlated amongst them, and this greatly affects the interpretation of the multiple regression analysis. Path analysis is the tool of choice for this type of situation. The first step in the analysis is the definition of a theoretical model, which specifies what directed binary relations between the variables will be countenanced. This theoretical model, illustrated in Figure 6.1, is based on a conceptual analysis of the variables in play, and on existing literature. The relations are to be read from right to left. Some of the relations incorporated are that demographic variables, which are unrelated, affect the knowledge level; the socioeconomic level affects the study section; age affects the allowance, participation in economic life and knowledge; receiving an allowance affects participation in economic life, but not

Table 6.1 Multiple regression analyses

Dependent variable	Independent variables	Beta	$p<$ per variable	R^2	F	df	$p<$ overall
1. Economic enterprise	knowledge	0.30	0.001	0.09	16.6	1,169	0.001
2. Business world	section	−0.29	0.001	0.08	16.9	2,168	0.001
	SES	−0.19	0.015				
3. Alienation	section	−0.23	0.003	0.06	5.66	2,168	0.004
	participation	−0.12	0.107				
4. Govt in welfare	age	0.21	0.019	0.04	3.23	2,168	0.042
	knowledge	−0.17	0.048				
5. Govt on prices	sex	−0.20	0.008	0.07	6.01	2,168	0.003
	allowance	−0.13	0.099				
6. Trade unions	section	0.22	0.005	0.08	6.55	2,153	0.002
	participation	0.15	0.063				
7. Workers' welfare	age	−0.26	0.001	0.08	7.21	2,160	0.001
	section	0.16	0.037				
8. Status quo	sex	0.14	0.076	0.04	3.15	2,164	0.045
	section	−0.13	0.096				
9. No opinion	sex	0.26	0.001	0.2	13.62	3,167	0.001
	age	−0.34	0.001				
	allowance	−0.20	0.007				

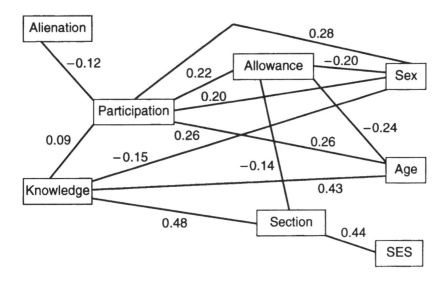

Figure 6.1

conversely; pocket money is affected by sex, age, socioeconomic status (SES) and school section.

As we saw above, the multiple regression did not confirm the hypothesis that younger children would express more extensive feelings of alienation towards the economic system than the older ones. However, it may be seen from the path analysis that there is an indirect link between lower age and support of this scale, since age affects participation in the economy (Beta = 0.26; $p < 0.001$), while those more involved in the economy feel less alienated.

The influence of section on the scale is interesting. We saw that students in the technical section feel more alienated from the economy. School section merely mediates the effect of SES. The relationship between section and alienation is composed of a direct effect and an indirect effect, which goes via pocket money and participation in economy. The sum of those effects is equal to the total effect, indicating that there are no additional unidentified variables. SES has no direct effect on alienation, but there are indirect effects. Age is another variable that has no direct effect on alienation, but there are indirect effects: age exerts an effect via participation in the economy, and by way of pocket money and participation in the economy, and the total of those paths is close to the strength of the relationship between them.

We conclude from this examination of scale three that young students, those in the technical section, who receive no allowance and are not involved in the economy feel alienated and helpless towards the economic system. Older respondents, those in the academic section, and those belonging to the middle class, tend to support liberal values characteristic of advanced western economies. At the affective level, those attitudes are accompanied by a feeling of control, and of satisfaction with the present economic order. With increasing knowledge in economics comes increasing support for liberal economic values, and trust in the individual's power to progress and succeed in the economic world. Adolescents actively engaged in economic life support free enterprise, limits on the power of trade union and restricted intervention in economic matters by the government. Older respondents, those economically active, and those possessed of more knowledge in economics express more definite and coherent attitudes.

Regarding economic behaviour, middle-class children, those studying in the academic section, and those economically active reported more saving (both in incidence and in amount), thus expressing better ability to delay gratification. Summarizing, upper- and middle-class students tend to work part-time, save more and have a more liberal, free market view of the economic system. Lower-class children tend to be given their allowance and favour a more controlled, interventionist economic system. Exploring the relationship between demographic variables and attitudes, we found that older respondents, those in the academic section and those in the middle class or higher (that is, those whose fathers graduated at least from high school) express support for those attitudes corresponding to western politico-economic arrangements and for liberal values, such as support for free enterprise, technological progress, limited state intervention and creation of opportunities for individuals to progress according to their abilities. Feelings of control and satisfaction with both the status quo and the treatment of workers are associated with these attitudes.

The relations between components of economic socialization (allowance and participation) and attitudes were also investigated. Economic knowledge strengthens support for the free enterprise, freedom of choice, competition in the business world and personal confrontation of difficulties while increasing opposition to state intervention, the hallmark of egalitarian planned economies.

An improved theoretical and cognitive ability, which was found more prevalent in the middle class, is related to support for liberal economic arrangements (such as opposition to strong trade unions and to state control of prices). Members of the lower class, who are generally in the technical school sections, oppose the status quo, feel there is no equality of opportunity and that the division of wealth is unequal, and that the situation of the average person in Israel is worsening, rather than improving. They feel that getting ahead in society is mainly a matter of luck, express feelings of exploitation by others and helplessness regarding the economic system. At the same time, these lower-class respondents support the business world. This unexpected effect is perhaps due to familiarity: many of the parents of the respondents are hard-working small shopkeepers or are employed in small workshops.

Economic knowledge is directly influenced by the young person's participation in economic life, which in turn depends on pocket money and control of expenses. While the effect of participation in economic life on economics attitudes is not significant, it does affect those feelings that are closer to home: feelings of personal efficacy, control of those economic aspects relevant to the young people's own lives, and faith in their ability to progress by their own effort if they set their mind to it. Those who regularly receive an allowance (two-thirds of the sample), who plan and budget their economic activity, take a markedly dim view of state intervention in setting prices. To them, objective market forces of offer and demand should determine price levels.

To summarize, those young people who have an economic role and express more knowledge express different views from those less exposed to economic activity. The more they know about economics and are involved in the economy, the more they will believe in personal efficacy and support liberal economic views. As we noted, the Israeli economy is mixed, and liberal–capitalist aspects coexist with the older egalitarian socialist views. It would therefore not be accurate to say that members of the more affluent classes support the existing economic state of affairs. Rather, they favour more systematic liberal views.

The Reluctance to Express a View

Older respondents and those more active economically express more definite views, choosing less frequently the 'don't know' option. Sex also has an influence: boys commit themselves more than girls.

Developmental cognitive research (Ng, 1983; Leiser, 1983; Leiser *et al.*, 1990; Furnham and Thomas, 1984; Berti and Bombi, 1988; Stacey, 1982) emphasizes the importance of adolescence as the age at which economic knowledge and attitudes become more systematic and better coordinated and, indeed, approach the level commonly found amongst adults. In the early part of their research, O'Brien and Ingels (1984) found a primitive, inconsistent system of attitudes amongst the younger subjects, whereas the organization of those attitudes, as extracted by factor analysis of the scales, became more sharply defined in the older age group. The attitudes of ninth graders, in both the academic and the technical section, are still in formation. Our findings are in keeping with these earlier ones. Only in late adolescence (age 17 and above) are the students capable of reasoning at the level required to understand modern economics. To grasp macroeconomic relationships, the child must have a notion of the structure and functions of society as a whole.

Developing attitudes towards many of these aspects are acquired in the course of involvement in economic life. The aspects of youthful economic activity we studied – pocket money and participation in economic life – fit in with the findings of previous investigators on the role of knowledge, participation and personal relevance in the formation of coherent positions in general (Sherif *et al.*, 1965; Petty and Cacioppo, 1981; Vaughn, 1980; Marshall and Magruder, 1960). Those of our subjects who participate in economic life proved more willing to expend the necessary cognitive effort to integrate their knowledge in order to take a personal stand.

Economic Behaviour of Youth

Table 6.2 gives a breakdown of the prevalence of work as a function of the independent variables. The significantly higher proportion of working youngsters amongst the medium/high SES group, despite the higher income of the household, suggests that children's work is encouraged in this group. The role of the parents in fostering economic autonomy is clear. This is very much in keeping with the work summarized in the introduction.

Table 6.2   Prevalence of work

Low SES	38
Medium/high SES	60
Ninth grade	27
Eleventh grade	65
Male	44
Female	58

The tendency to give an allowance is somewhat stronger in the lower class. This finding is in keeping with that by Furnham and Thomas (1984) in Britain. On the other hand, the effect of age is reversed: 77 per cent of ninth graders were receiving an allowance, as against 61 per cent of the eleventh graders. It seems that, in Israel, economic independence is encouraged via part-time work, rather than by giving an allowance.

The subjects were further asked whether they save some of their money and, if so, how much. The answers were analysed by a regression analysis.

Table 6.3   Factors affecting savings

	Independent variable	Beta	$p<$	R^2	F
Saving frequency	section	0.19	0.014		
	participation	0.16	0.05	0.10	8.89
Saving size	participation	0.26	0.001		
	sex	−0.22	0.007		
	section	0.18	0.021	0.11	6.5

Table 6.4   The uses to which money is put

	Independent variable	Beta	$p<$	R^2	F
Entertainment	sex	−0.27	0.001		
	allowance	0.16	0.05	0.10	8.89
Sweets	participation	−0.17	0.04		
	section	−0.16	0.057	0.05	3.7
Presents	sex	0.36	0.001	0.13	22.0

Significant factors are summarized in Table 6.3. These findings make it clear that students in the academic section, and those involved in economic life (working, buying for themselves, participating in discussions on family finances and so on) are those who save money. More of them save money and they save more. In addition, boys reports saving larger sums than girls.

The respondents were asked to describe how they would allocate a sum of NIS 100 (about US$40) to several goals. We suggested the following categories: entertainment, sweets, presents, savings and others. The answers were then analysed in a regression analysis. Table 6.4 summarizes this analysis, for those categories where independent variables proved statistically significant. Boys who receive an allowance will use a large portion of it for entertainment. Children who do not participate in economic life allocate more of the hypothetical sum for sweets. From the path analysis it emerged that these tend to be the younger ones who do not receive an allowance. Finally, girls are more likely than boys to buy presents for friends and relatives.

CONCLUSION

By adolescence, economic socialization follows a significantly different course in different socioeconomic strata and results in different attitudes. The most striking differences are seen in the extent of economic knowledge and in the feelings of alienation and helplessness as regards making progress in the economic world. It is therefore essential to develop a programme of school and parental education that will enable all young people to enter the economic world with more knowledge and to face the challenges of free enterprise with increased confidence.

REFERENCES

Abramovitch, R., Freedman, J.L. and Pliner, P. (1991), 'Children and money – getting an allowance, credit versus cash, and knowledge of pricing', *Journal of Economic Psychology*, **12** (1), 27–45.
Aries, Ph. (1973), *L'enfant et la vie familiale sous l'Ancien Régime*, Paris: Seuil.
Berti, A.E. and Bombi, A.S. (1988), *The Child's Construction of Economics*, Cambridge: Cambridge University Press.
Cummings, S. and Taefel, D. (1978), 'The economic socialization of children: A neo-Marxist analysis', *Social Problems*, **26**, 198–210.
Elder, G. (1974), *Chicago of the Great Depression*, Chicago: University of Chicago Press.
Elster, J. (1985), *The Multiple Self*, Cambridge: Cambridge University Press.
Emler, N.D.J. (1985), 'Childrens' representation of economic inequalities: the effect of social class', *British Journal of Developmental Psychology*, **3**, 191–8.
Furby, L. (1979), 'Inequalities in personal possession: explanations for and judgment about unequal distribution', *Human Development*, **22**, 180–202.
Furnham, A. (1982), 'The perception of poverty among adolescents', *Journal of Adolescence*, **5**, 135–47.
Furnham, A. (1984), 'Work values and beliefs in Britain', *Journal of Occupational Behaviour*, **5** (4), 281–91.
Furnham, A. and Thomas, P. (1984), 'Pocket money: A study of economic education', *British Journal of Developmental Psychology*, **2**, 205–2.
Furth, H.G. (1980), *The World of Grown Ups*, New York: Elsevier.
Goldstein, B. and Oldham, J. (1977), *Children and Work: a study of socialization*, New Brunswick, NJ: Transaction Books.
Goodnow, J.J., Cashmore, J., Cotton, S. and Knight, R. (1984), Mother's developmental timetables in two cultural groups', *International Journal of Psychology*, **19**, 193–205.
Goodnow, J.J. (1988), 'Children's household work: its nature and functions', *Psychological Bulletin*, **103**, 5–26.
Harris, D.B., Clark, K.E., Rose, A.M. and Valasek, F. (1954), 'The relationship of children's home duties to an attitude of responsibility', *Child Development*, 29–33.
Holmes, R. (1976), *Legitimacy and the Politics of the Knowable*, London: Routledge and Kegan Paul.

Jahoda, G. (1979), 'The development of thinking about reality by some Glaswegian children', *European Journal of Social Psychology*, **9**, 115–25.

Jahoda, G. (1983), 'European "lag" in the development of an economic concept: a study in Zimbabwe', *British Journal of Developmental Psychology*, **1**, 113–20.

Jahoda, G. (1984), 'The development of thinking about socio-economic systems', in H. Tajfel (eds), *The Social Dimension*, Cambridge: Cambridge University Press.

Leahy, R.L. (1981), 'The development of the conception of economics inequality: descriptions and comparisons of rich and poor people', *Child Development*, **52**, 523–32.

Leiser, D. (1983), 'Children's conceptions of economics – The constitution of a cognitive domain', *Journal of Economic Psychology*, **4**, 297–317.

Leiser, D. and Sévon, G. (1989), 'Economic Socialization: A comparison of Israeli and Finnish Children', in T. Tyszka (ed.), *Homo Oeconomicus* (IAREP proceedings), Kazimierz Dolny, Poland.

Leiser, D. and Zaltzman, J. (1991), 'Children's economic socialization, inside and outside the kibbutz', *Journal of Economic Psychology*, **11**, 551–66.

Leiser, D., Sévon, G. and Levy, D. (1990), 'Children's economic socialization: Summarizing the cross-cultural comparison of ten countries', *Journal of Economic Psychology*, **11** (4), 591–631.

Maital, S. and Maital, S.L. (1994), 'Is the future what it used to be? A behavioral theory of the decline of saving in the west', *Journal of Socio-Economics*, **23** (1–2), 1–32.

Marshall, H. and Magruder, L. (1960), 'Relations between parent money education practices and children's knowledge and use of money', *Child Development*, **31**, 253–84.

Newson, J. and Newson, E. (1976), *Seven years old in the home environment*, London: Allen and Unwin.

Ng, S.H. (1983), 'Children's ideas about the bank and shop profit: developmental stages and influences of cognitive contrast and conflict', *Journal of Economic Psychology*, **4**, 209–21.

O'Brien, M.U. and Ingels, S.J. (1984), 'The Development of the Economics Value Inventory (UVI)', *NORC*, Chicago: University of Chicago.

Petty, R.E. and Cacioppo, J.T. (1981), *Attitudes and Persuasion: classic and contemporary approaches*, Dubuque: Brawan.

Salter, W.J. (1986), 'Tacit Theories of Economics', PhD dissertation, Department of Psychology, Yale University. University Microfilm International, #8728393.

Sherif, C.M., Sherif, M. and Nebergall, R.E. (1965), *Attitudes and Attitude Change*, Philadelphia: Saunders.

Shorter, E. (1976), *The Making Of The Modern Family*, London: Collins.

Stacey B.G. (1982), 'Economic socialization in the pre-adult years', *British Journal of Social Psychology*, **21**, 159–73.

Straus, J.A. (1962), 'Work rules and financial responsibility in the socialization of farm, fringe and town boys', *Rural Sociology*, **27**, 257–74.

Vaughn, R. (1980), 'How advertising works: a planning model', *Journal of Advertising Research*, **20** (5), 27–33.

White, K.L. and Brinkerhoff, D.B. (1981), 'Children's work in the family: its significance and meaning', *Journal of Marriage and the Family*, **42**, 789–98.

Zelizer, V. (1985), *Pricing the Priceless Child*, New York: Basic Books.

7. Young people's understanding of private and public ownership

Fiona Cram, Sik Hung Ng and Nileena Jhaveri

INTRODUCTION

Ownership of property is an assortment of rights that include the rights of enjoyment, possession and transfer (Hollowell, 1982). Expressed differently, these are, respectively, the right to use the possession, the right to control use of the possession by others, and the right to transfer possession to someone else. It is only within the context of these conventions that ownership and property are feasible (Snare, 1972). For example, the majority of members in a society must be aware of the conventions and respect them. Without such common attitudes there can be no rights. Consequently, conventions of ownership of property hold an important place in the laws of a society, in the conduct of its citizens and in the social development of its children.

On the basis of a cross-cultural survey of penalties for property theft and robbery, Westermarck (1926) concluded that ownership rights existed among all societies then known. There is no reason to suspect that ownership is any less universal or important now than before (see, for example, Ellis, 1985; Furby, 1980). The importance of ownership can be seen from the legal codification and governmental protection of ownership, from the training of children from an early age concerning the respect for private and public properties (Dufty and Harrold, 1972) and also from the psychological meaning that emanates from owning possessions. *Owning* imparts a sense of personal control, whereas *possessions* enable owners to express their identities. These two aspects are intertwined in possessive behaviour throughout the life span (Furby, 1980). However, despite its importance in law, social conduct and human development, ownership has not been a well researched topic. The scarcity of relevant research is evident from standard references on economic socialization (Furnham and Lewis, 1986; Lea *et al.*, 1987; Stacey, 1987).

The first part of this chapter examines young people's understanding of private ownership, including their awareness of ownership, knowledge about the rights of ownership, and acceptance or rejection of various bases for acquiring possessions. The second part examines the development of children's understanding of public ownership. Relative to private ownership, public ownership is embedded in more complex social institutions and is more remote from the direct observation of young people. Understanding of public ownership is not a simple matter of extending the understanding of private ownership into the public arena. This is the main reason for separating private and public ownership in our discussion; it also underlies our experiment to be outlined at the end of the chapter, of applying peer interaction to facilitate the understanding of public ownership under experimental conditions.

AWARENESS OF PRIVATE OWNERSHIP

Parents often furnish babies and children with a variety of toys and other objects. These are progressively gazed at, reached for and, if possible, grabbed by young babies as they grow older (Stacey, 1982). When babies become mobile at around 6–9 months of age they can move towards these toys and more actively explore them as well as other interesting items in their environment. To prevent damage to objects or to the child, parents and older siblings may intervene in the baby's new-found activity and communicate to her or him what can be handled and explored and what is out of bounds. In this way children come to understand that the objects they are allowed to explore are theirs (Furby, 1980) and so begins their socialization of property concepts (Loewenthal, 1976).

Young children's rudimentary sense of owning is also reflected in their language development: by 24 months possessives such as 'mine' are well established in their vocabulary. By means of these possessives, children can point at an object and seemingly name its owner (Miller and Johnson-Laird, 1976). Object names that children learn are closely linked to the children's immediate environment and represent objects that can be manipulated in such a way as to provide the children with a feeling of efficacy. For example, a child is likely to acquire such words as 'toys' and 'shoes' earlier than 'trees' or 'table', as the former can be interacted with to produce an effect in the child's environment (Hetherington and Parke, 1986). Later, with the development of two-word phrases, children can express possession verbally by means of noun–noun ('mummy purse' for mummy's purse) and adjective–noun ('her purse') constructions, without having to rely on gesturing (cited in Furby, 1980).

As children grow older they increasingly respond to objects in a social fashion. Children's disputes over objects can be seen as an expression of their desire for control as they learn that their actions on objects (such as toys) can produce contingent actions by other children (Furby, 1980). These disputes are therefore more than an expression of their wish to temporarily use and control an inanimate object; their experience of having an effect on their environment now extends beyond the physical and into their social environment (Isaacs, 1936).

An early study by Dawe (1934) found that over half of the 200 disputes she observed among pre-school children involved possessions. She also noted that the frequency of these object disputes decreased with age. This latter finding has been confirmed by Bakeman and Brownlee (1982, p. 108) who proposed that the decrease in object disputes with age reflected 'a greater uncertainty [among toddlers as compared to preschool children] as to how possession [disputes] should be resolved and a need to explore each possible conflict to see how it would end'. In this way, children as young as two or three years are learning about their social world from object disputes with their peers (Bakeman and Brownlee, 1982). The knowledge they gain concerns the norms of possession and ownership: for example, the social rules governing sharing, lending, giving, and receiving possessions (Stacey, 1982).

One method of inquiring into children's awareness of private property is to simply ask them, 'What do you mean when you say that this is your property?' Such an approach was adopted by Furby (1978b) in one of her studies of ownership and possession among American and Israeli respondents. Content analysis of the responses revealed 290 categories, although only 30 of these were commonly used by respondents. The most salient defining characteristics of possession for the American sample at all ages were use of an object by the owner and the right to control use by others. These also featured in the responses of the Israeli sample. Other popular characteristics concerned the acquisition of possessions through gifts, purchase or making something. This acquisition process changed with age from a passive one among younger children (their possessions were bought or given by others) to an active one for older children whereby they bought or worked for their own possessions. These characteristics correspond to the conventions of ownership described by several authors (for example, Hollowell, 1982; Miller and Johnson-Laird, 1976; Snare, 1972) namely, the right to use the possession, the right to control use of the possession by others, and the right to transfer these rights to others.

When a similar question about the meaning of possession (What do you mean when you say that these things are yours, that they belong to you?) was asked of New Zealand children (Cram, 1990) the majority of the youngest children (5–6 years) and over 40 per cent of 8–9-year-olds were unable to answer. In addition, over 40 per cent of the 8–9-year-olds and 50 per cent of the 11–12-year-olds simply restated their claim to ownership (for example, 'They're my things'). This may suggest that understanding of private ownership develops late for New Zealand children compared to their American and Israeli counterparts. Alternatively, it is more likely that the direct questioning approach did not inspire the New Zealand children to reason actively about the nature of property rights (see also Burris, 1983) and therefore did not provide an accurate assessment of their understanding.

Rather than questioning children directly about ownership and property, Burris (1983) asked them why stealing is wrong. The result was a stage-like pattern for children's understanding of property rights. The reasons given by the youngest children (4–5 years) reflected a need to avoid punishment or disapproval by adults. Others responded that stealing was wrong simply because it was prohibited. Older children (7–8 years) judged stealing to be wrong because of the injury it causes the victim, thus reflecting reciprocity and empathy. Lastly, the majority of the oldest children (10–12 years) were able to conceptualize property within the total system of economic exchange and production. Stealing therefore contradicts principles of equity as one person procures for nothing what another person has worked for.

Furnham and Jones (1987) also asked children and young adults (7–17-year-olds) about theft and, interestingly, also whether or not theft could be mitigated by poverty, passion or brain damage. The youngest children (7–8 years) were the most lenient in their recommended punishments for thieving and were affected the most by mitigating circumstances. Furnham and Jones propose that theft is seen as less threatening by this age group because possessions are less integral to their self-identity. With increasing age the concept of possession becomes more structured and theft, in turn, becomes less tolerated. This coincides with an increase in the severity of the recommended punishment for theft.

Another, indirect approach was adopted by Furby (1978b) in one of her studies. She sought responses from American and Israeli children about their sharing decisions and experiences with peers or known adults. The youngest children (5–6 years) based their decisions on the perceived characteristics of the other person: for example, whether they were family members, or friendly, likable, and so on. These children were also concerned about whether the person in question would damage or destroy their possessions. The responses of older children (7–8 years) were similar, with negative reciprocity also frequently mentioned (for example, 'If she doesn't let me use her things, I don't let her use mine'). Negative reciprocity was also frequently mentioned by the 10- and 11-year-olds.

Children's understanding of others' perspectives showed up at this stage in their concern for the other person's welfare. That is, sharing decisions were frequently based on the other person's need for the object. However, a similar study of New Zealand children (Cram, 1990) found that older children (8–9 and 11–12 years) were not as concerned about the other's welfare as they were about the safety of their possessions; that is, the borrower had to be responsible.

RIGHTS AND BASES OF PRIVATE OWNERSHIP

As noted in the introduction, ownership entails the right to use the possession, the right to control the use of the possession by others, and the right to transfer the possession to someone else (Hollowell, 1982; Snare, 1972). The rights of use and control are well understood by children as young as 5 years, according to a study in which American and Israeli children were interviewed on what they owned and what owning these things meant to them (Furby, 1976). Less evident is children's knowledge of the right of transfer. This is not surprising because transfer implies the concepts of sharing and giving that are not part of the interviewing discourse on owning, having and receiving. Further, young children's possessions, mostly apparel and toys, are given for their use by adults who, for most practical purposes, retain the right of transfer. This makes it difficult for young children to connect the rights of use and control with the right of transfer in so far as these possessions are concerned. Older children, on the other hand, are more active in the acquisition of their own possessions and view possessions as being theirs to the extent that they have exerted an effort to gain them (Ellis, 1985). They also consider their ownership of such possessions as more absolute (Furby, 1978a) and presumably have a better understanding of the right of transfer.

Moessinger (1975) asked pairs of Swiss children aged 4 to 15 years to divide a gift of trees between themselves. There were already trees planted in their own gardens and one child had more trees than the other; these were represented by means of a model placed in front of the two children. The youngest children simply ignored the garden trees and divided the gift trees in a playful, give and take, fashion. Older children included the garden trees in the division and shared the aggregated trees equally. The oldest children (11 years on) divided the gift trees equally but *separated* the garden trees from the division. When questioned, they offered reasons to the effect that the garden trees, unlike the gift trees, were already owned and non-transferable.

The present authors developed Moessinger's (1975) allocation procedure with children's understanding of the non-transferable nature of private property. As children's allocations may be influenced when they are also a recipient (Streater, and Chertkoff, 1976), we looked at whether children would include or exclude private property in a reward allocation to two imaginary others, excluding themselves. A total of 120 New Zealand children, aged 8 to 15 years, were drawn from three urban schools. Each child was presented with a two-part scenario. In the first part, the child was told that twins, A and

B, were sent $4 as a birthday gift by their aunt. The child's task was to decide how to divide the gift money between the twins. As intended, all children invariably divided the gift equally. The interviewer then presented the child with the second, critical, part of the scenario. She – the interviewer – produced two piggy banks belonging to the twins and pointed out that A already had $2, and B $4 of pocket money in their respective piggy banks. She placed the $2 of gift money allocated by the child next to the piggy bank to show that A now had $4 whereas B had $6. Following this, she asked the child if it were all right to take one dollar from B's piggy bank and give it to A, so that they would have the same. In this way, the child was confronted with a decisional conflict between the ideal of equality, which would require a 'yes' answer, and the non-transferable nature of the initial possessions, which would require a 'no' answer. Criteria for the mastery of the transfer concept were a 'no' answer coupled with one or more relevant reasons such as 'the money belongs to B'.

We then repeated the study with an equal number of young Indian people in a Bombay school. The third author judged the responses given by the two samples in terms of mastering or failing to master the concept of transfer. Half of the responses from each sample were independently judged by a second person. There was total agreement between the two judges. The results (see Table 7.1) showed an age-related increase in the mastery of the transfer concept. The New Zealand sample up to 12 years lagged behind their Indian counterparts; by 14–15 years, however, they were on a par with them. Almost all children at 14–15 years showed mastery.

In a second study we inserted an input factor so that the money allocation was not a gift but a reward for work done. Children ($n = 140$) aged 8 to 11 years, were individually asked to divide a payment (60 cents) between two young workers, one of whom had more pocket money (40 cents) than the other (20 cents). In one scenario, the two workers had done equal work; in a

Table 7.1   Frequency of mastery of the concept of the right of transfer in private property (various age groups)

	New Zealand ($n = 120$)		Indian ($n = 120$)	
	Passed	Failed	Passed	Failed
8–9 years	7	33	14	26
11–12 years	22	18	32	8
14–15 years	37	3	38	2

second scenario, the worker with less pocket money had done more work than the other. Coins representing the payment were laid between the two piles of pocket money coins. The children were asked to indicate their answers by rearranging any of the coins. After this, they were asked why they had done it that way. The arrangement of coins and associated reasons were recorded by the interviewer for later classification.

The chief purpose of the classification was to ascertain whether the children recognized that the pocket money was different from the payment and should be separate from the payment. Children were initially classified as either including or not including the pocket money in their allocation. There were two main criteria for the '*include*' category, one physical and the other verbal. The physical criterion was met when the child mixed the pocket money and payment coins and then divided them between workers, as if the two sets of coins were equally transferable. The verbal criterion related to statements confirming the equivalence of the two sets of coins: for example, 'They should have equal pay and equal pocket money', 'Pocket money should be shared too'. Children who were not classified in the 'include' category were considered for membership in the '*separate*' category. Membership in this category required a clear recognition that the pocket money was different from, and should not be included in, the payment. This was indicated by such statements as 'One has more pocket money than the other, but this money should not count', and 'The pocket money is separate, it belongs to her'.

Children were given two separate classifications, one for each scenario, by two independent judges who were unaware of the children's age. This enabled consideration of the consistency of responses across scenarios. In Table 7.2, only those children who received 'separate' classifications in both scenarios were represented as such; and the same criterion of consistency applied

Table 7.2   *Frequency of children's awareness of private ownership (various age groups)*

	Age in years			
	8	9	10	11
Separate	4	10	20	17
Include	12	20	5	13
Other	18	6	9	6
Total	34	36	34	36

Note: 'Separate' = showed awareness; 'Include' = did not show awareness.

to the 'include' category. Children who were not classified under the 'include' or 'separate' category for whatever reason were lumped together in the 'other' category. The two judges agreed on the classification of all the 101 children in the 'separate' and 'include' categories. They also agreed on the classification of 12 children under the 'other' category. The remaining 27 children in the *'other'* category either gave inconsistent responses across scenarios, changed their answers when they were probed by the interviewer, or else gave incomprehensible responses. Using the 'separate' category as an indicator of awareness of private ownership, and the 50 per cent rate as the pass criterion, the results showed that a definite awareness emerged around 10–11 years, which was slightly ahead of Moessinger's Swiss children.

It was noticeable from our study that some children, especially the younger ones, changed their answers when asked a second time or when asked to explain their answer. Although we do not have information in support of any particular explanation, we think the change was probably due to the children inferring from the interviewer's inquisitive questioning that their answer must be wrong (see also Siegal, 1990). For this reason, our results do not give full credit to the children's awareness and should be interpreted as conservative.

What remains unclear from Moessinger's (1975) and our studies of children's understanding of the right of transfer is what attributes of garden trees and pocket money might have led the older children to regard these properties as private and therefore non-transferable. To answer this question we first compiled a list of attributes which children, rightly or wrongly, use to define a property as private. For example, a child may own a toy on the basis of current use, through purchase, or by some other means. Ownership based on use can justify only 'transitory' (Newman, 1978) or 'accidental' (Miller and Johnson-Laird, 1976) ownership: the child has no right – in the eye of an adult authority – of permanent ownership or transfer, even though the child has the rights of use and control as long as they are in physical contact with the object. Ownership based on purchase, on the other hand, justifies permanent ownership: the child does not have to stay in physical contact with the object to remain its owner and they also have the right of transfer.

Cram and Ng (1989) tested children's acceptance or rejection of 11 ownership bases that had been selected to represent contractual (for example, purchase, earned through work, inheritance), physical (for example, current use, forced appropriation) and egocentric (for example, liking, appearance) bases. The results showed a marked increase in the acceptance of contractual bases from 5–6 years to 8–9 years, and a further but less marked increase from 8–9 years to 11–12 years. A similar pattern of results was obtained for the rejection of physical bases. The age-related increase in the acceptance of contractual over other bases probably reflects, on the one hand, the increasing participation of older children in economic exchange as customers and workers, and, on the other hand, the older children's greater understanding of how ownership can be acquired indirectly without physical contact and in a deferred fashion through the media of money and labour.

PUBLIC OWNERSHIP

In private ownership, the owner–object relationship can be indirect and the owner difficult to identify. Public ownership is embedded in an even more complex social institutional setting that is remote from the direct observation of young people. For example, despite the child's experience of actually using public buses for transport, that experience alone is unlikely to lead to a mature understanding of the public ownership of buses. In Dunedin city these buses are not owned by any single individual, but are vested in a local government department accountable to the city council whose members are elected by residents. To understand this, the child must transcend the person-alized focus of private ownership, grasp the social institutional context of public ownership, as well as develop constructs relating to positional power (for example, boss, mayor), social sub-systems (for example, transport de-partment, city council) and such like.

Developmental Sequence

Few studies have looked at children's conceptions of public ownership. Furth (1980) asked children questions about ownership of buses ('To whom does the bus belong?', 'Who paid for it?') as part of a larger interview exploring under-standing of society. However, his interest lay in describing a comprehensive scheme of stages of societal understanding rather than reporting the details of children's understanding of any particular issue. What children thought about the buses is therefore not retrievable from this stage description.

   One study that has examined children's understanding of public ownership is that of Italian researchers Berti *et al.* (1982). They examined children's ideas about the means of production and the function and ownership of those means. The children interviewed resided in a working-class community; their fathers were factory workers and their mothers housewives. The factory, the countryside and the public transport bus service were chosen to represent principal productivity areas in society (industry, agriculture, services) and children (aged 4–13 years) were interviewed about the ownership and econ-omic exchanges occurring in relation to these producing means. In the case of ownership, five levels of awareness were identified with respect to whom the child recognized as the owner. These are summarized below (Berti *et al.*, 1982, p. 227).

1. Children either do not know who the owner is or they identify the owner as the person who is in close spatial contact with the object (for example, bus passengers).
2. The owner is identified as the person who uses or controls the use of the object (for example, the bus driver).
3. Children identify the owner as the person who controls the use of the object by others (for example, the 'boss').
4. The owner is identified as the council or the state, but children do not know how these institutions come into being.
5. Children identify the owner as the council or state and, in addition, they can describe the rudiments of the election process.

With increasing age the children passed from realistic or physical (concrete) conceptions of the owner, in which spatial contact with or use of the producing means identified a person as the owner, to abstract conceptions, with the owner no longer having to be in close proximity to the property. Furnham and Jones (1987) found a similar trend for British children's understanding of bus ownership. Berti *et al.*'s (1982) developmental sequence of public ownership understanding also fits in with a more general sequence of children's understanding of economics (Berti and Bombi, 1988).

The present authors adopted the Berti et al.'s (1982) sequence to classify New Zealand children's levels of understanding of bus ownership and of school ownership. The subjects were 172 children (5–6, 8–9 and 11–12-year-olds) from three state-owned schools in Dunedin. During individual interviews children were asked several questions relating to ownership of the city's buses ('Who owns the buses that carry people around Dunedin?' 'Who paid for the buses?'). Children's responses were classified into five levels of understanding. Levels 1 to 3 were the same as Berti *et al.*'s (1982) scheme. Children at level 4 identified the owners of the buses as the city council but were unable to explain where the money came from for purchasing the buses. At level 5, children also responded that the city council owned the buses and, in addition, were able to explain that the money for purchase came from taxes.

The children were also asked questions concerning the ownership of the school they were in ('Who owns your school?' 'Who pays your teachers?'). Their responses were classified into five levels of understanding that closely corresponded to the bus ownership levels. Table 7.3 shows the distribution of children by age group and level of understanding. As the age of children increased there was a general increase in the level of understanding of the ownership of the bus as well as of the school.[1] The change was faster in the case of the school than of the bus, probably because of the children's greater personal experience with the functioning of the former. By the age of 11–12 years, most children no longer inferred ownership from adults (bus drivers

Table 7.3   Percentage of children understanding bus and school ownership (various levels and age groups)

	Level of understanding[1]				
	1	2	3	4	5
Bus					
5–6 years	43.9 (25)[2]	50.9 (29)	5.2 (3)	0.0 (0)	0.0 (0)
8–9 years	39.3 (22)	23.2 (13)	19.6 (11)	14.3 (8)	3.6 (2)
11–12 years	5.1 (3)	0.0 (0)	0.0 (0)	44.1 (26)	50.8 (30)
School					
5–6 years	33.3 (19)	36.8 (21)	29.9 (17)	0.0 (0)	0.0 (0)
8–9 years	30.4 (17)	7.1 (4)	50.0 (28)	12.5 (7)	0.0 (0)
11–12 years	13.6 (8)	0.0 (0)	5.0 (3)	40.7 (24)	40.7 (24)

Notes:
1. Level 1 = person seen in spatial contact with object (e.g. passenger, school children); level 2 = person who exercises appropriate use/control over object (e.g. driver, teachers); level 3 = person who controls use of the object by others (e.g. 'boss', principal); level 4 = governing body but no idea about where money to buy object comes from (e.g. city council, government); level 5 = governing body and knowledge that money to buy object comes from taxes.
2. Frequency in parentheses.

and school teachers) who outwardly had the most observable contact with and control over the objects. Instead, the children were able to connect ownership with the corresponding political institution. The concept of the 'boss' provides the children with a clutch for making that connection.

The five-level sequence of development is reliable for classificational purposes, generalizable across domains and correlated with age. It provides a tool for measuring changes in understanding that may be induced under experimental conditions, as we shall show in the next section.

EFFECTS OF COGNITIVE CONFLICT

Damon (1981) has argued that, in order to examine more fully the process of social understanding, it is necessary to carry out social interactive studies to complement descriptive surveys of the kind reviewed above. Attempts have been made in this direction in some areas of children's economic understanding (for example, Jahoda, 1981; Ng, 1983), but no attempt has been made in the area of ownership understanding.

The general idea underlying our experimental hypothesis is that, when children encounter information that is incongruent with their current conception of a topic, they will experience cognitive conflict and as a result are motivated to resolve this conflict by reconstructing their knowledge about the topic. The conflict can be thought of in terms of 'the dynamics of the conflict between schemes' (Inhelder *et al.*, 1974, p. 265). A conflict between schemes, according to Piaget's (1977) equilibration factor of cognitive development, upsets the child's cognitive equilibrium and activates attempts to resolve the conflict. Such an attempt may lead to the construction of a more mature solution representing a new equilibrium. The benefit of conflict for cognitive development has been demonstrated in the domains of logicomathematical cognition (Inhelder *et al.*, 1974), spatial coordination skills (Emler and Valiant, 1982) and definite descriptions (Deutsch and Pechmann, 1982). A similar gain was found in the understanding of the bank (Jahoda, 1981).

The new information causing cognitive conflict may come from a book or a video (that is, intra-individually induced cognitive conflict) or from an interactional setting, that is, when the child's response is contradicted by the response of another person (inter-individually induced cognitive conflict). One comparison of inter- and intra-individual cognitive conflicts has been carried out by Doise and his colleagues (for example, Doise and Mackie, 1981) using spatial coordination and conservation tasks. The conclusion they have reached is that peer-induced inter-individual cognitive conflict promotes more cognitive development than its intra-individual counterpart. Doise's sociocognitive theory of cognitive development therefore endorses interactional sources of conflict. According to this theory, inter-individual coordinations that occur within a social interaction facilitate intra-individual coordinations by the individual participants, which in turn facilitate cognitive development (Doise, 1978; see also Vygotsky, 1978).

Other research has also examined the efficacy of inter-individual vis-à-vis intra-individual sources of conflict in promoting cognitive development. Studies by Mackie (1980), using a spatial transformation task, and Emler and Valiant (1982, experiment 1), using a spatial representation task, have found that both types of conflict (inter- and intra-individual) are effective in producing post-treatment gains in children. Mackie (1980) explains the disparity between her findings and those of Doise and his colleagues as due to differences in experimental manipulations which resulted in a stronger intra-individual conflict condition in Mackie's experiment. Emler and Valiant (1982, experiment 1) offer a similar explanation.

Roy and Howe (1990) attempted to extend the research on inter- and intra-individual sources of conflict into the social sphere with their research on children's sociolegal thinking. Their findings support those of Mackie (1980, 1983) and Emler and Valiant (1982), in that children experienced similar gains in understanding as a result of inter-individual and intra-individual conflict. However, Roy and Howe's intra-individual conflict condition had a strong social component in that children were required, first, to accept or reject a conflicting response and then to explain their decision to the experimenter.

In the experiment below, the present authors also looked at the role of conflict in promoting children's understanding in a social sphere, namely children's understanding of public ownership. We endeavoured to make our intra-individual conflict condition truly 'non-interactional' by having the children watch a video presentation that would induce intra-individual conflict, but in a non-interactional setting. The video was specially prepared for the experiment by two professional actors and showed a male bus driver requesting and receiving specific verbal instructions from another man on the routing of the bus he would drive for the day. Care was taken when writing the script to ensure that no reference was made to the 'boss' or other concepts associated with the higher levels of understanding. By showing the driver – who the child believed owned the bus – receiving instructions from another person, we hoped to present to the child one aspect of reality that might call into question the validity of that belief.

In order to allow for changes in either direction that might result from the experimental treatment, and also to maximize the availability of subjects, we chose level 2 children as subjects (that is, children who thought that the bus driver owned the bus, $n = 68$). They were selected from a sample of 180 children (7–8 years) who had been tested on the bus ownership question. They were paired to form friendship dyads on the basis of prior information they had given concerning names of their best friends in class.

One child in each dyad viewed the bus driver video prior to interaction. The second child in the dyad viewed a neutral video of comparable length depicting traffic scenes unrelated to bus ownership in any conceivable way. In the peer interaction phase that followed the viewing, half of the dyads discussed the bus ownership issue and the remaining dyads discussed a neutral topic ('Who is the best person on television?'). The discussion was recorded and later transcribed for analysis. Following the discussion (which was one week after the pre-treatment interview) the children were individually interviewed again on the bus ownership questions. Their responses were classified to provide the post-treatment level of understanding.

The above procedure created three conflict conditions: (1) *intra- and inter-individual conflict conditions* (children who saw the bus driver video and discussed the bus ownership issue); (2) *inter-individual conflict condition* (children who saw the neutral video and discussed the bus ownership issue); (3) *intra-individual conflict condition* (children who saw the bus driver video and discussed the neutral topic). In addition there were two other conditions for comparison that did not involve conflict. In one of the non-conflict conditions children saw the neutral video and discussed the neutral topic (non-conflict/interaction condition). In the second non-conflict condition children neither saw the video nor participated in the discussion (non-conflict/non-interaction condition). Children in the last condition were interviewed again at the same time as the experimental children, in order to provide some indication of any 'natural' changes in the level of understanding during the testing period.

The post-treatment levels of understanding were analysed by a one-way analysis of variance with the five experimental conditions as a between-subjects variable. The main effect of condition was significant (F (4, 63) = 2.79 p < 0.05). As shown in Table 7.4, the means in the two non-conflict conditions both remained at the pre-treatment level. The non-conflict/interaction condition was contrasted with each of the three conflict conditions by means of a Dunnett test, which corrected for multiple comparisons. With the p level set to 0.05, the results showed a significant contrast in the inter-individual conflict condition only: the mean here (2.46) was significantly higher than that in the baseline condition.[2]

The transcripts of the bus ownership discussions in conditions 1 and 2 were content-analysed to throw light on reasons for some dyads making post-treatment progress whereas others did not. Specifically, we wanted to find out if there was any relationship between progress and the number of active conversational attempts at resolving interpersonal disagreements over the bus ownership. (Disagreements over the neutral topic, which was unrelated to the topic of bus ownership, were not analysed.)

Two categories of statements were coded according to Damon's (1978) and Berkowitz and Gibbs's (1985) coding schemes. These were 'rejection' (that is, direct disagreement with partner's previous statement, other contra-

Table 7.4   Post-treatment levels of understanding (various conditions)

Condition	n	Mean	s.d.
1. Intra- and inter-individual conflict	13	2.23	0.44
2. Inter-individual conflict	13	2.46	0.52
3. Intra-individual conflict	13	1.85	0.56
4. Non-conflict/interaction	13	2.00	0.58
5. Non-conflict/non-interaction	16	2.00	0.52

Note: A one-way ANOVA (Analysis of Variance) showed a significant main effect of condition, F (4, 63) = 2.79 p < 0.05, MS_{error} = 0.27. A Dunnett test was used to compare the nonconflict/interaction condition with each of the three conflict conditions. With a-level set at 0.05, the only significant difference was for the inter-individual conflict condition.

dictory statement, ridicule, or stating a new solution that was not in agreement with partner's previous solution) and 'transaction' (that is, integration of partner's previous statement with other expressed ideas). These two categories of utterances were taken as an indication of conversational attempts to resolve conflict. To correct for the length of discussion, the sum of rejection and transaction utterances was expressed as a ratio of the total number of utterances made by the dyad.

In seven of the 13 dyads, neither child progressed; in the remaining dyads, either one child (three dyads) or both children (three dyads) progressed. Note that no children who discussed the bus ownership issue had regressed, and the vast majority of those who progressed were only one level above their pretreatment level. Dyadic discussions in which one or both children progressed contained a greater proportion of active conversational attempts to resolve interpersonal disagreements than dyadic discussions in which neither children progressed (means = 0.12 v. 0.03). However, this difference did not reach significance ($F(1,11) = 3.72$, $p = 0.08$).

Children might derive different benefits from attempts to resolve interpersonal disagreements depending on whether they were expressing or hearing these resolution attempts during a discussion. To examine this, children's post-treatment level of understanding following bus discussion was correlated with conversational attempts (that is, the rate of rejection plus transaction/statements) expressed by (1) self and (2) partner. Progress was significantly correlated with attempts by self ($r = 0.43$, $p < 0.05$) but not with attempts by partner ($r = 0.37$, $p = 0.06$). It appears that progress resulted more from the production than the hearing of conversational attempts.

Contrary to an imitation hypothesis the present study demonstrated that progress following social interaction on the bus ownership issue was possible when both partners were initially at the same level of understanding. This study also provided some support for the notion that interactional style had a strong influence on whether or not social interaction will stimulate cognitive development. This result from a sociocognitive domain supplements similar findings in the cognitive (for example, Mackie, 1983) and moral (for example, Berkowitz, 1980) domains.

CONCLUDING REMARKS

In examining young people's understanding of private ownership, we have focused on awareness, ownership rights and bases for acquiring ownership. A rudimentary awareness of private ownership begins early in the lives of children, probably prior to their acquisition of possessive words such as 'mine'. Children fight over and learn to share possessions with their peers, they receive gifts from friends and relatives, and they purchase items from a shopkeeper. Ownership is also featured in the media, especially advertising, and in the stories, proverbs and tales that are told to children (Stacey, 1987). Children are therefore able to form an understanding of ownership within this matrix of social influence (cf. Damon, 1981). From this awareness develops the recognition that the owner has certain rights. The rights of use and control, but not the right of transfer, are relatively easy for children to grasp, for these two rights alone are congruent with the nature of their possessions – toys and apparel – acquired from their parents.

Children's understanding of private ownership has mainly been examined by observing younger children, especially their object disputes, or interviewing children once their verbal skills are adequate. To overcome the difficulty of children's tautological responses to direct interview questions about the meaning of ownership, several researchers have resorted to indirect questions about, for example, sharing and theft of possessions. However, children do not spontaneously divulge all they know in an interview setting (Leiser, 1983). Their verbal skills may hinder them from expressing a 'correct' or 'mature' response, or their attention may simply be focused on some other aspect of the question or situation.

Our research on awareness and rights has been oriented towards the use of behavioural measures that would complement the children's verbal responses. Thus, by asking children to divide a sum of payment between two workers who had different amounts of savings, we have observed the ability of children to recognize the distinction between the payment and the private savings. Similarly, by assigning children a task that involved a decisional conflict between equality and transfer, we have created a realistic situation for assessing how well they understood the right of transfer. In both studies we found age-related increases in the criterion variable. Furthermore, specific to the study of transfer right, we found a country difference that favoured the younger Indian children over their New Zealand counterparts.

With increasing age there was a corresponding increase in the number of children who accepted the contractual bases of ownership and rejected the physical and egocentric bases. From this and the age-related changes in awareness and transfer, it appears that, at around 11 years of age, the awareness of private ownership is firmly established and the right of transfer well understood. This understanding, in turn, is almost certainly tied to the age-related increase in children's active acquisition of their own possessions.

We assessed young people's understanding of public ownership in two areas that are already familiar to them, namely, the bus and the school. In both areas there was an age-related trend for conceptions to change from the more concrete and more directly observable to the more abstract and less directly observable. The change was faster in the case of the school than of the bus, probably owing to the children's greater personal experience with the functioning of the former. By the age of 11–12 years, most children no longer inferred ownership from adults (bus drivers and school teachers) who outwardly had the most observable contact with and control over the objects. Instead, the children were able to connect ownership with the corresponding political institution. The concept of the 'boss' provides the children with a clutch for making that connection, and it would be worthwhile for future research to examine how children acquire this concept.

Children in our experiment who thought the bus driver owned the bus were likely to have already known the concept of the 'boss', even though they were yet unable to envisage a boss other than the driver. What was difficult for them was not so much the absence of the concept, but the inability to apply the concept to somebody not seen to be in control of the bus or the driver. Even when information about such a boss was available from a video, children did not benefit from it directly. Instead, they tended to become confused by the information and regress to a less mature level of understanding. It would appear that to be able to deal with the initially confusing information was of critical importance to the children. They could do this more effectively when they had the chance of talking to their peers about the information. In so doing, they also stimulated their peers to reconstruct their knowledge. At the end, the effectiveness of the dyadic discussion in promoting progress was related to children's own attempts to resolve interactional conflict. Such attempts indicate that the children were trying to coordinate their perspectives on the problem with conflicting information arising in the interaction. These cognitive coordinations between individuals, in turn, provide one basis of individual cognitive coordination (Perret-Clermont and Brossard, 1985). This kind of social talk, which may be triggered by various means and occur in various occasions, is perhaps the most natural and common avenue for children to develop an understanding of the social world.

NOTES

1. Analysis by Pearson's correlation showed a significant positive correlation between the understanding of bus and school ownership ($r = 0.63$, $p < 0.001$).
2. It is acknowledged that the above ANOVA (Analysis of Variance) may not be strictly appropriate, given the statistical non-independence of data, arising from the pairing of subjects. A further analysis of the 26 dyads in conditions 1–4 (see Table 7.4) was therefore carried out using the dyad as the unit of analysis. The mean post-treatment level of understanding of each dyad was calculated and then analysed according to a one-way analysis of variance design comprising discussion topic (bus versus neutral) as a between-subjects variable. As may be recalled from Table 7.4, this variable contrasted dyads who experienced inter-individual conflict with those who did not. There was a significant main effect for discussion topic ($F (1, 24) = 8.96$, $p < 0.01$, $MS_e = 0.13$). Dyads discussing bus

ownership made more post-treatment progress than dyads discussing the neutral topic (means 2.35 v. 1.92).

REFERENCES

Bakeman, R. and Brownlee, J.R. (1982), 'Social rules governing object conflicts in toddlers and preschoolers', in K.H. Rubin and H.S. Ross (eds), *Peer Relationships and Social Skills in Childhood*, New York: Springer-Verlag, pp. 99–111.

Berkowitz, M.W. (1980), 'The role of transactive discussion in moral development: The history of a six-year program of research – Part I, *Moral Education Forum*, **5**, 13–26.

Berkowitz, M.W. and Gibbs, J.B. (1985), 'The process of moral conflict resolution and moral development', in M.W. Berkowitz (ed.), *Peer Conflict and Psychological Growth*, San Francisco: Jossey-Bass.

Berti, A.E. and Bombi, A.S. (1988), *The Child's Construction of Economics*, Cambridge: Cambridge University Press/Paris: Editions de la Maison des Sciences de l'Homme.

Berti, A.E., Bombi, A.S. and Lis, A. (1982), 'The child's conceptions about means of production and their owners', *European Journal of Social Psychology*, **12**, 221–39.

Burris, V. (1983), 'The child's conception of economic relations: A study of cognitive socialization', *Sociological Focus*, **15**, 307–25.

Cram, F. (1990), 'Children's social understanding and the effects of peer interaction', unpublished PhD thesis, University of Otago.

Cram, F. and Ng, S.H. (1989), 'Children's endorsement of ownership attributes', *Journal of Economic Psychology*, **10**, 63–75.

Damon, W. (1978), *The Social World of the Child*, San Francisco: Jossey-Bass.

Damon, W. (1981), 'Exploring children's social cognition on two fronts', in J.H. Flavell and L. Ross (eds), *Social Cognitive Development: Frontiers and possible futures*, Cambridge: Cambridge University Press.

Dawe, H.C. (1934), 'An analysis of two hundred quarrels of preschool children', *Child Development*, **5**, 139–57.

Deutsch, W. and Pechmann, T. (1982), 'Social interaction and the development of definite descriptions', *Cognition*, **11**, 159–84.

Doise, W. (1978), *Groups and Individuals: Explanations in social psychology*, Cambridge: Cambridge University Press.

Doise, W. and Mackie, D. (1981), 'On the social nature of cognition', in J.P. Forgas (ed.), *Social Cognition: Perspectives on everyday understanding*, London: Academic Press.

Dufty, N.F. and Harrold, R. (1972), 'Economic socialization', in F.J. Hunt (ed.), *Sociology in Australia*, Sydney: Angus and Robertson, pp. 260–87.

Ellis, L. (1985), 'On the rudiments of possessions and property', *Social Science Information*, **24**, 113–43.

Emler, N. and Valiant, G.L. (1982), 'Social interaction and cognitive conflict in the development of spatial coordination skills', *British Journal of Psychology*, **73**, 295–303.

Furby, L. (1976), 'The socialization of possessions and ownership among children in three cultural groups: Israeli city and American', in S. Modgil and C. Modgil (eds), *Piagetian Research: Compilation and Commentary*, **8**, 95–127, Windsor: NFER Publishing.

Furby, L. (1978a), 'Possession in humans: An exploratory study of its meaning and motivation', *Social Behaviour and Personality*, **6**, 49–65.

Furby, L. (1978b), 'Sharing: Decisions and moral judgements about letting others use one's possessions', *Psychological Reports*, **43**, 595–609.

Furby, L. (1980), 'The origins and early development of possessive behaviour', *Political Psychology*, **2**, 30–42.

Furnham, A. and Jones, S. (1987), 'Children's views regarding possessions and their theft', *Journal of Moral Education*, **16**, 18–30.

Furnham, A. and Lewis, A. (1986), *The Economic Mind: The social psychology of economic behaviour*, Brighton: Wheatsheaf Books.

Furth, H.G. (1980), 'The world of grown-ups: Children's conceptions of society', New York: Elsevier.

Hetherington, E.M. and Parke, R.D. (1986), *Child Psychology: A contemporary viewpoint*, 3rd edn, New York: McGraw-Hill.

Hollowell, P.G. (1982), 'On the operationalization of property', in P.G. Hollowell (ed.), *Property and Social Relations*, London: Heinemann.

Inhelder, B., Sinclair, H. and Bovet, M. (1974), *Learning and the Development of Cognition* (translated by S. Wedgewood), London: Routledge and Kegan Paul.

Isaacs, S. (1936), 'Property and possessiveness', *British Journal of Medical Psychology*, **25**, 69–78.

Jahoda, G. (1981), 'The development of thinking about economic institutions', *Cahiers de Psychologie Cognitive*, **1**, 55–73.

Lea, S.E.G., Tarpy, R.M. and Webley, P. (1987), *The Individual in the Economy*, Cambridge: Cambridge University Press.

Leiser, D. (1983), 'Children's conceptions of economics – The constitution of a cognitive domain', *Journal of Economic Psychology*, **4**, 297–317.

Loewenthal, K. (1976), 'Property', *European Journal of Social Psychology*, **6**, 343–51.

Mackie, D. (1980), 'A cross-cultural study of intra-individual and inter-individual conflicts of centrations', *European Journal of Social Psychology*, **10**, 313–18.

Mackie, D. (1983), 'The effects of social interaction on conservation of spatial relations', *Journal of Cross-Cultural Psychology*, **14**, 131–51.

Miller, G.A. and Johnson-Laird, P.N. (1976), *Language and Perception*, Cambridge: Cambridge University Press.

Moessinger, P. (1975), 'Developmental study of fair division and property', *European Journal of Social Psychology*, **5**, 385–94.

Newman, D. (1978), 'Ownership and permission among nursery school children', in J. Glick and K.A. Clarke-Stewart (eds), *The Development of Social Understanding*, New York: John Wiley, pp. 213–50.

Ng, S.H. (1983), 'Children's ideas about the bank and shop profit: Developmental stages and the influence of cognitive contrasts and conflicts', *Journal of Economic Psychology*, **4**, 209–21.

Perret-Clermont, A.-N. and Brossard, A. (1985), 'On the interdigitation of social and cognitive processes', in R.A. Hinde, A.-N. Perret-Clermont and J. Stevenson-Hinde (eds), *Social Relations and Cognitive Development*, Oxford: Clarendon Press.

Piaget, J. (1977), 'Problems of equilibrium', in M.H. Appel and L.S. Goldberg (eds), *Topics in Cognitive Development, Vol. 1*, New York: Plenum, pp. 3–14.

Roy, A.W.N. and Howe, C.J. (1990), 'Effects of cognitive conflict, socio-cognitive conflict and imitation on children's socio-legal thinking', *European Journal of Social Psychology*, **20**, 241–52.

Siegal, M. (1990), *Knowing Children: Experiments in conversation and cognition*, Hillsdale, NJ: Lawrence Erlbaum Associates.

Snare, F. (1972), 'The concept of property', *American Philosophical Quarterly*, **9**, 200–206.

Stacey, B.G. (1982), 'Economic socialization in the pre-adult years', *British Journal of Social Psychology*, **21**, 159–73.

Stacey, B.G. (1987), 'Economic socialization', in S. Long (ed.), *Annual Review of Political Science, Vol. 2*, Norwood: Ablex Publishing, pp. 1–23.

Streater, A.L. and Chertkoff, J.M. (1976), 'Distribution of rewards in a triad: A developmental test of equity theory', *Child Development*, **47,** 800–805.

Vygotsky, L.S. (1978), *Mind in Society: the development of higher psychological processes*, Cambridge, Mass.: Harvard University Press.

Westermarck, E. (1926), *The Origin and Development of the Moral Ideas, Vol. 2*, 2nd edn, London: Macmillan.

8. Consumer education in French families and schools

Dominique Lassarre

INTRODUCTION

Socialization can be defined (Ziegler and Child, 1969) as 'a broad term for the whole process by which an individual develops through transaction with other people, his specific pattern of socially relevant behaviour and experience'. No doubt children have a very active role in their own social development and there is a great deal of research on cognitive development in economic psychology. One of the main aspects of children's socialization in any society is education: the purposive behaviour of parents and teachers in order to influence children and adolescents' understanding, attitudes and behaviours. Education can be based on practical experience (savoir-faire) as well as on the acquisition of some abstract operations and knowledge (savoir). Most of the know-how acquisitions are made at home and basic knowledge is acquired at school.

In European countries, children and early adolescents' economic activities are mainly reduced to consumption, and budgeting purchases with income and saving strategies. Parents who are the main purveyors of pocket money are also the most important educators of consumer behaviour. But the educative practices in this area are still little known because, as with other familial habits, they are not organized and are mainly unconscious. The first part of this chapter comprises a review of the scattered knowledge on consumer education at home informed by the results of a specific study among teenagers of a small French town (Lassarre *et al.*, 1992).

French teachers are encouraged to deal with everyday life: this part of their teaching is called 'éveil' (awakening) in primary schools and 'enseignement transversal' (transversal teaching) in secondary schools. It is a voluntary and autonomous activity under the control of each teacher. In 1989, the French state secretary for consumer affairs asked for a national survey in order to evaluate the amount of teachers' involvement in the area of consuming education. Following this study, the Ministry of Education published a new circular in order to promote consumer education at school (1990). The results of this national survey will be the main topic of the second part of this chapter.

CONSUMER EDUCATION AT HOME

Most data on the consumption and budgeting of young people comes from market research. The problem is that this does not tell us much about the educative process at home which is the origin of the acquisition of economic habits. To understand whether the teenager's consumption is predictive of the consumption of the adult he or she is going to be, we must know what are the constraints, rules and freedoms in their budget.

A sample of young adolescents born in 1977 and 1978 (14–15 years old), comprising 50 boys and 50 girls, were interviewed in the two secondary schools (collèges) of a small French town (19 000 inhabitants) in Champagne. The questionnaire was constructed in such a way as to collect information about four variables: sources of income; the amount of income from each different source; the different uses of money (saving, spending); and parental control over finances. In order to avoid fallacious generalizations from the respondents, the questions always concerned 'the last time' the teenager received money from different sources. The purpose of this research was to study the structure of parental education: is the supervision of finances related to their amount, to their purpose and/or to the origin of the money? Are there different types of education? Are boys and girls educated the same way? The findings of this study will be used for comparisons with some national marketing surveys.

Children and Primadolescents' Incomes

As they grow older, children have more and more money at their disposal. This money comes from different sources, including pocket money. Pocket money or allowances will be defined as money regularly (weekly or monthly) given by parents. There are apparent contradictions in studies of the amounts of allowance given to children and teenagers. Parents tend to cite much smaller amounts than children. For instance, comparing two surveys carried out in the same year (1986) on national samples for 12–14-year-olds, SOFRES found a monthly mean of 60 francs when asking parents and the Institut de l'Enfant found a monthly mean of 152 francs when asking children. This discrepancy is probably due to parents only counting pocket money and children counting the money they have 'in their pocket'. We will assume that children are more valid informants about their own money than their parents.

According to Institut de l'Enfant, when they are 13–14 years old, children's monthly income amounts to 578 francs and it comes from four different sources (see Table 8.1). A major part of this money is received as gifts for Christmas, birthdays or other festive occasions by parents and other members of the family. Teenagers from Champagne received a mean of 645.67 francs for Christmas 1991 or their birthday if it occurred during the first term of 1992.

Table 8.1   The different sources of income

Pocket money	84F
Gifts (monthly mean)	268F
Payment for household chores	58F
Small jobs	168F

Source: Institut de l'Enfant.

Paid work outside the home and small jobs are another source of more or less regular income. Paid work is encouraged by 70 per cent of parents during holidays and by 19 per cent of parents during school time, a low proportion compared to the USA: where 40 per cent of the boys and 63 per cent of girls of 14–15 are working outside home during school time (Mortimer *et al.*, 1991). The monthly income from paid work amounted to a mean of 233.77 francs in Champagne, with 53 per cent of children working – the boys mainly working in the vineyards and the girls baby-sitting.

Part of the income comes from parents who pay for household chores (washing up, washing the car, change left over after shopping for the family), as revealed by a national sample of 492 parents of children aged 6 to 18 interviewed in France (IPSOS, 1991). This practice is admitted by 29 per cent of parents, compared to 87 per cent in the USA (Mortimer *et al.*, 1991). In Champagne, 63 per cent of the sample received a mean of 63.25 francs for payment for household chores on the latest occasion.

Many parents (42 per cent – IPSOS, 1991) give more money for good results at school, and 22 per cent admit they give less pocket money in the case of bad results. In Champagne, 32 per cent of the adolescents received a mean of 67.46 francs on the last occasion they had good school marks. Educators would certainly not approve of this extrinsic reward, but in fact we have little idea of the real function of incentive rewards (money) in educa-tion. According to GSI-CFRO (1989) some children and adolescents also get their money from legitimate selling of items (such as school books or old records) or from illicitly selling stolen things (cosmetics, confectionery, stationery, leather jackets, hifis, and so on).

A recent survey (1992) of the Institut de l'Enfant shows that the amount of money handled by children grows as they get older and the proportion of pocket money in this amount decreases at the same time (see Table 8.2). In the Champagne survey, the numbers of boys and girls receiving an allowance are similar, and so are the monthly amounts of pocket money (boys: 107 francs, girls: 104 francs). These figures are consistent with national polls. According to different marketing surveys, 25–30 per cent of young people aged 6 to 18 do not receive an allowance. The figure was 40 per cent in the Champagne survey: 33 per cent are given money irregularly and 7 per cent are never given money by their parents (5 per cent of boys and 2 per cent of girls).

Table 8.2   Amounts of income and proportion of pocket money

Age	Income	Pocket money
4–7 years	46F	46F
8–10 years	201F	
11–12 years	340F	
13–14 years	578F	84F
15–16 years	607F	

Source: Institut de l'Enfant (1992).

A survey of 431 'lycéens' aged 15 to 20, from middle and upper classes in Paris suburbs, showed that giving pocket money generally depended on the social class of parents: 15 per cent of children in the upper economic classes did not receive pocket money, but the proportion was doubled (30 per cent) in the lower economic classes. To have no pocket money does not mean for either children or adolescents that they have no money at all. Some of them (34 per cent of boys and 32 per cent of girls in Champagne) receive money 'when they ask for it', with a mean amount of 84 francs for boys and 108 francs for girls.

Money Education

The practice of giving an allowance is the sign of an economic education within the family. In a recent study (Lassarre, not published) among a population of girls aged 16–17, still at school, from a low economic class in a big town near Paris, 44 per cent declared they did not receive any pocket money, but said 'I get money from my parents when I need it', which meant that in fact they received daily a variable amount for buying sandwiches, bus tickets, a sweater or school books. In fact, those who received a mean of 33 francs pocket money a week also received in the same week a mean of 21.5 francs for their everyday expenses, while those who received monthly pocket money, received a weekly mean of 51 francs without daily extras.

Giving an allowance is recommended as an educational practice partly because it is assumed that parents who give pocket money also discuss family budget issues with the children, who are also given more autonomy and trust. Some of the consequences of parental educational practices have been studied, but results are somewhat dissimilar and even contradictory. After interviewing both parents and children (aged 7 to 12), Marshall and Magruder (1960) found that four recommendations in particular regarding parents' money education practices were supported by the data: if children are given wide experience in the use of money, they will have more knowledge of money and its use than when lacking such varied experience; children will have more knowledge of money use if they are given money to spend; children will have more knowledge of the use of money if they save money; they will have more knowledge and experience with money if their parents handle the family income wisely.

Marshall and Magruder's findings did not, however, support other recommendations: for example, that children will have more knowledge when they are given an allowance or when they are given opportunities to earn money; and that rewarding or punishing with money have bad effects on money use. Also the practice of giving an allowance to children and adolescents did not seem to affect the cognitive aspects (knowledge about money) of economic socialization. But four years later, one of the authors (Marshall, 1964) after a similar study with 90 children aged 10 to 12, concluded that:

> allowance parents differed from non-allowance parents in (a) providing their children with a wider variety of experiences in the use of money, (b) making the purposes of spending money clearer to their children, (c) stating that their children received more spending money, and (d) permitting or encouraging their children to earn money away from home.

More recently, Abramovitch *et al.* (1991) and Pliner *et al.* in Chapter 3 of the present volume gave children aged, 6, 8 and 10 four dollars in cash or in the form of credit card to spend in an experimental store. Those who did not receive pocket money at home spent more with their credit card than in the cash conditions, but this was not the case for those who received pocket money. Children who got allowances had a better knowledge of pricing and in general 'were more sophisticated about money than those who do not'. Mortimer *et al.* (1991) in a longitudinal study of adolescents of 14–15 years found that economic exchanges of services for pay at home were correlated with a weaker intrinsic orientation towards work in relation to jobs both before and after finishing school.

In terms of social class there is some evidence of a lack of budgeting education. Michaud and Bourdy (1991) carried out a survey among young prisoners in Fleury-Merogis Prison (near Paris). For these teenagers, the 'cantine' rules (a kind of mail-order selling inside the penitentiary system) are their first experience of a budget; they had never counted their money or anticipated their expenses before going to jail. Delarue (1991) emphasizes the total lack of realism of young people facing unemployment without any professional skill. They ask for a job with monthly wages of 10 000 francs when the national mean is about 7000 francs (see also Dickinson and Emler in Chapter 4 of the present volume).

These results show that the family arrangements of the sources of children and adolescents' money is more important than the knowledge of monetary value. For children who do not receive pocket money, there is no possibility of provisional strategies, no money management, no responsibility and the feeling of 'never having any money'. These facts are a good example of the reproduction of social handicaps: parents who ignore budget management cannot give any economic education to their children.

Parental Influences on Children's and Adolescents' Consumption and Savings

Parents' motivation for giving an allowance changes during the years of education. In the early years pocket money is given to the children to be spent. Parents start giving an allowance when they are annoyed to hear their children requesting an increasing variety of goods when they are shopping. This increasing desire on the part of the child leads to disputes with the parents. Initially, therefore, pocket money is a way to avoid disputes. At this stage children tend to buy unnecessary gadgets, low quality or even harmful products (such as sweets), so there is generally no educative purpose before children are 11 and enter the 'college' (secondary school). Then comes the time of negotiation where a portion of pocket money must be used to cover certain school expenses, for example, transport or books (13 per cent) or personal expenses (12 per cent) (for items such as clothes or cosmetics). Among parents, 81 per cent induce their children to compare prices in different stores, 81 per cent urge theme to make sure they buy good quality and 44 per cent suggest they avoid expense and save their money (IPSOS, 1991). We can conclude, with Marshall (1964), that for many parents 'giving an allowance may be a relatively easy or frictionless way to handle children's spending money'.

Table 8.3 shows the different areas of adolescents' expenditures as they appeared in a national poll. Spending increases with age: an average of 330

Table 8.3   Structure of monthly consumption of 15–20-year-olds (in French francs)

Clothes and shoes	110
Records and cassettes	59
Other outings	55
Cinema	47.5
Books and magazines	46
Transport	45
Cafes	35.5
Sport	31.5
Tobacco	30
Concerts	28.5
Hairdresser	28
Restaurants	24
Driving licence	22
Cosmetics	21

Source: GSI-CFRO (1989).

francs at 15 525 francs at 18 and 1000 francs at 20 (GSI-CFRO, 1989). The Champagne findings are that, when children are 14–15 years old, main consumption sectors for both boys and girls, are clothes, outings (restaurants, cinemas), books and magazines, records and cassettes, sweets, pastries and cigarettes. Boys also bought petrol for motorbikes and girls bought cosmetics and gifts. Money is given to children and adolescents for everyday expenses. The amount increases as the teenager's everyday activities become more autonomous.

Parents encourage saving. Most children and adolescents 88 per cent (IPSOS, 1991) have an account in a savings bank; some of them (34 per cent) have a current account, 23 per cent a cash card and 17 per cent a cheque book (these last two categories apply to children aged 15 to 18). According to the savings banks ('Caisses d'Epargne'), 42 per cent of holders or 'livret A', the most popular savings account, are under 17, which means about six million such accounts with an average of 2000 francs in each. In Champagne, only two boys did not save money; the others saved by putting money in a savings account (74 per cent), in a money box (68 per cent) or by giving money to their parents (6 per cent), with different combinations. Neyrand and Guyot (1990) interviewed adolescents aged 11 to 15 living near Marseille. They found that only 16 per cent of them did not save. Half the savings were for a specific purchase (hifi, computers, holidays, a motorbike), the other half was just for 'later on'. Savings decrease when they get older. By the time they are

20, they are constrained to spend all their money on everyday purchases (GSI-CFRO, 1989).

Educational Styles in French Families

We have very little idea of the different styles of economic education in French families. National surveys find a strong tendency towards liberalism. Even in the lower classes, most adolescents and young adults keep the money they earn from their jobs and are not contributing to the family income. Only a few children or adolescents must report to their parents hope they spend their money. But are all educational practices consistent?

Lautrey (1980) described three types of education (Table 8.4) which are strongly correlated with children's success at school: low structuration of education (no rules), flexible structuration (correlated with success) and rigid structuration (correlated with failure). The two last types are correlated with the educational level of parents (how long the parents went to school). So Lautrey emphasizes the sociocognitive aspects of social 'reproduction' (Bourdieu and Passeron, 1970).

Table 8.4   Educational styles (per cent)

Educational style	High educational level	Low educational level
Low structuration	17	16
Flexible structuration	47	33
Rigid structuration	36	51

Source: Lautrey (1980).

We used various categories to interpret interviews with parents about the influences of television advertising on their children: 61 per cent of them were pessimistic, feeling that television adverts were bad and that therefore the only thing to do is to keep children away from their influence (rigid structuration); 23 per cent were optimistic, feeling that there is no danger because children are able to form their own opinions and to choose (low structuration); 11 per cent were voluntarist – they had discussions with their children as they watched television in the evenings; they asked their children more often to run errands, although they agreed to discuss such requests and they gave more pocket money for personal purchases.

In a different approach to parental economic education, we studied the structure of parents' behaviour (according to their teenagers' answers) by means of a correspondence analysis. The first factor (18 per cent of the total variance) is concerned with the general supervision of the way children spend their money wherever it comes from. The minority of parents who supervise the use of pocket money do not give it regularly; they also supervise the use of money given for school results, household chores, gifts and money earned from small jobs. No wonder their children do not feel free. At the other end of the spectrum there is a larger group of more liberal parents.

The second factor (11 per cent of the total variance) reveals a supervision of income: on one side money is given without any conditions (regular allowance and gift for Christmas or birthday); on the other it is given as a reward for school results or household chores. In the first case, savings are more autonomous (money box) while in the second parents decide the amount to save and take care of the savings.

The third factor (10 per cent of the total variance) opposes a regular allowance to money given irregularly. In the first case the amount of savings is under control and all purchases, even those of less than 300 francs, are supervised, as is the money earned from small jobs. In spite of this supervision, the children feel free.

The fourth factor (9 per cent of the total variance) opposes the rewarding of household chores to the rewarding of school results; the fifth factor (7 per cent of the total variance) concerns an absence of money education: no pocket money, no supervision, no savings.

The main conclusions of the Champagne study are as follows: there is no prototype of money education as it takes five factors to account for only 55 per cent of the total variance. Supervision of savings and expenses is well accepted by children when a regular allowance is given. The gender of the child has no influence on any of these results. The lack of money education is a concern to less than 7 per cent of the children. In order to fit Lautrey's structuration types, we used a gradation of supervision extending from nought to 133: 20 subjects have nought (low structuration); four subjects have 133 (rigid structuration); the rest can be divided between a flexible liberal structuration (35 subjects between 8 and 60) and a flexible authoritarian structuration (41 subjects between 66 and 116), in both of which children are given a regular allowance with more or less supervision of the use of the money. Thus the allocation of regular pocket money is the main indicator of economic education at home.

Parent–Child Interaction when Shopping

Consumer education also implies the learning of the ability to choose products according to their utility, quality and price. A great part of this education certainly takes place at home during everyday conversations. Another part is a 'training' that occurs during shopping.

Parents often go shopping with their young children. In 1979 (study not published), we observed 40 mother–child and eight father–child couples in supermarkets (22 boys and 26 girls, aged 9 to 10). They were followed in three departments: toys, sweets and milk products. Then, after they went through the cash register, they were surveyed separately by short question-naires. We observed purchase requests and parents' answers. Children were asked about the products they wanted and we asked the parents for the same information: 71 per cent of the children asked verbally and/or by gestures at least once for something in the three departments; 16.6 per cent of the parents yielded, but in 39.5 per cent of incidents they bought another product as a substitute after a discussion. Childrens' answers to the questionnaire were correlated with observations, but 16.6 per cent expressed some self-censor-ship: they wanted something but they did not ask for it as they knew their parent would refuse. Parents noticed only 45.5 per cent of their children's wishes and 50 per cent said they yielded. In this case there was no correlation between interviews and observations. To learn to purchase supposes that parents are open-minded and children expressive when going shopping.

A second study (Lassarre and Roland-Levy, 1989) relied on observation followed by an interview of 49 children aged 11 to 12. These children were alone (17), with a friend of the same age (10) or with an adult (22). They were observed during a visit to a supermarket. The interviewer also tried to find out the motives for the observed behaviour. Before buying, the principal activity of children in the supermarket was to seek information. It included seeking the advice of the accompanying person about school stationery or biscuits or asking shop assistants for more information on fresh food (meat and vegetables) when they were on their own. They also read labels, tried out products and looked at prices. The motives for this behaviour are various: when they go shopping for the family, they try to find the right product, but buying things for themselves is an entertainment they enjoy, especially when they are with a friend. When parents let their children go shopping, they give them the opportunity for pleasant consumer training.

Buying clothes, in particular, implies a whole process of interactions be-tween parents and adolescents. Clothes are expensive. Table 8.3 shows ex-penditure on clothing in the adolescent's budget; although it is the highest in the list, it is below 200 francs. This implies that parents are financing or cofinancing the purchase of clothes, even among late adolescents.

In a small exploratory survey, Fosse-Gomez (1991) distinguished three economic roles: the buyer who goes shopping, the payer who finances the purchase and the user of the product. She studied the last clothing purchase of 46 adolescents aged 14 to 16. It appeared from her results that only the mother was intervening in the process of purchasing clothes. She only found four combinations of the three economic roles: (1) the adolescent was the buyer, the user and the payer (two girls and a boy); they bought odd clothes or expensive brands that their mother did not want to pay for. (2) The adolescent was the buyer and the user and the mother was a co-buyer and the payer: this was the case in most families (23 cases); the purchase was decided by both, the mother paid and the adolescent went shopping accompanied or not by the mother in order to try the clothing on; (3) the adolescent was the buyer, the user and the payer and the mother was sometimes a co-buyer but always a co-payer: in this widespread case (18) the purchase was cofinanced in order for the adolescent to afford the brand he or she asked for; (4) the adolescent was the user and the mother was the buyer and the payer (two boys of 14): the continuation of the process of purchasing clothes during the childhood. Excepting the first case, the choice of the purchase was discussed between the mother and the teenager with different criteria: the 'image' encoded in the garment, the comfort of the product, its quality, its price and the opportunity of a bargain.

To summarize economic socialization at home, parents educate their children and adolescents by (1) giving them money regularly, (2) encouraging saving and budget planning, (3) delegating the responsibility of buying products for themselves and for the whole family, and (4) helping them to choose expensive products.

CONSUMER EDUCATION AT SCHOOL

At present, economics is not a school subject for children before the age of 16 in France. When interviewing children (Lassarre and Roland-Levy, 1989), it appeared that the main sources of economic information were television, parents, friends and stores. School was not considered a primary source of information but teachers were taken as experts for verifying information collected somewhere else.

As early as 1989, consumer education was encouraged in French schools but there were no specific recommendations from the Ministry of Education. A survey was carried out in order to describe and estimate the number of spontaneous initiatives in this area. The survey started with a qualitative study extended to different types of institutional educators. The subjects were 34 teachers and other education staff in primary schools (16), secondary schools (7) and children's leisure organizations (11). These organizations (Centres de loisirs) have charge of children during their days off (Wednesdays and holidays). The interviewees were aged 20 to 50, men and women, from different parts of France. They were asked to describe precisely the different opportunities they had had recently to talk about consumption with children. What were the topics? Was the discussion spontaneous or did they prepare a lesson? Where did they get their information? Did they use any documents? How did the children react? They were then asked to describe their projects on consumption, if they had any.

Next, a national survey on representative samples of the same population was carried out, with 5720 questionnaires being sent with a freepost return envelope. The answering rate was 22.3 per cent (1276 questionnaires) which was the same in different regions but smaller in private schools (9.8 per cent) and much higher among the leisure organization staff (45.9 per cent). Comparing the sample with the actual figures, the poll rate was also variable according to the category of educator (see Table 8.5).

Table 8.5   Poll rates in the different categories of education

	Sample	Population	Poll rate(*)
Primary schools			
Headmasters	398	28 325	1.4
Schoolmasters	390	171 120	0.2
Secondary schools			
Head teachers	38	4 435	0.8
Teachers	178	73 237	0.2
Librarians	118	4 795	2.4
Leisure companies	154	n/a	

Note: *   per thousand.

Headmasters often answered for the rest of the school (most primary schools have only one or two forms) and the respondents were highest poll rates were headmasters and librarians. This response bias made the sample slightly older and more masculine than the actual population.

Motives and Obstacles to Consumer Education at School

The interviews expanded out of the frame so that the analysis does not directly reflect the questions mentioned. Principles of an education in consumption can be differentiated from actual practice. The link between them seems to be ideology as well as pedagogical skill. There were strong motives for educating children in consumption:

1.   Communication motives: 'it is a means of letting the children talk about their everyday life'; 'It's entertaining, especially for those who have difficulties at school'.

2. Moral motives: 'When they are young, they can learn not to be spoiled'; 'They can learn to know the value of money'.
3. Practical motives: 'Children must be aware of their consumers' role'; 'They can be taught to think, decide and choose one product rather than another'; 'They will be more autonomous'.
4. Intellectual motives: 'Consumption is an introduction to economics'; 'They know a lot of things ... all we have to do is to organize their knowledge'.
5. Social motives: 'Children are the go-between for reaching parents'.

These motives were independent of the age or the gender of the children, but they changed in their specification with the children's social class: for the lower class, 'You have to explain that the most expensive rubber is not necessarily the best one', and for the upper class, 'They must learn solidarity and to help one another'.

Consumption was defined by products and by economic topics. The first reaction of the subjects was to deny that they talk at school about consumption or economics; then they came up with a topic and asked, 'Is that consumption?' and the interview could start. Topics which emerged in the interviews were classified into 11 categories:

1. Consumption is 'everyday life'; 'We live in a world of consumption'.
2. It is the study of goods that children consume: sweets, food, clothes, school equipment, toys; 'They try everything they can see. At the moment, the fashion is cereals'.
3. A special category can be created for food products and 'nutritional education': many children take their lunch at school with their teachers; this gives them the opportunity to learn what a well balanced meal is.
4. Safety and prevention of disease: education for preventing home or street accidents, dangers of alcohol, tobacco, drugs or AIDS. 'We organized with the children an exhibition on safety from prams to airplanes'.
5. It is the study of mass communication, especially advertising (television, newspapers): 'We collected ads from different magazines and we used them in many different ways'.
6. Production is the story (evolution) of products from the farm or the mine to the shop: 'They studied cocoa, how and where it grows and all the way until processing; reading labels'.
7. Public and private services, such as banks, EDF (electricity production and distribution) or the mail, are studied.
8. Prices, value of goods and money: 'How to save their pocket money'; 'We studied inflation by comparing the prices of CARAMBARS (sweets) over the last ten years!'

9. Macroeconomy: employment, EC, developing countries: 'Children are really concerned about helping poor countries'.
10. Ecology – the protection of the natural environment: 'We spent the whole year on water: irrigation, visiting a dam, a refining plant, following a river'.
11. Consumers' rights are studied with reference to specific examples: buying a second-hand car, excessive rent increases.

With such motives and such a broad definition of consumption, the subjects felt guilty that they did not offer more lessons or activities on this topic. This was the turning-point of the interviews. Respondents justified their 'inaction' by citing various kinds of obstacles.

First, children are 'too young'. This statement has different consequences. 'They can't understand'; 'They are not interested'; 'They are not involved. For them consumption is pleasure, that's all ... and it's OK: don't frustrate children by stealing their childhood.' The paradox is that this kind of point of view is developed for any topic and any age: in primary schools, the young ones are six years old, in secondary schools, they are eleven, but the same justification is used. Educators felt personally involved. This opinion came only from leisure staff but it is implicit in the teachers' words too: 'It's a dangerous topic'; 'You must be brave, it's a personal commitment.' School organization and rules did not work for this topic: there was no time, no resources, because 'It is not a school subject'. Parents appeared to be hostile to consumer education.

Leisure staff related a number of problems with parents: 'The day after, parents came and told me to mind my own business!'; 'They think we are evaluating their family life.' Teachers did not give precise examples, but they had assumed a defensive position as regards parents' reactions and feared being misunderstood. The last difficulty was intrinsic to the institution they worked in because the school had not enough links with the rest of society. It could be a specific problem: 'After making a rationalization of meal balance, I realized that the meals cooked in the school kitchens were really bad and it was impossible to change them.' It could also turn into a very pessimistic attitude towards education: 'and when they are 18, they'll do what they want to do.'

Returning to actual practices, all subjects admitted after a while that they develop some kind of pedagogical activities to do with consumption with the children. Facing the difficulties identified, economic education appeared to some of them as an ideological involvement. We noticed three tendencies: ecology ('green movements'), socialism and Christian humanism, justifying consumer education. In fact, most respondents used consumption to 'change school', but they refused to admit they were doing so. Their major stated purpose was 'to use consumption to illustrate core subjects' (that is, French and maths), showing their pedagogical skill.

To study consumption and economics implied opening school to the real world. It offered a double opportunity: to admit somebody 'from the outside world' into the classroom and to go outside with the pupils: 'A store manager came: someone who is in the real world'; 'We went to the market-place, to a post office, to a supermarket, to an industrial bakery'. A danger was that children's opinions and knowledge were considered equal to or even more important than the teacher's: 'They know more than I do about fashion'; 'When he talked about his father's unemployment, it was better than anything I could explain'. Modern media, videos and microcomputers were introduced at school but teachers were not at ease with them. As consumption was not a school subject, it gave the opportunity to test these media without any risk.

Through the pedagogic documents they published, economic agents such as firms or public services penetrate the world of education. Teachers had ambivalent feelings about this: they admitted that these documents were well produced, that they were free (and schools are poor!), but they feared advertising motives. Some of them thought they were not strong enough to protect children and they preferred to reject that kind of document. Others tried to counterbalance the influence of advertising by using documents published by consumers' lobbies.

RESULTS OF THE NATIONAL SURVEY

In the national survey, we proposed 17 items or topics. The subjects answered whether they had already dealt with each of them during the present school year (the survey took place in May) and what kind of information they had used. They were asked if they would like to do them (or do them again) and what kind of pedagogical instrument they would like to use. Finally, they had to answer questions related to seven attitude scales on consumer education at school.

Table 8.6 shows a grouping of the different topics into five categories, with two criteria: the topics already introduced and future interests according to requests for information. All topics can be talked about very early (8.3–9.7 year-olds). The first category contains topics which were talked about by more than 75 per cent of the subjects and for which more than 50 per cent were asking for pedagogical documents. These included environment (energy, pollution), food, health and hygiene.

The second category contains topics introduced by 50–75 per cent of the subjects, who were asking for documents in the same proportion (they included safety and waste). These were the most popular themes which could

Table 8.6   Classification of consumption topics

environment (8.8)

food (8.7)	safety (8.3)			
health (8.6)	waste (8.7)			
		advertising (9.2)		
		public utilities (8.8)		
		economics (9.4)		
		leisure (8.4)		
		tourism (8.7)		
		quality (9.2)	consumer support (9.7)	
		money (9.3)	insurance (9.3)	
				housing (8.5)
				clothing (8.6)
				school stationery (8.5)

Notes:
1. In columns: according to the actual activity. In rows: according to information requests.
2. Numbers: lowest age at which the topic was introduced.

be dealt with very young children. The third category comprises topics which were introduced by 25–50 per cent of the subjects, who were asking for documents in the same proportion: advertising and the media, public utilities, economic problems and trade, leisure, toys, audiovisual and microcomputing equipment, tourism and holidays, quality of products, labelling, budget, prices, money. In this category respondents asked for documents for themselves in order to prepare lessons.

The fourth category contains topics which were introduced by less than 25 per cent of the respondents. With older children they include consumer support, access to justice and insurance. Documents were requested for respondents themselves. Teachers do not feel at ease with these two categories, for technical reasons: they are difficult topics for which they need information or training.

In the last group, the topics were rarely introduced and no pedagogical documents were requested although they concerned children and adolescents' everyday life. The topics were housing, clothing and fashion and school stationery. These are typical themes that can create problems with parents or children. Respondents avoid them for interpersonal rather than technical reasons.

There were seven four-point 'agree–disagree' attitude scales: (1) that studying consumption is useful for making basic lessons more attractive; (2) that consumption is a strictly family educational topic; (3) 'discovery' lessons and holidays are the preferred contexts for consumer education; (4) to study consumption is to open schools to everyday life; (5) consumer education should be included in school programmes; (6) consumer education is more useful than the study of history of natural sciences; (7) one should not bother children with consumer education.

The results showed that the opinion that consumer education is an open door to everyday life was the strongest and the most frequently expounded (see Table 8.7); that discovery lessons and holidays are the preferred contexts for this education, being attractive ways to teach basic lessons; that consumption should be included in school programmes; that it cannot be considered as a strictly family issue; and that the child must be educated as a consumer. But more than 10 per cent of the respondents replaced 'more useful than' with 'as useful as' history and natural sciences, showing they were enthusiastic, but reasonable.

The national survey of educators has shown that in 1989 most respondents were favourable to consumer education at school. The Ministry of Education published in 1990 a circular outlining purposes, methods and topics in order to encourage teachers to introduce consumer education at different levels:

Table 8.7   Attitudes towards consumer education at school

	Mean	No answers %
Basic lessons	1.74	7.9
Family education	3.44	4.2
Preferred contexts	1.77	7.3
To open schools	1.36	2.5
School programmes	1.75	6.1
More useful	3.14	12.4
No bother children	3.64	4.2

'The acquisition of thoughtful and critical behaviour should enable the pupil to react responsibly in everyday life situations which bring consumption out.' There were no constraints on school programmes; schoolmasters 'must integrate [economic concepts] in all school activities, when this is possible ... This education also implies an opening to the outside world.' The different topics studied in the survey are proposed, with a progression according to the age of the children, from perception (taste, smell, touch and so on) at the nursery school (3 years old) to an introduction to economics in the lycée (16 years old). The possibility of training is offered to teachers.

Policy, context and implications

'Everyday life affords a mass of opportunities for economics lessons' (Webley and Lea, 1991). Parents as well as teachers are certainly conscious of this and most of them recognize that consumer education is useful and even necessary. The main purpose of parental education is to rear autonomous individuals who will be able to face the complexity of their society. At the moment, their main concern is the success of their children at school that will give them a better chance to find a job.

Young people know a lot about the economy and much more about consumption. The main concern of teachers is to change this everyday know-how into scientific knowledge, namely economics. This is why social scientists (Kokosowski, 1978; Verges, 1989) and economists try to discover 'spontaneous knowledge' or social representations of economics.

Nowadays, consumer education is entering school not only as an introduction to economics lessons or as an attractive way of presenting basic lessons, but for itself. New issues of everyday life, such as indebtedness, protection of natural resources and limitation of refuse and pollution make consumer education necessary at school when parents are themselves uneducated. Finally, consumer education can also be useful for social integration; for example, when someone is confronted by numerous social and educational problems (no job, no skill, no diploma) it appears that consumption is still a way of participating in the social world. Social workers are beginning to use this motivation for integration instead of rejecting the way of life of some categories of young people.

In conclusion, we may say that consumer education is no longer a private problem; it concerns all social actors and thus becomes a political concern.

REFERENCES

Abramovitch, R., Freedman, J.L. and Pliner, P. (1991), 'Children and money: getting an allowance, credit versus cash, and knowledge of pricing', *Journal of Economic Psychology*, **12**, 27–45.

Bourdieu, P. and Passeron, J.C. (1970), *La reproduction. Eléments pour une théorie du système d'enseignement*, Paris: Minuit.

Delarue, J.M. (1991), 'Banlieue en difficultés', *La rélégation*, Paris: Syros.

Fosse-Gomez, M.H. (1991), 'L'achat de vêtements de l'adolescent: est-ce encore un achat familial?', Colloque Européen sur les Modes de Vie et de Consommation des Jeunes, Paris.

GSI-CFRO (1989), 'L'argent des jeunes', *Sciences et Vie Economie*, **52**, 12–17.

Institut de l'Enfant (1992), 'L'argent de la poche à la banque', *Libération*, 22 January.

IPSOS (1991), 'Argent de poche, l'apprentissage', *Budgets Famille, Mars 1991*, 16–23.

Kokosowski, A. (1978), *Enseigner les Sciences Economiques et Sociales*, Paris: PUF.

Lassarre, D. and Roland-Levy, C. (1989), 'Understanding Children's Economic Socialization', in K. Grunert and F. Olander (eds), *Understanding Economic Behavior*, Dordrecht, Boston, London: Kluwer Academic Publishers, pp. 347–68.

Lassarre, D., Maurice, R. and Lance, B. (1992), 'Economic education at home', IAREP/GEW Joint Conference, Frankfurt/Main, August.

Lautrey, J. (1980), *Classe Sociale, Milieu Familial, Intelligence*, Paris: PUF.

Marshall, H. (1964), 'The relation of giving children an allowance to children's money knowledge and responsibility and to other practices of parents', *The Journal of Genetic Psychology*, **104**, 35–51.

Marshall, H.R. and Magruder, L. (1960), 'Relations between parent money education practices and children's knowledge and use of money', *Child Development*, **31**, 253–84.

Michaud, P. and Bourdy, M.C. (1991), 'La consommation des jeunes détenus', Colloque Européen sur les Modes de Vie et de Consommation des Jeunes, Paris.

Ministère de l'Education Nationale (1990), *Education à la consommation*, Circulaire numéro 90-342 du 17 décembre.

Mortimer, J.T., Dennehy, K. and Lee, C. (1991), 'Economic Socialization in the American Family: the Prevalence, Distribution and Consequences of Allowances Arrangements', Colloque Européen sur les Modes de Vie et de Consommation des Jeunes, Paris.

Verges, P. (1989), 'Représentations sociales de l'économie: une forme de connaissance', in D. Jodelet (ed.), *Les Représentations Sociales*, Paris, PUF, pp. 387–405.

Webley, P. and Lea, S. (1991), 'Towards a More Realistic Psychology of Economic Socialization', Colloque Européen sur les Modes de Vie et de Consommation des Jeunes, Paris.

Ziegler, B. and Child, I. (1969), 'Socialization', in G. Lindzey and E. Aronson (eds), *Handbook of Social Psychology, Vol. 3*. Reading, Mass.: Addison-Wesley, pp. 450–555.

9. Playing the market: the autonomous economic world of children

Paul Webley

INTRODUCTION

Most research into children's economic socialization has concentrated on children's understanding of aspects of the adult economic world (Burris, 1983; Furnham, 1986; Berti and Bombi, 1988; Roland-Levy, 1990; Leiser *et al.*, 1990). This has given us valuable descriptions of the stages children pass through in achieving adult conceptions of work, money, value, price and so on. By contrast, the focus of the recent research carried out at Exeter has been on children's economic behaviour (for example, Webley *et al.*, 1990; Sonuga-Barke and Webley, 1992a) and the question of how they solve the wide range of economic problems they face. Much of the economic behaviour of children is, of course, part of the adult economic world. The most obvious example is pocket money, where children are given money so they can participate as consumers in the economy (Furnham and Thomas, 1984; Webley *et al*, 1988; Hill, 1992). Children also do household work (Goodnow, 1988), work part-time for money and exchange gifts (Eimers, 1992). But in addition to this explicitly economic behaviour, children construct their own autonomous economic world involving bargaining, bartering, swopping and betting.

Unfortunately, very little is known about these kinds of activities. There are a number of valuable descriptions of playground life, though these tend to concentrate on games and their associated rituals (for example, Opie and Opie, 1969; Sluckin, 1981). There is also some research on the language of trading (Mishler, 1979) and a certain amount on the precursors to gambling (Griffiths, 1991; Ide-Smith and Lea, 1988; Smith and Abt, 1984). The picture this research paints is engaging but frustrating. Clearly, there is an autonomous economic world (as Smith and Abt, 1984, put it, 'While marbles were not the coin of the realm, they were a form of currency among those who played with them') but we learn more about the language associated with it than the economic substance. For example, Sluckin (1981) refers to the need to say 'Tin tacks, no backs' to ensure that a child does not change his mind about a swop and Mishler (1979) describes the language in which rules of equivalence are put forward and discussed ('Those are smaller, so if I give you one, you'd hafta give me like five'). One conclusion that can be drawn is that the economic sub-culture is likely to vary enormously from school to school and region to region since this is the pattern found for games, rules and rituals. According to Blatchford *et al.* (1990), none of their sample of 175 London schoolchildren reported playing marbles in the playground, whilst from the studies of Sluckin (1981) and Linaza (1984) it is clear that marble playing was alive and well in Oxford and Spain in the early 1980s.

THEORETICAL AND METHODOLOGICAL ISSUES

One could conclude that the lack of attention given to swopping and related activities is entirely appropriate. Surely these are trivial activities and so of little interest to psychologists? I think not. I would argue that activities like swopping and bargaining are more real for children than the adult world of working, investing and spending. As Furth (1978) wrote:

> We should recognize that children's peer relations are bound to be more real and their relations to the adult world more playful. Sitting quietly next to dad on a bus is for the 4-year-old girl a play that she chooses to enact ... In contrast, the girl's interactions with a friend ... are for real: Here the two children are literally constructing their social life and fashioning themselves into socialized persons. (Furth, 1978, p. 103)

So it is at least arguable that children's notions of value, for example, owe as much to their experience of swopping a football card for a marble as to their experience of buying sweets in a shop and it is almost certainly true that their bargaining skills are honed in the playground rather than in negotiations about pocket money with their parents.

But an apparently 'trivial' activity like swopping raises a far more important issue for researchers, namely to what does the 'economic' in economic socialization refer (Webley and Lea, 1993; Sonuga-Barke and Webley, 1992b)? For the most part researchers have adopted a nominal definition of economic activity and the term has served simply as a label for that part of the social world concerned with the acquisition, management and distribution of wealth. So the child's understanding of buying, banking and borrowing have all been seen as legitimate areas of study. However, taking the meaning of 'economic' for granted is probably unjustifiable. We cannot rely, as we can in other areas of economic psychology, on the fact that researchers and the researched share assumptions about the nature of economic activity. Children do not, in general, use the word 'economic'.

What definitions of economic behaviour could, then, be used? One possibility is to consider behaviours that involve maximizing utility. The problem with this is that any behaviour that is consistent can be described as maximizing something (Rachlin, 1980), which means that economic behaviour would include nearly all behaviour. This problem could be resolved if we used Simon's (1957) idea that economic behaviour involves action where the individual intends to maximize, but this raises problems of its own. Another option is to consider behaviours which are generally labelled 'economic' (the approach that has usually been followed). This is fine as far as it goes, as long as we recognize that the concept of economic behaviour is culturally and historically determined and, more importantly, that the boundary between the economic and the non-economic is inevitably poorly defined. I would tentatively propose that all economic behaviour has something to do with exchange and the division of labour. Note that it is not necessary for money to be exchanged (there are plenty of examples of economic systems where money was unknown).

This definition shifts our attention somewhat. Whether studying adults or children we should be concerned not only with the cash economy; it is legitimate, for example, to ask questions about the economic psychology of the norms governing neighbourly help (Webley and Lea, 1992) and similarly to investigate swopping, bargaining and using marbles as 'coins of the realm'. Though these behaviours may seem trivial to adult bystanders they are certainly not for the participants.

We can reach this same point by another route. The Maussian approach to objects identifies two distinct types of social relations: commodity relations and gift relations (Carrier, 1991). Put simply, commodity relations are impersonal; there is a transfer of an object or service from A to B and countertransfer of money (usually) from B to A. By contrast, although gift relations also consist of a transfer and a countertransfer, the relationship is not transient and the object continues to be identified with the giver. Thus the area of life which involves the household, family, friends and neighbours is likely to be characterized by gift relations and that associated with work and shops by commodity relations. The study of economic socialization, like economic psychology generally, has clearly been overconcerned with the commodity domain (children's understanding of money, work and so on). Investigating aspects of gift relations (in this case, economic relationships with friends) is long overdue.

Does this concentration on real economic behaviour have any implications for methodology? There are two important points. First, we should expect to find considerable variability in the forms of 'indigenous' economic culture among children (as we have already seen in the case of marbles). This suggests that we need to ground our investigations in a firm knowledge of the particular culture and use different experimental materials in different schools. This is to use a form of 'individualized' experiments, to use the term coined by Greenfield and Zukow (1978). In these, what is held constant across subjects is not the physical characteristics of the stimuli but the functional relationship between the subject and the stimuli. They give the example of researchers interested in the effect of how familiar an object is on lexical overgeneralization. They might show children photographs of objects from their own environment which were classified as to their degree of familiarity; thus the pictures would be different but their functional relationship with the child equivalent. Similarly, in investigating children's understanding of the relationship between rarity and value, one would use examples of tradeable objects from their own playground that differed in rarity; in one school this might be marbles, in another, football cards.

Second, investigating the economic culture of children is clearly a kind of ethnography. Childhood is another country and they do things differently there. What is required to interpret this culture are local informants. This suggests that child collaborators are vital, and that without them we may find ourselves left outside the gates of the playground, staring in.

Initial inquiries revealed that there is considerable informal economic activity at schools, though much of it has the flavour of the underground economy. Swopping, for example, is banned at many schools because of complaints by parents and the exploitation of younger children by older children. Betting, though common (Ide-Smith and Lea, 1988) is also frowned on by the school authorities. Activities that are permitted, such as the swopping of football cards, are often confined to one sex.

SWOPPING

Swopping has been investigated by two of my students, Bardill (1985) and Traub (1991). Bardill used unstructured interviews and investigated the current swopping activities of 30 children from a social priority school aged between 6 and 8, and swopping as remembered by adults. Traub used more structured interviews and scenarios involving swopping and had a larger, and more middle-class, sample: 60 children with equal numbers from the three age groups 8, 10 and 12. This gives us a fairly clear picture of swopping, although we should be cautious about generalizing our findings to other times and other places.

Swopping seems to be most popular among 8–10-year-olds and generally takes place at school (though a third of swops reported to Traub took place at home). The most common response of the adults when asked how old they were when specific incidents of swopping took place was nine and those who could not remember specific incidents suggested ages between seven and ten, with nine being the most popular response. Perhaps surprisingly, the recollections of adults correspond with current self-reports by children. According to their own accounts, swopping is most frequent for 8-year-old boys and 10-year-old children of both sexes. Most of the 12-year-olds reported that they had not swopped anything in the last term and several said that they had given up swopping for good. So swopping is clearly an activity of middle childhood.

Again, the recollections of adults and the accounts of children as regards what was swopped are very similar. The adults remember swopping pencils, stickers, conkers, erasers, marbles, top trump cards, sweets, stamps, toy cars, beads, football and sweet cigarette cards; the children reported swopping all kinds of stationery (pens, pencils and erasers), toys, football cards, stickers, games and books and food (crisps and sweets). There seemed to be a consensus among children that swopping items should be of low value, one reason mentioned being parental disapproval of high value swops. Maternal disapproval was a feature of the specific swopping incidents remembered by adults: one respondent remembered swopping a pencil set for something inferior and her mother being very angry and insisting that the swop be reversed.

The usual swop is fairly straightforward and immediate (I'd like one of your crisps; do you want a Smartie for it?') but some swops take a long time and may involve days of arguing and negotiation. For some children, this period of negotiation seemed to be the most meaningful part of swopping. The usual swapping partner was a fellow class member, most often a friend, though most children had no favourite swopping partner. If they did, it was because the other child was trustworthy and their friend.

The children's accounts of why they swopped fell into three groups. First, there were economic justifications, such as 'getting better things', 'getting rid of something you don't want any more and getting something back' and 'it is cheaper than buying'. In some cases the economic motive was starkly stated: 'Get rid of rubbish and get other things free.' Second, there were a group of accounts centred around the idea of friendship. Several children said that they would swop 'because you do it with a friend' and pointed out that 'If we swop we become best friends.' Third, there was the idea that swopping was simply enjoyable; as one child commented, 'swopping is fun'.

To tease out the role that economic and social factors play in swapping, Traub presented her respondents with three scenarios. In the core of the first, the children were told: 'The first child is a good friend of yours and the pen s/he offers you is, well, alright, it's OK. But the other child, who you only know a little bit, s/he offers you a really great pen ... What would you do?' The answers varied between the age groups but essentially most children chose the friend. Two-thirds of the 8-year-olds and three-quarters of the 12-year-olds made this choice, though the split was 50/50 with the 10-year-olds. In the second scenario, the children had to imagine how they would react if a friend refused a swop. The preferred strategy of the 8 and 10-year-olds was to find another swopping partner, whereas the 12-year-olds mostly preferred just not to swop. This probably reflects the diminishing interest in swopping at that age. In the final scenario, the children had to decide whether they would agree to a poor swop with a pleasant child who was new to the class. Again, the 10-year-olds appeared to have a more economic approach; most would not agree to such a swop, whereas two-thirds of the 8-year-olds would.

A Hidden Economy

The picture of swopping that emerges from these studies corresponds in a number of ways to Henry's (1978) analysis of part-time trading (dealing in goods that have 'fallen off the back of a lorry') in his book, *The Hidden Economy*. He discusses the customs, norms and motives involved in part-time trading which distinguish it both from normal trading and from normal crime. He claims that the transactions which occur are meaningful in terms of the social relationships between members of trading networks rather than in terms of monetary benefits; put simply, that part-time trading is more social than economic; or, in Maussian terms, that it is concerned with gift relations. The parallels between part-time trading and swopping are intriguing; those involved in trading admit that it is illegal but see it as a good thing and trading usually takes place openly but carefully. Similarly, swopping has an illegal air with parents and teachers vetoing certain kinds of transactions and often banning it altogether. At a more fundamental level, Henry identifies two kinds of social rewards in trading, 'competitive play' and 'reciprocal favours'. The former, which involves ideas of beating the system, corresponds with children's acquisition of things through swopping that they otherwise could not get hold of. For example, a child who is not allowed crisps by his parents can easily swop things for them at school. The latter, involving the norms and expectations of a friendly relationship, is clearly comparable for most swopping. Finally, Henry points out how easy it is to misunderstand part-time trading if it is seen from the perspective of economic rationality (as it is in courts of law). Just as the hidden economy is 'mystified and transformed in the court setting', so may swopping be distorted and misunderstood by a parent. Though the evidence is not overwhelming, it is arguable that swopping is essentially an act with an economic form but a social function.

SOCIOECONOMIC ASPECTS OF MARBLE PLAYING

Marble playing in England seems to be unique in appealing to both sexes across a reasonable age range and involving a variety of interesting activities (though this has not always been the case: Sutton-Smith, 1982, shows how marbles were originally played mainly by boys). Some children collect marbles in the same way as they collect coins or stamps. For others, playing marbles is an important activity and one that involves considerable skills, technical, social and economic.

Marbles are made in a wide variety of sizes and colour combinations. These cost different amounts in the shops but, more important, have different values and names within the school context. The unit of value in the playground is not the cost in pennies but the number of 'goes' that a marble player can have in the various games. A 'bonker cats-eye', for example, is usually valued at ten, which means that in the standard game (described below) a player could have ten attempts at hitting the target marble, if the target was an 'ordinary'.

In Exeter, marbles come in five basic sizes, though there is considerable variation within each category. The main sizes are miniatures (7 mm diameter), standard (1.5 cm), bonkers (2 cm), grannies (2.8 cm) and granddads (3+ cm). Various colorations (spotted, striped, opalescent and so on) are found in most of the different sizes and so there are a large number of different types of marble. Each coloration has an appropriate name, though these vary from school to school. At one school in Exeter the names in use are ordinaries, pixies, cats-eyes, frenchies, bare ladies, petrols, squids, jinks, galaxies, oilies (and dutch oilies), pirates, spotted dicks and misties. A granny spotted dick is thus a large clear marble with spots of different colours which is worth 15–20 and a miniature jinks is a small plain marble all of one colour which is worth roughly three.

In Exeter, there appear to be four different ways of playing marbles. The simplest involves rolling a marble from a distance towards the target marble. If the player hits the target marble he wins it. The number of 'goes' depends on the value of the marble being rolled (this is the standard game described by Piaget, 1932, as 'courate'). The second way is to make a hole or small ditch in the ground and to designate a marble as a prize. The other player tries to roll their marble into the hole. If they succeed within a negotiated number of 'goes' (dependent on the value of the marble being rolled and the value of the prize marble) they win the prize marble. The third way involves one player 'setting out' two marbles with a small gap between them. The other player attempts to roll their marble through the gap without hitting either of the marbles. In this case, if the player succeeds they win both marbles. The number of goes depends on the value of the marbles involved and the size of the gap. The final way is an elaboration of the first and is called 'choices'. Three (or more) marbles are set out and the person shooting chooses which to aim at. If he hits it within the negotiated number of goes he chooses another one to aim at and so on until he has no goes left.

From this brief description it should be apparent that it is possible to win marbles even if one lacks technical skill. A player 'setting out' his or her marbles has to assess the skills of the shooter and adjust the difficulty of the game or the terms offered.

Marbles are not just a game. Just as there were cigarette economies in prisoner of war camps (Clarke, 1946; Einzig, 1945) so is there a marble economy in the playground. Marbles have an exchange value; they can be swopped as well as won and lost. One obvious question, then, is how far children understand the relationship between scarcity and value. This phenomenon of 'scrambling' (scattering marbles for others to collect and keep) has parallels with potlatch (Codere, 1950) which are interesting. Perhaps the most striking discovery is that children will 'work' for other children. This involves one child providing the capital (the marbles) while another provides his or her labour (playing the game). The winnings (earnings) are then divided between the two children.

Although, as was pointed out above, there is little psychological research into the informal economic activities of children, two areas of research do provide some background to these features of the marble economy: children's notion of value and children's notions of fairness. Berti and Bombi (1988) and Burris (1983) have investigated children's understanding of value. Burris, for example, reports that 4–5-year-olds explain the value of an object by referring to its physical size. Thus a diamond does not cost much 'because it is so tiny'. For 8-year-olds value is explained in terms of usefulness or function. A wristwatch costs more than a book because 'you can tell the time on a watch but a book you can just read'. By contrast, the 10–12-year-old group understand value from the point of view of production. Value is put into the object during production and its magnitude depends on the type or cost of the inputs. So a wristwatch is worth more than a book because 'it has glass and motors in it and it comes with a band and that's leather and it usually has silver or gold framing and ... it's just got more'. Berti and Bombi studied children across the same age range and conclude: 'Taking our own results with those reported by Burris it seems reasonable to conclude that before 10 or 11 years, and even later for many children, price appears to be an intrinsic property of goods, something directly derived from its characteristics' (p. 113). On these grounds we might expect children to believe that some marbles are more valuable than others because they are bigger or more beautiful and not because of the relative supply and demand for different marbles. With regard to the division of the proceeds between the marble capitalist and the marble worker, such research as there is suggests a developmental shift from judgements of fair division based on parity to those based on investment (Eiser and Eiser, 1976; Moessinger, 1975). For young children the simplest solution to resource allocation (that all participants should receive the same) is regarded as fair; older children take the participants' inputs into account.

The Study

The approach used to investigate the marble economy was exploratory. First, six children of middle school age were individually interviewed about all aspects of playing marbles to obtain background information. From these interviews three topics were identified for further study: children's understanding of the relationship of scarcity and value; the phenomenon of 'scrambling' (scattering marbles for others to collect and keep); and the rules governing working for other children. Five scenarios involving these topics were then presented to 34 children aged between eight and eleven.

Two contrasting scenarios about scarcity were presented, counterbalanced for order and separated by the other scenarios. In one, 'St Thomas' school won a marble competition and every child got 100 or a new type of marble called metal spotted dicks. There were thousands of them in the school'; in the other, 'At another middle school in Devon a child brought along some of the new metal spotted dicks. There were only two of them in the whole school.' In each case the child was asked what they thought their value in terms of goes would be and why. This revealed that there was widespread recognition of the relationship between scarcity and value. A partial repeated-measures ANOVA (Analysis of Variance) was carried out on the values given by the children for the 'metal spotted dicks' in the two conditions of scarcity and abundance. There was no effect of sex but scarcity had a significant effect (see Table 9.1).

When the children were questioned as to why they gave the marbles different values in the scarce and abundant conditions, 31 said it was due to

Table 9.1   Mean value of 'metal spotted dicks' in terms of goes as a function of scarcity and sex

	Rare	Common
Girls	11.93	5.43
Boys	12.36	5.50
Both	12.17	5.47

rareness, one that it was because 'big ones' were worth more and two gave the marbles the same value in each condition.

The scenarios elicited various reasons for scrambling (see Table 9.2), and it seems as if scrambling may be a reputation-enhancing act (as with the potlatch). Scrambling remains something of an enigma, though this interview extract gives some hints:

I. Why do you scramble marbles?
C. Because you don't want them. If you don't want them you just throw them away for other people to have.
I. Because you don't want them any more?
C. Because it is a waste of time to get rid of them by shooting 'cos you end up winning more.
I. Does it make you very popular if you scramble?
C. Sometimes. I had about 150 marbles and I got them all in my box and I flung them across the playground. There were all these marbles everywhere, all over the playground. It was really funny.

Table 9.2   Reasons given for scrambling

He had too many, was bored, did not want them
He wanted to be more popular
He was showing off to get noticed
He wanted to be able to play with those who got them
He did not want them
No one would play with him
He was angry
He wanted other people to think he was popular

The final scenario looked at the phenomenon of working and examined how the spoils should be divided between owner and worker: 'Jane had no marbles and asked Tom if she could work for him. She took one of his marbles and went and played. It was Jane's lucky day and she won ten marbles. Jane went back to Tom with her winnings and Tom gave her a chipped pixie'. The children were asked how many marbles they thought Tom should have given her and what they would have done if they were Tom.

There was a professed belief that any marbles won should be roughly equally divided between the child providing the capital (the marble) and the child supplying the labour (the play), though there was a bias in favour of the capitalist. The modal answer to the question of how many marbles Jane should have received was 5 (that is, a 50/50 split) though the mean was rather lower (see Table 9.3)

Table 9.3   Fair distribution of marbles between owner and worker

Number of marbles worker should get	1	2	3	4	5	6	7	8	9	10
Number of children	2	3	10	1	13	0	0	2	0	3

To try and get opinions that were less influenced by social desirability, my daughter (a 10-year-old at the time) interviewed a large number of children in the playground about working for people. She found that, despite the commonly expressed belief that in working the winnings should be equally divided, in practice the marble capitalist always took a bigger share than the marble worker. Thus we see in the marble economy what appears to be a genuinely autonomous economic world. Though it intersects with the adult world (after all, marbles can be bought in the shops) it has its own norms and rules. It was evident from the interviews, for example, that it is local scarcity that determines the value of a marble in the playground and not its price in the shops. How far this economic world depends on the adult world is debatable. I suspect that working for someone is a direct copy of the outside economy; the origins of scrambling are rather more obscure.

CONCLUSIONS

Although I am well aware of the limitations of this research (notably the small samples and relatively primitive data collection), it is clear that there is considerable potential for research into the autonomous economic worlds of children. I would argue that this area is not only engaging (there is a certain nostalgic charm in studying playground behaviour) but has a serious contribution to make to our understanding of economic socialization. There are a number of issues that need to be tackled. First, there is the question of how far the playground economy is a precursor of the adult economy. Harre (1974) argued, in another context, that it is the autonomous social world of the child that is the true precursor of adult social relationships and not the attachment relationship formed between parent and child. If this is true in the economic world, we need to concentrate more on marbles and less on pocket money. Second, there is the question of realism. I suspect that, paradoxically, it may be through what seems to us play that children derive a firm grasp on economic reality. My impression is that children's understanding of the marble economy is considerably more sophisticated than their understanding of the adult economy: this impression needs to be put on a firm empirical footing. Finally, there is the issue of taking economics for granted. This has meant that researchers interested in economic socialization have neglected certain kinds of behaviour – but have also neglected other disciplines with something to offer, most obviously economic anthropology. So a change of emphasis is needed in research in economic socialization in the future.

ACKNOWLEDGEMENTS

I would like to thank the staff and pupils of various primary schools in Exeter for their help over the years and my daughter Elizabeth, Katie Banham, Jeremy Bartlett, Michele Hopwood and Kirsten Storry for collecting some of the data.

REFERENCES

Bardill, J. (1985), 'Swopping', BSc project, University of Exeter.

Berti A.E. and Bombi, A.S. (1988), *The Child's Construction of Economics*, Cambridge: Cambridge University Press.

Blatchford, P., Creeser, R. and Mooney, A. (1990), 'Playground games and playtime – the children's view', *Educational Research*, **32**, 163–74.

Burris, V. (1983), 'Stages in the development of economic concepts', *Human Relations*, **36**, 791–812.

Carrier, J.G. (1991), 'Gifts, commodities and social relations: a Maussian view of exchange', *Sociological Forum*, **6**, 119–36.

Clarke, G.B. (1946), 'The experiment', *Clare Market Review*, **41**, 27–31.

Codere, H. (1950), *Fighting with Property: a study of Kwakiutl potlatching and warfare 1792–1930*, New York: J.J. Augustin.

Eimers, Y. (1992), 'Gift Evaluation by Children', unpublished report, University of Exeter Economic Psychology Research Group.

Einzig, P. (1945), 'The cigarette standard', *The Banker*, **75–6**, 148–50.

Eiser, C. and Eiser, J.R. (1976), 'Children's concepts of a fair exchange', *British Journal of Social and Clinical Psychology*, **15**, 357–64.

Furnham, A. (1986), 'Children's understanding of the economic world', *Australian Journal of Education*, **30**, 219–40.

Furnham, A. and Thomas, P. (1984), 'Pocket money: a study of economic education', *British Journal of Developmental Psychology*, **2**, 205–12.

Furth, H.G. (1978), 'Children's societal understanding and the process of equilibration', in W. Damon (ed.), *New Directions for Child Development, Vol. 1*, San Francisco: Jossey-Bass, pp. 101–22.

Goodnow, J. (1988), 'Children's household work', *Psychological Bulletin*, **103**, 5–26.

Greenfield, P.M. and Zukow, P.G. (1978), 'Why do children say what they say when they say it?', in K. Nelson (ed.), *Children's language, Vol. 1*, New York Gardner Press.

Griffiths, M.D. (1991), 'The acquisition, development and maintenance of fruit machine gambling in adolescence', PhD thesis, University of Exeter.

Harre, R. (1974), 'The conditions for a social psychology of Childhood', in M.P.M. Richards (ed.), *The Integration of the Child into the Social World*, Cambridge: Cambridge University Press.

Henry, S. (1978), *The Hidden Economy*, London: Martin Robertson.

Hill, M. (1992), 'Children's role in the domestic economy', *Journal of Consumer Studies and Home Economics*, **16**, 33–50.

Ide-Smith, S. and Lea, S.E.G. (1988), 'Gambling in young adolescents', *Journal of Gambling Behavior*, **4**, 110–18.

Leiser, D., Sevon, G. and Levy, D. (1990), 'Children's economic socialization: Summarizing the cross-cultural comparison of ten countries', *Journal of Economic Psychology*, **11** (4), 591–631.

Linaza, J. (1984), 'Piaget's marbles: the study of children's games and their knowledge of rules', *Oxford Review of Education*, **10**, 271–4.

Mishler, E.G. (1979), '"Wou' you trade cookies with the popcorn?" Talk of trades among six-year-olds', in O. Garcia and M. King (eds), *Language, Children and Society: the effects of social factors on children learning to communicate*, Elmsford, NY: Pergamon, pp. 221–36.

Moessinger, P. (1975), 'Developmental study of fair division and property', *European Journal of Social Psychology*, **5**, 385–94.

Opie, P. and Opie, I. (1969), *Children's Games in Street and Playground*, Oxford: Oxford University Press.

Piaget, J. (1932), *The Moral Judgement of the Child*, London: Routledge and Kegan Paul.

Rachlin, H. (1980), 'Economics and behavioral psychology', in J.E.R. Staddon (ed.), *Limits to Action*, New York: Academic Press, pp. 205–36.

Roland-Levy, C. (1990), 'Economic socialization: Basis for international comparisons', *Journal of Economic Psychology*, **11**, 469–82.

Simon, H.A. (1957), *Models of Man*, New York: Wiley.

Sluckin, A. (1981), *Growing Up in the Playground*, London: Routledge and Kegan Paul.

Smith, J.F. and Abt, V. (1984), 'Gambling as Play', *Annals of the American Academy of Political and Social Sciences*, **474**, 122–32.

Sonuga-Barke, E.J.S. and Webley, P. (1992a), *Children's Saving*, Hove: Erlbaum.

Sonuga-Barke, E.J.S. and Webley, P. (1992b), 'Toward a development economic psychology' (unpublished manuscript).

Sutton-Smith, B. (1982), 'Sixty years of historical change in the game preferences of American children', in R.E. Herron and B. Sutton-Smith (eds), *Child's Play*, Malabar, Fla.: Krieger.

Traub, A. (1991), 'Swopping and economic socialization', Testamur project, University of Exeter.

Webley, P. and Lea, S.E.G. (1991), 'Towards a more realistic psychology of economic socialization', *Journal of Economic Psychology*, **14**, 461–72.

Webley, P. and Lea, S.E.G. (1992), 'The partial unacceptability of money as repayment for neighborly help', *Human Relations*, **46**, 65–76.

Webley, P., Levine, R.M. and Lewis, A. (1988), 'Money for saving and money for spending: parental views about children's saving', in P. Vanden Abeele (ed.), *Psychology in Micro- and Macro-economics* (Proceedings of the 13th IAREP colloquium), Leuven: IAREP.

Webley, P., Levine, R.M. and Lewis, A. (1990), 'A study in economic psychology: children's saving in a play economy', *Human Relations*, **44**, 127–46.

10. Economic knowledge and the formation of economic opinions and attitudes

William Walstad

INTRODUCTION

People are confronted daily in the news media and by personal experience with the world of economics. The wide variety of economic topics that are discussed includes unemployment, inflation, personal income, taxes, poverty, budget deficits, monetary policy, economic growth, regulation, profits, trade policy, exchange rates, and many others. As people think about economics and economic issues, they develop economic opinions and attitudes. This affective process of making sense of the economic world and its complex and wide-ranging economic issues starts at an early age and continues throughout the years of formal schooling. Even after leaving a secondary school or graduating from a university, indeed over a lifetime, economic opinions and attitudes are forming and changing.

This chapter reviews American research on the development of economic opinions and attitudes, as found in the literature on economics education (Siegfried and Fels, 1979; Schug and Walstad, 1991; Walstad, 1992). The review is divided into seven sections. The chapter first describes the broad interest in economic opinions and attitudes by many groups in American society and, consequently, why the topic is worthy of study. The second section makes several critical distinctions between the terms 'attitudes' and 'opinions' because these distinctions have implications for the way knowledge affects them. In the third section, selected results from a national survey of American economic literacy are presented to illustrate the relationship between economic opinion and knowledge. The fourth section discusses the problems of measuring economic attitudes and the desired psychometric properties in an attitude instrument. The fifth and sixth sections report major findings from economics education studies that have been conducted on attitudes toward economics and on attitudes toward economic issues at the pre-college and college levels. The final section derives implications for education and for the conduct of future research.

At the risk of overstatement, the basic conclusion that emerges from this chapter is that economic knowledge is a key factor in shaping opinions and attitudes about economics and economic issues. Personal and social characteristics, such as sex, race, ethnic origin, education or income, are also important and certainly have some sort of influence on economic opinions and attitudes, but these characteristics either cannot be changed or change slowly, and they affect attitudes and opinions in uncertain ways. Economic knowledge is perhaps the only factor affecting attitudes and opinions that is most susceptible to change and also has the greatest potential for altering economic opinions or attitudes over time. The positive effects of economic knowledge on the formation of economic opinions and attitudes are significant, and consistently found throughout American research in economics education.

INTEREST IN OPINIONS AND ATTITUDES

Economic opinions and attitudes are of great interest to many different groups in American society – politicians, economists, business leaders, academics and educators – despite the mercurial nature of these affective constructs. Presidential elections in the USA, for example, are directly affected by the public's perception of the state of the economy, especially when economic problems seem to be greater or when they are given more attention by the media. Ronald Reagan's defeat of President Jimmy Carter in the 1980 election was based in large part on public opinion, due to the economic conditions resulting from high inflation and a recent recession, that Americans were not better off economically than they had been four years earlier. Similarly, in the 1992 election, widespread public dissatisfaction with the state of the economy (higher unemployment, limited new job creation and slow growth in personal income) eroded the previously strong support for President George Bush and led to the election of Bill Clinton as the candidate representing economic change. Public concerns about the national debt, large federal budget deficits and the economic future of the nation also fuelled the stronger than expected showing of third-party candidate Ross Perot in that election.

Economists also track economic opinions and attitudes to assess their effects on the economy (Leeper, 1992; Throop, 1992). The Index of Consumer Expectations produced by the University of Michigan is used by the United States Department of Commerce as one of its 11 leading economic indicators about the direction of economic activity. Another measure of consumer confidence is reported monthly by the Conference Board, a business organization, and there are several similar measures regularly reported by other organizations. These public opinions about the state of the economy are given careful attention by government and business economists because they may signal changes that directly affect macroeconomic variables such as aggregate expenditures.

Public views on economic issues are regularly assessed by polling firms for the news media, government officials or business executives. These public surveys are valuable to decision makers as a means of following the changing course of public opinion on business and economic issues and for assessing when public opinion on an issue represents public judgement (Yankelovich, 1991). Surveys can cover a short or long list of issues – taxes, regulation, economic competitiveness, health care financing or protectionism (for example, *Business Week*, 1992). The news media conduct polls to obtain news information and to monitor the direction of public opinion. Politicians follow survey data to identify pressing public concerns and the need for legislative or other governmental actions. Business executives use surveys to get ideas for new products or to gauge the need for change in business practices. Business organizations have also sought to shape public opinion through advertising campaigns to promote more positive general attitudes towards business or selected issues of concern to business (Bach, 1979).

Academics in different disciplines study economic attitudes and opinions to improve our understanding of public perceptions of economic topics. In economics, a study of popular attitudes towards free markets in the USA and the former Soviet Union found strong similarities among Soviets and Americans on their attitudes towards fairness, income inequality and incentives, and less similarity on attitudes towards money exchange or towards business (Shiller *et al.*, 1991). An extensive study in political science examined attitudes towards capitalism and democracy using public opinion polls and attitude surveys over a 40-year period and argued that these attitudes were the major components of what the authors called 'the American ethos' (McClosky and Zaller, 1984). In psychology, Kerlinger (1984) developed a structural theory of attitudes and presented empirical methods for studying liberalism and conservatism in American society. The above are just three examples of topics in economic attitude research that have been investigated.

Teachers are also interested in affective domain in economics. On the one hand, it is sometimes observed that, even when students understand the economic consequences of an economic decision, they may still act 'irrationally'. That is, despite what they know about an economics issue, they may act or behave differently, perhaps because their attitude towards or opinion about an issue runs counter to their economic knowledge. On the other hand, economic knowledge may be the most vital factor in shaping attitudes towards economics and economic issues. If this is true, then teachers should consider ways to increase economic knowledge, either through more coursework in economics or better instruction, to promote more positive attitudes toward economics and more thoughtful opinions about economics issues. In either case, there is now a greater recognition of the role of the affective as well as the cognitive domain in the learning of economics.

For many different reasons, economic attitudes and opinions command the attention of individuals and organizations in American society. A common problem with much survey work, however, is the failure to account for the influence of knowledge in shaping public opinions or attitudes. Knowledge plays a key role in this process, as described in the next and subsequent sections of the chapter.

ATTITUDES AND OPINIONS: SOME DISTINCTIONS

'Attitude' and 'opinion' are terms that often are used interchangeably. This lack of precision needs to be avoided because there are major distinctions which have implications for understanding how economic knowledge directly affects them.

Attitudes

Attitudes are more difficult psychological constructs to define and to measure than opinions. A definition of an attitude offered by Triandis (1971) states that 'an attitude is an idea charged with emotion which predisposes a class of actions to a particular class of social situations' (p. 21). In this definition, attitudes are thought to consist of three components that interrelate to shape the idea. The first component is *cognitive* and helps the person categorize the topic or issue. The second component is *affective* and includes the emotional or motivational evaluations of the topic or issue. The third component is *behavioural* and indicates the tendency or the predisposition to behave or act in a certain way towards the topic or issue. What should be noted is that the general definition of an attitude indicates that the cognitive component is almost a prerequisite for holding an attitude. Knowledge directly changes attitude through this cognitive dimension.

The operation of the three components can be illustrated with a brief explanation of the formation of an economic attitude. Taxes are an economic idea about which an attitude might develop. Before a person can have an attitude towards taxes, the person must know what taxes are, or at least have some idea about what taxes mean to them. Knowing about taxes establishes the cognitive component for holding an attitude about taxes. Should the concept of taxes have little connection to a person, either because the person does not know what taxes are or because the person never thinks about taxes, the person is not likely to hold a defined attitude about taxes. This situation might arise with younger students for whom a category such as taxes simply has no meaning. If the cognitive dimension is missing, a study of a young person's attitude about taxes is more questionable because it has limited validity.

When an idea does have significant meaning for a person, the person may develop an emotional or valuative reaction to the idea based on how it affects the person, or how it affects other people that the person knows. A negative attitude toward taxes, for example, might develop when a person feels that the requirement to pay taxes is a major burden, or when a person perceives that there are few benefits from tax expenditures because of government support of 'welfare' programmes. By contrast, a more positive attitude towards taxes might emerge in situations where a person understands and appreciates the public programmes that taxes support, or a person feels that there is fairness in sharing the tax burden to support public programmes. In either case, the affective component of an attitude 'charges the idea with emotion' in a positive or a negative direction.

The behavioural component predisposes a person to act in ways consistent with the emotional direction of the attitude. A person who holds a negative perspective on taxes is likely to take actions, such as voting or campaigning, to oppose tax increases. A person who views taxes more positively, because of perceived benefits from government activity the taxes support, may be willing to pay more taxes if asked to do so. Even if a person opposes taxes in general, the person may vote for a tax increase if there are other perceived benefits that outweigh the costs. For example, voting for a school bond issue may increase taxes, which a person might oppose in principle, but if it also leads to educational benefits for the person's children, then the person might vote for the bond issue. In this case, the person was predisposed to oppose the bond issue because of an underlying negative attitude towards taxes, but did not actually behave that way because of other mitigating circumstances (greater perceived educational benefits than costs). Although the example shows that attitudes may not always be consistent with actions, they still predispose a person to behave in an expected way.

Opinions

Economic attitudes combine with economic facts or knowledge to produce economic opinions. Economic attitudes influence what facts will be selected or what economic knowledge will be used in forming opinions. This process suggests that economic attitudes are broader and less well understood by a person than an opinion. Holding an opinion on an economic issue does not mean that a person is fully aware of his or her underlying attitude towards the issue; for example, a person can oppose a tax proposal even when the person is unable to describe his or her attitude toward taxes.

Economic opinions are also more transitory and held less strongly than economic attitudes. Opinion may change as more facts become known or as economic knowledge increases about the topic, whereas an economic attitude is less likely to shift with more facts or information. An economic opinion, therefore, can be described as being a *tentative* conclusion because new facts or information about the issue can change the conclusion. Whether the opinion varies also depends on the source and quality of the information or knowledge, and on the person's capacity to evaluate it.

Similar economic opinions about related topics often reflect an underlying economic attitude. Consider the following three statements: (1) the federal government should provide medical care for all citizens; (2) high salaries for top business executives should be limited by the federal government; and (3) the federal government should limit imports from other nations to correct a trade deficit. The views expressed about each statement reflect an economic opinion about each issue, be it medical care, business salaries or the trade deficit. Taken together, however, the set of responses may reflect an underlying attitude towards the role of government in the economy. An attitude supporting federal government intervention in the economy would be suggested by agreement with the three statements. Agreement with other opinion statements about federal involvement in an area of the economy would provide further evidence of an underlying positive attitude towards federal government intervention in a market economy.

ECONOMIC OPINIONS AND KNOWLEDGE: SOME FINDINGS

Economic opinions differ from economic attitudes as psychological constructs, so it should not be surprising that the measurement of each should be different. Opinions on economic topics are assessed more often than economic attitudes because instruments to measure opinions are relatively easy to prepare and administer. The major measurement problem is the potential bias from wording of questions. Limited study is given to psychometric properties in survey work.

Questionnaires on economic topics are administered mostly by polling firms in the USA. Some surveys include a few questions while others contain many. A recent comprehensive telephone survey of economic knowledge and opinion was conducted by the Gallup Organization (Walstad and Larsen, 1992). The survey instrument contained 48 items: 12 questions asking for background information about the respondent (such as age or sex); eight questions seeking opinions on economic issues; 19 items assessing knowledge of economic topics, and nine questions probing for sources of economic information. Four drafts of the questionnaire were prepared and each was reviewed for economic content and for suitability of use with the public by a national advisory committee of ten economists drawn from education, business and labour. Questions were field tested with several small samples to check for potential bias and to determine the time needed for the survey.

The final survey instrument was administered by telephone in March 1992 to three representative national samples – 1005 adult heads of households, 300 high school seniors and 300 college seniors. The sampling procedures meant results from the adult sample would not differ from those found with the adult population by more than plus or minus three percentage points. The maximum margin of error for responses from the high school and college seniors samples from their respective populations was plus or minus 5.6 percentage points.

The results from the 19 economic knowledge questions on the survey are reported in Table 10.1. These questions covered basic economic ideas reported regularly by the news media, such as unemployment and inflation rates, economic growth, supply and demand, monetary and fiscal policy, and the value of the dollar. Significant deficiencies in basic economic knowledge were found in all three groups. The general public was able to answer correctly only 39 per cent of the questions. High school seniors were correct on only 35 per cent of the items. College seniors performed better, in large part because of more economics education for some in that group, but they still only gave correct answers to 51 per cent of the questions.

The definition of opinions suggests that they will be greatly affected by economic knowledge. The influence of economic knowledge, either specific or general, can be illustrated with an example drawn from the Gallup data. One knowledge question asked: 'What is an example of monetary policy? Would it be a change in: (a) the discount rate; (b) a change in Federal government spending; or (c) a change in corporate profits?' Only 21 per cent of the general public, 17 per cent of high school students and 42 per cent of college students knew that a change in the discount rate was an example of a change in monetary policy. Most respondents in each group answered the following opinion question: 'Who should set monetary policy? Should it be: (a) the President; (b) the Congress; (c) the Federal Reserve; or (d) the United States Treasury?' Their opinions were offered despite the fact that the majority in each group did not know what monetary policy was.

When responses from the monetary policy knowledge and opinion questions are cross-tabulated, they show that there were significant differences in the support for the current institution that controls monetary policy in the USA – the Federal Reserve – on the basis of the respondents' correct or incorrect responses to the knowledge question. Among adults who could give a correct example of a change in monetary policy, 53 per cent thought it

Table 10.1 Percentage of correct responses to economic knowledge
questions in a national survey of American economic literacy

Response	General public ($n = 1005$)	High school seniors ($n = 300$)	College seniors ($n = 300$)
Unemployment rate	22	10	26
Inflation rate	11	4	12
Measure of inflation	35	35	56
Measure of economic growth	40	37	56
Budget deficit definition	51	38	66
Budget deficit size	19	22	24
Federal Reserve purpose	46	38	58
Monetary policy set by	33	25	47
Monetary policy example	21	17	42
Fiscal policy set by	50	50	55
Fiscal policy example	23	28	48
Economic policy	48	39	55
Productivity/wages	68	69	77
Purchasing power/inflation	60	53	81
Purpose of profits	36	42	52
Profit rate on investment	13	12	22
Supply and demand	64	72	79
Value of dollar/exports	50	38	61
Quotas and employment	49	37	50
Mean percentage correct	39	35	51

Source: Walstad and Larsen (1992).

should be set by the Federal Reserve, but among adults who gave incorrect examples only 20 per cent thought that monetary policy should be set by the Federal Reserve. The respective percentage for college seniors showed a greater difference, 71 per cent versus 15 per cent. The difference was less and the percentages lower for high school students, 32 per cent versus 15 per cent, but still sizeable. These percentages for all groups are reported in the upper half of Table 10.2.

Shown in the lower half of Table 10.2 is the cross-tabulation of results from the monetary policy opinion question with overall knowledge scores based on the 19 content questions. The responses are shown when the knowledge scores are divided at the mean for each group. A total of 70 per cent of adults with scores above the mean compared with only 25 per cent of adults with scores at or below the mean thought that the Federal Reserve should set monetary policy. Similar differences were found with college seniors (66 per cent versus 23 per cent). High school seniors again showed less difference

Table 10.2   Opinions on what institution should set monetary policy, by knowledge question and knowledge score (per cent)

	Overall	Correct	Incorrect
		By knowledge question	
Adults			
Federal Reserve	28.8	53.1	20.3
Other institutions	71.2	46.9	79.7
N	(819)	(213)	(606)
College seniors			
Federal Reserve	42.4	71.3	14.8
Other institutions	57.6	28.7	85.2
N	(264)	(129)	(135)
High school seniors			
Federal Reserve	17.9	32.0	14.7
Other institutions	82.1	68.0	85.3
N	(274)	(50)	(135)
		By knowledge score	
Adults			
Federal Reserve	39.9	70.0	24.5
Other institutions	60.1	30.0	75.5
N	(819)	(277)	(542)
College seniors			
Federal Reserve	42.4	65.8	22.9
Other institutions	57.6	34.2	77.1
N	(264)	(120)	(144)
High school seniors			
Federal Reserve	17.9	23.2	13.4
Other institutions	82.1	76.8	86.6
N	(274)	(125)	(149)

Source: Walstad and Larsen (1992).

and lower percentages (23 per cent versus 13 per cent), which is most likely because of maturity, education, income or other factors influencing that age group. Nevertheless, for all groups, the differences in opinions between high and low knowledge scores parallel the differences in opinions based on the correctness of response to a single knowledge question related to the issue. Both analyses demonstrate that there are significant effects of knowledge on opinion, whether the knowledge is specific or general.

Similar cross-tabulations of opinion and knowledge questions on such topics as unemployment, the federal budget deficit, economic growth, profits or trade protectionism could be performed with this survey data to demonstrate the same point, but for the sake of parsimony they will not be presented. The findings from the survey of American economic literacy suggest that knowledge factors must be used in interpreting public opinion on economic issues. Most economic issues require a minimal amount of economic knowledge for people to understand, but too often survey results are presented only in the aggregate. Analysis of economic opinions on issues is perhaps best performed by sorting responses by using a knowledge variable and by showing both the informed and the uninformed opinions about the economic issue rather than only overall responses. Among the informed, of course, there will still be differences of opinion about what should be done on an issue, as the monetary policy example above illustrates. Further study should then be conducted to identify how other variables contribute to informed opinion.

THE MEASUREMENT OF ECONOMIC ATTITUDES

Developing an instrument to assess economic attitudes presents more measurement problems than writing an opinion questionnaire. The awareness of these and other problems led to calls for the construction of better attitude and cognitive measures for research in economics education (Becker, 1983). In some respects, the procedures for the development of attitude measures need to be as rigorous as those used for the development of standardized achievement tests. Items need to be carefully written, selected and field tested with a variety of students, so that they contribute to reliability and validity. These psychometric properties should also be well documented for each measure. In essence, attitude instruments are similar to cognitive achievement tests because both are based on responses to a related set of individual items. Just as it would not be valid or reliable for an economic knowledge test to assess knowledge across a random collection of items, it is not valid or reliable for an attitude instrument to measure perceptions with a set of random or unrelated collections of opinion statements. When responses to these related items are summed in some scoring scheme they generally produce a reliable and valid score that represents a person's position on the measured dimension.

The Survey on Economic Attitudes

An example of an economic attitude instrument that meets psychometric standards for construction is the *Survey on Economic Attitudes* (SEA). The SEA consists of two attitude measures, one assessing attitudes towards the subject of economics (ATE) and the other measuring economic attitude sophistication (EAS). The ATE and EAS were developed by a national committee of economists and educators who followed measurement guidelines to ensure that each instrument possessed good reliability and validity. The ATE and EAS were first nationally normed with 1797 senior high school students in 67 schools in 35 states in 1979. They were nationally normed again in 1986 with larger samples: 7181 students for the ATE and 6109 students for the EAS. Summary statistics for each measure are reported in Table 10.3, but more psychometric documentation can be found in several other publications (Soper and Walstad, 1983, 1988).

The ATE is composed of 14 Likert-type statements; students are asked to check whether they strongly agree, agree, are uncertain, disagree or strongly disagree. Points from 1 to 5 are assigned for each response category. For example, a student who strongly agrees with the statement 'I hate economics' would receive a score of 1 for that item. If the student strongly disagrees, he or she would receive a score of 5. Scores of 2, 3 and 4 would be assigned, respectively, for the agree, uncertain and disagree categories. Higher scores on an item would indicate a more positive attitude towards economics.

Eight of the ATE items need to be reverse coded so that a more positive feeling about economics gets a higher score: for the fifth item, 'I enjoy economics', a strongly agree would receive a score of 5 and a strongly disagree, a score of 1. The reason for the use of reverse coding on some items

Table 10.3   SEA norming results

Characteristics	ATE scale		EAS scale	
	1986	1979	1986	1979
Sample sizes	7 181	1 747	6 109	1 747
Overall mean	4 364	4 641	4 701	4 701
Alpha reliability	0.87	0.88	0.67	0.66

is to safeguard against response sets by students, such as a tendency to agree strongly to all items. Once the items have been scored, they can be summed to obtain the attitude score. On the ATE, scores range from 14 to 70, with a 14 representing a very negative view of economics and a 70 representing an extremely positive view of economics. The ATE statements and item means and standard deviations are reported in Table 10.4

Caution must be exercised in the interpretation of scores on the ATE and EAS measures. Although a positive attitude towards economics may be a desirable goal for students taking an economics course, a low ATE score should not be viewed as being 'bad'. The ATE provides an index of student or class sentiment on the subject of economics. Unlike economic opinions, attitudes are more resistant to change, so that it is quite possible to have no change in student attitudes even after some instruction in the subject.

The EAS portion of the *Survey* is perhaps more controversial because it attempts to measure the extent to which high school student views are in agreement or disagreement with the 'consensus' view of economists on the 14 opinion statements in that part of the survey. Most economists, for example, would disagree with the statement: 'Government should control the price

Table 10.4   Survey on economic attitudes: attitudes towards economics

Code	Items		Mean	s.d.
(+)	1.	I enjoy reading articles about economic topics	2.95	1.08
(−)	2.	I hate economics	3.40	1.12
(+)	3.	Economics is easy for me to understand	2.94	1.10
(−)	4.	Economics is dull	2.98	1.15
(−)	5.	I enjoy economics	2.95	1.08
(−)	6.	Studying economics is a waste of time	3.80	1.08
(−)	7.	Economics is one of my most dreaded subjects	3.33	1.13
(+)	8.	On occasion, I read an unassigned book on economics	2.26	1.13
(+)	9.	I would be willing to attend a lecture by an economist	2.87	1.57
(−)	10.	Economics is a very difficult subject for me	3.23	1.13
(+)	11.	Economics is one of my favourite subjects	2.62	1.09
(+)	12.	I use economics concepts to analyze situations	2.84	1.07
(+)	13.	Economics is practical	3.20	1.01
(−)	14.	Economic ideas are dumb	3.80	1.03

Notes:
1. Written directions were: 'Please indicate your opinions about the following statements. Mark 1 if you strongly agree; mark 2 if you agree; mark 3 if you are undecided; mark 4 if you disagree; mark 5 if you strongly disagree.'
2. In scoring, a (+) item indicates the positive response is to agree strongly, while a (−) item indicates the positive response is to disagree strongly. Scores are summed across items, but plus (+) items are also reverse coded (1 = 5, 2 = 4, 4 = 2, 5 = 1) before summing.
3. $N = 7181$.

of gasoline.' If the student also disagrees, he or she will receive a higher score on that item than if the person agrees with the statement. The total score ranges from 14 to 70, with higher scores indicating stronger agreement with the economics profession. Item statements and item means and standard deviations are reported in Table 10.5.

The EAS is not a score representing a 'correct' set of opinions on 14 statements, nor is it designed to force students to adopt or conform to the consensus views of American economists on these economic issues. The EAS simply assesses the degree or tendency of students to hold a set of opinions on economic issues that are consistent with the generally accepted or consensus view of the economics profession on different issues. Although arguments are sometimes made in the popular press that there is a lack of consensus in economics, in many areas of economics there is a great deal of consensus among professional economists. This consensus view can be supported by survey work that was used to validate the EAS and by a national survey of economists (Soper and Walstad, 1988; Alston *et al.*, 1992). Obviously, in the

Table 10.5   Survey on economic attitudes: economic attitude sophistication

Code	Items		Mean	s.d.
(–)	1.	Government should control the price of gasoline	3.26	1.19
(–)	2.	Inflation is caused by greedy business and union leaders	3.15	1.08
(–)	3.	Business makes too much profit	3.34	1.03
(–)	4.	People should not have to pay taxes	3.50	1.18
(–)	5.	Free medical care should be provided for all Americans	3.00	1.20
(–)	6.	Banks should not charge interest on loans to customers	3.47	1.12
(–)	7.	Most people who don't have jobs are too lazy to work	3.20	1.24
(–)	8.	When a business gets big, it should be controlled by government	3.56	1.11
(–)	9.	New factories are not needed	3.68	1.05
(+)	10.	People should not be told how to spend their money	3.89	1.11
(–)	11.	If everybody had more money, we'd all be better off	3.22	1.13
(+)	12.	Profits should not be regulated by government	3.28	1.06
(–)	13.	Most unemployed people are lazy	3.35	1.18
(–)	14.	When a strike occurs, government should step in and settle the dispute	2.98	1.10

Notes:
1. Written directions were: 'Please indicate your opinions about the following statements. Mark 1 if you strongly agree; mark 2 if you agree; mark 3 if you are undecided; mark 4 if you disagree; mark 5 if you strongly disagree.'
2. In scoring, a (+) item indicates the sophisticated response is to agree strongly, while a (-) item indicates the sophisticated response is to disagree strongly. Scores are summed across items, but plus (+) items are reverse coded (1 = 5, 2 = 4, 4 = 2, 5 = 1) before summing.
3. $N = 6109$.

norming process, the more extreme views of the profession are 'washed out', so that the instrument certainly does not represent the complete spectrum of the economics profession. A high degree of EAS may not and probably should not be an expressed outcome from an economics course, but whether intended or not, economics instruction will have an effect on students' views of economic issues. The EAS is an attitude measure that permits researchers to assess that dimension of instruction.

Achievement Tests

Research in economics education in the USA has also been advanced by the development of a battery of standardized multiple-choice tests of economic knowledge or understanding. The three published pre-college tests are: (1) the *Test of Economic Literacy* (TEL) for senior high students (17–18-year-olds) (Soper and Walstad, 1987); the *Test of Economic Knowledge* for junior high school students (13–14-year-olds) (Walstad and Soper, 1987); and (3) *Basic Economic Test* for intermediate elementary students (10–11 years old) (Walstad and Robson, 1990). These tests were constructed on the basis of a widely-used framework outlining the basic economics content that should be taught in American schools (Saunders *et al.*, 1992). Also available for research work is the *Test of Understanding of College Economics* (TUCE) which is designed for students taking a principles of economics course at the college level (Saunders, 1991). These reliable and valid measures of economics achievement, particularly the TEL and TUCE, together with such affective measures as the ATE or EAS, have permitted researchers to conduct national and local research studies of the relationship between economic knowledge and economic attitude using common measures.

RESEARCH ON ATTITUDES TOWARDS ECONOMICS

One research topic that has drawn much attention over the years is the nature of the relationship between economic knowledge and attitudes towards economics. The first possibility is that a more positive attitude towards the subject of economics would improve student understanding of the subject. If this were true, a teacher seeking to increase student achievement in economics would be wise to spend time employing educational strategies that contribute to the development of a more positive student attitude towards economics as a subject. This extra classroom time spent on attitudinal development would pay for itself in increased learning. The second possibility is that achievement in economics affects attitudes towards economics. If increased economic knowledge improves student attitudes towards the subject, more instruction or teaching strategies that improve the learning of the subject are likely to contribute to more positive attitudes towards economics. The third possibility, of course, is that there is a simultaneous relationship between economic achievement and attitudes towards economics. That is, increasing economics knowledge improves attitude towards the subject and, in turn, a more positive attitude contributes to increased economics knowledge. This scenario of mutual reinforcement is perhaps most appealing to educators since it would justify classroom time spent in both the affective and cognitive domains.

The direction of the relationship between economic knowledge and attitude towards economics was first examined in two studies involving a total of 896 students, aged nine to 11 years (Walstad, 1979, 1980). In each study, a two-equation regression model was specified that allowed for the simultaneous relationship between economic knowledge and attitudes towards economics and also controlled for personal, social and classroom variables and prior knowledge of economics. The model was estimated using two-stage least-squares (TSLS) regression procedures that corrected for the possible simultaneous equations bias that was characteristic when ordinary least-squares (OLS) regression procedures were used to estimate each equation. The results showed that student knowledge of economics contributed positively and significantly to improvement of attitude towards the subject after controlling for other background factors, but that there was no significant or necessarily positive effect of attitude on achievement.

Research with students at other levels of education supports these initial findings. In each study, a similar simultaneous two-equation model of economic achievement and attitude was specified and estimated using TSLS, and economic knowledge and attitude towards economics were measured by standardized instruments: the TEL or TUCE, and the ATE. A study of 642 senior high school students and 247 teachers in Louisiana showed that economic knowledge improved student and teacher attitude towards economics, but not the converse (Schober, 1984). Four college studies involving 1275 students taking principles of economics courses showed similar results (Hodgin, 1984; Charkins *et al.*, 1985; Fizel and Johnson, 1986; Walstad, 1987).

The previous research hypothesis has been extended by examining the simultaneous relationship between economic knowledge and student interest in taking another economics course (Beron, 1990). A national, representative sample of 1054 senior high school students taking an economics course was used for the study. The model was estimated using TSLS procedures to correct for a simultaneous equations bias, and with probit analysis because the variable measuring student interest in taking more economics was dichotomous. The study found that economic understanding had a significant effect on interest in taking another course, but not vice versa.

RESEARCH ON ATTITUDES TOWARDS ECONOMIC ISSUES

Many studies have examined the effect of economic knowledge on views of economic issues. Three lines of research can be identified in the area. The first line examined the effects of economic understanding on economic attitude sophistication, or the extent to which student views on selected economic issues are in agreement with the consensus view of economists on those issues. Mann and Fusfeld (1970), who originally defined the term 'economic attitude sophistication', found that college students exposed to economics instruction and who had more economic knowledge showed greater sophistication about economic issues than those college students without economics instruction. This basic finding is supported in two national studies with 3427 senior high school students. The regression results from those two studies showed that, on average, each point a student scored on the TEL contributed about a fifth of a point to the prediction of the EAS score, after accounting for personal, social and other factors in the model (Walstad and Soper, 1982, 1989). Further evidence of the direct effect of economic understanding on EAS was reported in a study of 204 pre-college teachers and college students (Walstad, 1984).

The second line of research has studied factors affecting attitudes towards various economic topics. One high school study used path analysis to explore senior high school student attitudes towards the American economic system, business and labour unions (Jackstadt and Brennan, 1983). The authors constructed three attitude instruments that each contained 30 Likert-type statements on each topic. The alpha reliability estimates for the instruments were in the ranges of 0.65 to 0.74. Economic understanding was measured by scores on the TEL. The results showed that the level of economic knowledge, and also whether the student had taken a previous economics course, were significant predictors of improved positive attitudes towards the American economic system and towards business. No significant relationship was found between the knowledge or course variables and attitudes towards labour unions, which were mostly influenced by parental membership of a labour union.

Further support for the influence of both economic knowledge and instruction on economic attitudes was reported in a study of 1457 junior high school students (14–15-year-olds) (Ingels and O'Brien, 1988). This study used the *Economic Values Inventory*, an attitude instrument that contained 44 statements that were sorted into eight scales. The results from a two-way analysis of variance of economic knowledge and economics instruction showed that more economic knowledge was a 'powerful predictor of statistically significant attitude differences' (p. 285). The knowledge factor contributed to (1) more support for the American economic system; (2) less thought of economic alienation and powerlessness; (3) more support for government welfare as a 'safety net' for the poor and the unemployed; (4) less support for government price fixing; (5) less support for powerful unions; (6) more support for the view that workers receive fair treatment from business; and (7) less support for changing the distribution of wealth and income. The only odd result was for the scale measuring trust in business because greater economic knowledge contributed to less trust. This result may have been an artifact of measurement problems with that scale because the other cognitive influence, economics instruction, had a positive effect on student attitudes towards trust in business. Economics instruction also had a positive influence on three other attitude scales: support for the American economic system; viewing workers as receiving fair treatment from business; and less expression of equality in the distribution of income.

Both the junior and senior high school studies reinforce the conclusion from an earlier national study of adult attitudes towards the economic system and towards business (Barlow and Kaufman, 1975). The research measured the level of economic knowledge of the public and the attitudes that people held towards the economic system and business, based on a mail questionnaire to a representative national sample of about 2000 adults. The researchers found strong support for the capitalist economic system and concluded that public relations programmes conducted by business to convince people to support the American economic system were unnecessary. They also discovered that 'the best predictor of attitude toward business is the score people make on the test of economic knowledge' (p. 20), not variables such as income, education or sex. They concluded that the most effective way, although by no means guaranteed way, to develop more positive public attitudes towards business was to increase knowledge about basic economics through educational programmes.

Some educators have contended that economics education is ideological and that it indoctrinates students (Watts, 1987). Although it would be easy to interpret the findings from the previous three attitude studies as evidence to support this contention, the process of economics education is more subtle and complex. Economic knowledge does have the potential to change economic opinions and attitudes because it makes people more aware and gives them greater understanding of issues. More awareness and understanding of any issue, be it social, political or economic, usually leads people to develop more appreciation of other points of view, and perhaps changes their opinions or attitudes. Consequently, it should not be surprising that more economics knowledge and instruction leads to more positive views of the American economic system or of business positions on economic issues. More economics knowledge or education, however, offers no guarantee that people will hold the 'desired' opinions or attitudes. Even among people who are knowledgeable and informed about economics, there will be differences of opinion on economics issues, often reflecting underlying differences in attitudes that are less susceptible to change.

Ironically, scepticism about the position that economics education is ideological or indoctrinating finds support in a third line of attitude research on the effects of economics on political orientation. Four college-level studies of the effect of taking economics courses on student liberalism or conservatism on economics issues were reviewed by Siegfried and Fels (1979). They tentatively concluded that college economics instruction had a liberalizing influence on views of economic issues. Later college studies concluded the opposite: economics instruction and learning shifts students' views on economics issues in a conservative direction (Luker and Proctor, 1981; Jackstadt *et al.*, 1985). Thus the research findings are too conflicting, and the number of studies too limited, to draw any firm conclusions about political orientation.

What may be contributing to these results is that 'liberalism' or 'conservatism' are difficult terms to define and the definitions change over time. This situation makes it difficult to judge whether agreement on an issue statement represents a conservative or a liberal position. When asked, for example, whether 'government should own and operate all public utilities' or whether 'there should be public ownership of oil and other natural resources', both liberals and conservatives might generally disagree, so that these items would contribute little information to the scale. If this problem is present with many items, the total scores will have little validity as an index of liberalism or conservatism. Compounding the problem has been the use of different measurement instruments, some with unknown psychometric properties. These problems combine to make measurement of political orientation especially problematic.

IMPLICATIONS

Two implications can be drawn from the wide range of research reviewed in this chapter. The first applies to economics education. Students develop perceptions of their economic world at an early age that form into attitudes and opinions about the subject of economics and about economics issues. Strong support is found in this review that increased economics knowledge and more instruction in the subject significantly influence that attitude development. Educators and others contribute to improved student attitudes towards the subject by increasing economics knowledge. More economics instruction and increased economics knowledge provide a foundation for more informed student opinions about economics issues, and may improve decision making about those issues. This process of economics education is not simply indoctrination because differences of opinions still remain on many economic issues, even after economics instruction or after accounting for the effects of economics knowledge on the issues.

Although the research shows that, the more economics students know, the more they like the subject and the more information they have for assessing economic issues, the problem in the USA is that most students receive little formal instruction in economics. Only about half of American high school students take a separate semester-length course in economics before high school graduation. Students who do not have the opportunity to learn economics and improve their knowledge of economics will probably never take much interest in the subject or in many economics issues. Of course, they will still form opinions and attitudes about economics matters, but these are likely to be ill-informed and simplistic. When this happens, the educational system is producing less knowledgeable and interested consumers, workers and citizens. Ensuring that students have the opportunity to learn economics throughout a formal education, from early years to adulthood, creates a positive learning environment for the formation of economics attitudes and opinions.

The second implication applies to the conduct of future research. Most surveys and attitude studies assume that all expressions of opinion or attitude are equally valid, without regard to what the respondent knows about the topic. The mixing of informed and uninformed opinion or attitude, and the failure to analyse results without taking into consideration the knowledge of respondents, have the potential to mislead researchers and to distort findings. This problem should be a concern for research on economic opinions or attitudes, given the complexity of the economics issues that students or adults are asked to evaluate. Definitions of opinions and attitudes plus research in economics education with pre-college and college students show that knowledge plays a critical role in forming economics opinions and attitudes. This knowledge factor should not be neglected in future studies.

REFERENCES

Alston, R.M., Kearl, J.R. and Vaughan, M.B. (1992), 'Is there a consensus among economists in the 1990's?', *American Economic Review*, **82**, 203–9.
Bach, G.L. (1979), 'Economic education and America's love–hate affair with big business', *Journal of Economic Education*, special supplement, 1–7.
Barlow, W. and Kaufman, C. (1975), 'Public relations and economic literacy', *Public Relations Review*, **1**, 14–22.

Becker, W.E. (1983), 'Economic education research: Part I, issues and questions', *Journal of Economic Education*, **14**, 10–17.

Beron, K.J. (1990), 'Joint determination of current classroom performance and additional economics classes: A binary/continuous model', *Journal of Economic Education*, **21**, 1–7.

Business Week (1992), 'Who will raise taxes? Try Clinton, Bush, and Perot', 19 October, 32.

Charkins, R.J., O'Toole, D.M. and Wetzel, J.M. (1985), 'Linking teacher and student learning styles with student achievement and attitudes', *Journal of Economic Education*, **16**, 111–20.

Fizel, J.L. and Johnson, J.D. (1986), 'The effect of macro/micro course sequencing on learning and attitudes in principles of economics', *Journal of Economic Education*, **17**, 87–98.

Hodgin, R.F. (1984), 'Information theory and attitude formation in economic education', *Journal of Economic Education*, **15**, 191–6.

Ingels, S.J. and O'Brien, M.U. (1988), 'The effects of economics instruction in early adolescence', *Theory and Research in Social Education*, **26**, 279–94.

Jackstadt, S.L. and Brennan, J. (1983), 'Economic knowledge and high school student attitudes toward the American economic system, business, and labor unions', *Theory and Research in Social Education*, **11**, 1–15.

Jackstadt, S.L., Brennan, J. and Thompson, S. (1985), 'The effect of introductory economics courses on college students' conservatism', *Journal of Economic Education*, **16**, 37–51.

Kerlinger, F.N. (1984), *Liberalism and Conservatism: The nature and structure of social attitudes*, Hillsdale, NJ: Lawrence Erlbaum.

Leeper, Eric M. (1992), 'Consumer attitudes: king for a day', *Economic Review* (Federal Reserve Bank of Atlanta), **77**, 1–15.

Luker, W. and Proctor, W. (1981), 'The effect of an introductory course in microeconomics on the political orientation of students', *Journal of Economic Education*, **12**, 54–7.

Mann, W.R. and Fusfeld, D.R. (1970), 'Attitude sophistication and effective teaching in economics', *Journal of Economic Education*, **1**, 111–29.

McClosky, H. and Zaller, J. (1984), *The American Ethos: Public attitudes toward capitalism and democracy*, Cambridge, Mass.: Harvard University Press.

Saunders, Phillip (1991), *The Test of Understanding of College Economics*, 3rd edn, New York: National Council on Economic Education.

Saunders, Phillip *et al.* (1992), *A Framework for Teaching the Basic Concepts*, 3rd edn, New York: National Council on Economic Education.

Schober, H.M. (1984), 'The effects of inservice training on participating teachers and students in their economics classes', *Journal of Economic Education*, **15**, 282–96.

Schug, M.C. and Walstad, W.B. (1991), 'Teaching and learning economics', in James P. Shaver (ed.), *Handbook of Research on Social Studies Teaching and Learning*, New York: Macmillan, 411–19.

Shiller, R.J., Boycko, M. and Korobov, V. (1991), 'Popular attitudes toward free markets: The Soviet Union and the United States compared', *American Economic Review*, **81**, 385–400.

Siegfried, J.J. and Fels, R. (1979), 'Research on teaching college economics: A survey', *Journal of Economic Literature*, **18**, 923–69.

Soper, J.C. and Walstad, W.B. (1983), 'On measuring economic attitudes', *Journal of Economic Education*, **14**, 4–17.

Soper, J.C. and Walstad, W.B. (1987), *Test of Economic Literacy: Examiner's manual*, New York: National Council on Economic Education.
Soper, J.C. and Walstad, W.B. (1988), 'Economic attitudes of high school students: New norms for the *Survey on Economic Attitudes, Theory and Research in Social Education*, **26**, 295–312.
Throop, Adrian W. (1992), 'Consumer sentiment: Its causes and effects', *Economic Review* (Federal Reserve Bank of San Francisco), **1**, 35–59.
Triandis, H.C. (1971), *Attitude and Attitude Change*, New York: Wiley.
Walstad, W.B. (1979), 'The effectiveness of USMES in-service economic education program for elementary school teachers', *Journal of Economic Education*, **11**, 1–12.
Walstad, W.B. (1980), 'The impact of *Trade-offs* and teacher training on economic understanding and attitudes', *Journal of Economic Education*, **12**, 41–8.
Walstad, W.B. (1984), 'The relative effectiveness of economics instruction for teachers and college students', *Journal of Economic Education*, **15**, 297–308.
Walstad, W.B. (1987), 'Applying two-stage least squares', in W.E. Becker and W.B. Walstad (eds), *Econometric Modeling in Economic Education Research*, Boston: Kluwer-Nijhoff, pp. 114–34.
Walstad, W.B. (1992), 'Economics instruction in high schools', *Journal of Economic Literature*, **30**, 2019–51.
Walstad, W.B. and Larsen, M. (1992), *A National Survey of American Economic Literacy*, Lincoln, Nebraska: The Gallup Organization.
Walstad, W.B. and Robson, D. (1990), *Basic Economics Test: Examiner's manual*, New York: National Council on Economic Education.
Walstad, W.B. and Soper, J.C. (1982), 'A model of economic learning in the high schools', *Journal of Economic Education*, **13**, 40–54.
Walstad, W.B. and Soper, J.C. (1989), 'What is high school economics? Factors contributing to student achievement and attitudes', *Journal of Economic Education*, **20**, 23–38.
Watts, M. (1987), 'Ideology, textbooks, and the teaching of economics', *Theory into Practice*, **26**, 190–97.
Yankelovich, D. (1991), *Coming to Public Judgment: Making democracy work in a complex world*, Syracuse, NY: Syracuse University Press.

11. Social factors of economic socialization

Anna Silvia Bombi

THE DIFFERENT MEANINGS OF 'SOCIAL ENVIRONMENT'

The first studies on children's economic ideas were conducted with the main purpose of demonstrating that children indeed had such ideas; hence many of them were descriptive works focusing on age comparison, broadly interpreted in a cognitive–developmental perspective (see a critical review in Chapter 2 of the present volume). While these studies were successful in illustrating the relationship between age and development of economic notions, they explored only the individual side of economic socialization, leaving unanswered the questions about the role of experience and different information available to the subjects.

Thus successive studies which attempted to validate and refine the results of the earlier ones, as well as those aiming to support new theoretical concepts, gave more consideration to the social factors that contributed to the shaping of economic socialization processes. Before briefly reviewing this literature, it is useful to distinguish three meanings of 'social environment' that seem to be implied by some writers. First, a number of studies addressed the classical cross-cultural question: how do children from different countries conceive of economic reality? From this perspective, social environment is a very wide concept, and it may be considered a synonym for nation. On the contrary, a very specific, restricted meaning of the term is adopted in a second, smaller group of studies, whose authors examined children from comparable sociocultural contexts, only differing in one or two specific dimensions, relevant to the investigated notion(s); from this perspective, social environment is the experiential field in which children's particular ideas develop. Third, social environment may coincide with social class, when researchers try to determine how children from different socioeconomic conditions view economic reality.

CROSS-CULTURAL STUDIES

The purpose of cross-cultural studies is to compare the economic conceptions of children from different countries, to validate the sequence of developmental levels found in the European and American groups, and to verify whether specific ideas characterize children raised in different cultures. Several economic notions (buying and selling, banks, wealth and poverty, ownership) were considered from this perspective, more to take advantage of the peculiarities of the country in which the studies took place, than to follow a predetermined general research plan.

Overall, these studies confirm the impression of homogeneity conveyed by the previous investigations, which were conducted independently, but nevertheless gave very similar results. Hong Kwan and Stacey (1981) found in Chinese Malaysian children the same developmental stages of the notions about buying and selling previously indicated by Furth (1980) and Jahoda (1979), the only difference being the more or less precocious age at which the understanding of profit is reached. The same result emerged in the study of buying and selling conducted by Jahoda in Zimbabwe (1983). The ideas about the functioning of the bank, originally studied by Jahoda in Great Britain (1981), were investigated in the Netherlands (Jahoda and Woerdenbagch, 1982) and in Hong Kong (Ng, 1983). Similar developmental sequences were found, with different rhythms of progress towards the more complex notions.

Other cross-cultural comparisons were performed by Ng, who replicated in New Zealand a study conducted in Italy by Berti *et al.* (1982) on the notion of ownership (Ng and Cram, 1990). He also repeated in New Zealand and India two American studies of Leahy (1981, 1983) on the notions of wealth and poverty (Ng and Jhaveri, 1988). These comparisons again confirmed the sequence of levels emerging from the previous studies, with interesting peculiarities in the different groups (for example, Indian children are more prone than New Zealanders and Americans to fatalistic explanations). Giving a systematic support to the indicated developmental sequences, these studies were more successful in demonstrating the cross-cultural similarity of some basic features of economic knowledge than in explaining the emerging differences, in particular the non-coincident ages at which the same developmental levels are attained by children of various countries. The compared countries differ from each other in so many parameters that it is very difficult, if not impossible, to indicate which aspects are really influential. The overall 'cultural distance' between two countries is not predictive per se of the variance in results: the differences between two European samples are sometimes wider than those between European and African samples (as in the case of the British and Dutch children compared with those from Zimbabwe). In fact, only those differences in the children's answers are interpretable that can be related to strong and pervasive characteristics of cultures, as in the above-mentioned case of Indian children's fatalism (Ng and Jhaveri, 1988). To explain more subtle differences it would be necessary to reduce the 'noise' in the comparisons.

EXPERIENCE AND ECONOMIC KNOWLEDGE

The need for a greater degree of control over the variables does not mean abandoning the analysis of natural contexts, as would be the case in experimental studies. A clear example of the reason for this choice is a study by Bellelli, *et al.* (1984) comparing the concept of work in two groups of Neapolitan children: school children (8–14 years old) and subjects of the same age who went to school but also worked. It is evident that a real and direct experience of working is not an experimentally manipulable variable, though it may be extremely interesting to know how such experience affects children's economic notions. In general, this kind of research is based on the analytic examination of the developmental steps of single economic notions, and of the potentially relevant social variables; it tries to identify in the children's 'living space' (family, neighbourhood, school) the opportunity for specific experiences (to see exchanges, to hear conversations, to notice facts) which are hypothesized as important for the construction of a specific notion in a determined age range. While these studies maintain a precise connection between social variables and children's economic conceptions, their explanatory range is clearly restricted. The underlying developmental mechanisms can be conceived differently according to the chosen theoretical frame. In the study mentioned above, Bellelli *et al.* (1984) considered the social interactions involved in each working situation as the determining factor for children's understanding. In other studies about payment for work (Berti and Bombi, 1988) and the origins and distribution of goods (Berti and Bombi, 1990) the authors adopted a cognitive–developmental perspective, interpreting children's answers as the result of an interaction between age and specific experiences relevant to the concept being studied. Subjects from different social environments provided answers reflecting their opportunities for direct experience as well as their age: after the age of 5–6 years (but not earlier) children of blue-collar workers proved less competent about work payment than their peers who had self-employed fathers. Urban children knew more about shops than their peers living in a mountain community, but appeared prone to invent fantasies about the origin of goods, reflecting their lack of first-hand experience; and here, too, the difference between groups appeared only after the age of six.

Berti and Bombi found many similarities between the compared groups; we will come back later to the coexistence of similarities and differences across subjects, examining Emler's contribution. The school is a particularly relevant environment for economic socialization, especially in those countries (like Britain or the USA) in which the state school system is paralleled by a significant number of privately run schools. In these countries the option for a particular kind of school corresponds quite strictly to the family socioeconomic class, and was used by authors such as Emler and Dickinson (1985) and Furnham (1982) to select their samples in studies where the socioeconomic variables were of pre-eminent interest. Nevertheless, it is important to note that the values transmitted in school may be influential independently of the pupil's social class, as shown in a study by Roker (1990). She interviewed middle-class British adolescents (15–17 years old) from a public and a state school about work, unemployment and poverty. Even though in both groups the subjects' fathers were professionals or managers, the two groups' answers differed significantly: in the state school work was considered a need for everybody and a means of supporting oneself, while in the public school it was viewed as the access to a career and a source of satisfaction; unemployment and poverty were attributed in the first school to government policy, in the second to individuals' laziness or insufficient abilities.

STUDIES ON THE INFLUENCE OF SOCIAL CLASS

These studies have in common a more or less explicit dissatisfaction with the Piagetian or neo-Piagetian approaches, which are limited to age comparisons. Emler (1986) observes that Piaget-inspired approaches, while rightly emphasizing the child's role in his or her economic socialization, give an incomplete picture of socialization itself. Socialization is not only a process of cognitive growth, but also an acculturation process; it is possible that acculturation was not taken into account by Piagetian scholars, because it was historically associated with a conception of the child as a passive and irrational being (Turiel, 1983). Focusing only on structural characteristics of social cognition (which do not vary across cultures), these scholars leave aside the representational contents and values in which societal influences can be better demonstrated.

Not all the economic concepts appeared equally suited for demonstrating the influence of social class; in fact, while the functioning of economic exchanges (in shops, wholesale markets, banks and so on) was initially chosen to trace the construction of economic knowledge, topics more· evidently connected to moral judgements and values (such as those related to the payment of work and the resulting social inequalities) were preferred by the critics of the earlier research.

The emergence of the understanding that work is remunerated was seldom studied, especially in young children (Berti and Bombi, 1988; Furth, 1980; Goldstein and Oldham 1979), while more effort was devoted to questions concerning economic inequalities: when are they discovered and how they are explained and evaluated by children?

The first of these was investigated by Danziger (1958), Connell (1977) and Leahy (1981) who asked subjects of various ages to describe verbally wealth and poverty. Only Danziger found subjects who had no idea of what 'rich' and 'poor' meant, though he did not specify how many and in what age groups. Leahy and Connell, instead, both reported their younger subjects (6 and 5 years old, respectively) to be able to differentiate rich and poor people, even if in more generic and superficial terms than those typical of later ages. In particular, Leahy found a trend from descriptions based on 'peripheral' characteristics to descriptions based on 'central' and 'sociocentric' elements. Connell (1977) found that younger children conceived wealth and poverty in terms of a 'dramatic contrast', while older children recognized the existence of an intermediate condition between rich and poor. Other researchers asked children to match jobs and adjectives from a list (Fabbri and Panier Bagat, 1989) or to classify jobs on the basis of income, as perceived from photos, drawings and verbal descriptions (Goldstein and Oldham, 1977a; Mookherjee and Hogan, 1981; Siegal, 1981; Duveen and Shields, 1984, 1986; Emler and Dickinson, 1985). Children as young as $3^{1}/_{2}$ were able to recognize that not every activity receives the same payment, even if only at around the age of 8 does a correct ordering of income appear.

Explanations and evaluations of economic inequalities also change as children grow older. Danziger (1958), Connell (1977), Burris (1983) and Berti and Bombi (1988) reported that only a few of their youngest subjects (pre-school children) believed in magical means for obtaining money; from about age 8, children connected income with work, initially considering rich those people who worked 'harder' or 'longer' or 'better'; similar results were found in elementary school children by Furby (1979), Siegal (1981) and Emler and Dickinson (1985). Older subjects understand that wealth does not always depend on such simple criteria: for instance, Leahy (1983) found that, while younger children only refer to concrete, personal factors to explain wealth and poverty, adolescents also take into account societal factors. The adolescents' attitudes are not uniform: while some still believe in 'individualistic' causes of poverty (laziness, lack of skills), others are 'fatalistic', blaming the unfortunate circumstances (sickness, accidents) in which some people found themselves; only a few of the adolescents look at poverty as being caused by exploitation, prejudice or insufficient opportunities provided by society (Furnham, 1982).

While the age changes are so pervasive, not every study has demonstrated differences related to class or social environment, even though this was a primary concern in many of them; moreover, the reported differences have not always been easily interpreted as a coherent trend. Emler and Dickinson (1985) found lower-class children more inclined than middle-class children to admit the perspective of equal payment for all jobs; but no differences emerged between groups in accepting unequal payment as right, and their meritocratic explanations of it. Connell (1977), who compared children from three socially differing neighbourhoods in an Australian city (lower-, middle- and upper-class), concluded that no consistent differences in the perception of social class were evident between the three groups.

Fabbri and Panier Bagat (1989), who also examined children of three socioeconomic levels, reached the conclusion that the representation of work is very homogeneous in the compared groups, with differences that can be better explained as a developmental delay of children from a less favoured social background. Leahy too (1981, 1983) considers this explanation valid for one part of his data; only some of his findings reveal genuine attitudinal differences. One is that lower-class subjects identify more intimately with the condition of the poor; another is the tendency of middle- or upper-middle-class subjects to justify income differences on the basis of merit, and to consider it impossible to eliminate poverty, a result that parallels those obtained by Furnham (1982). Leahy concludes that there is more consensus than opposition in the perspectives about wealth and poverty yielded by different social classes. Another American study (Goldstein and Oldham, 1979) did not reveal any differences in the ability of middle- or lower-class children to recognize and describe economic inequalities, and little difference in the explanations given for such inequalities.

In the light of Emler's distinction between the *structural* aspects of economic cognition (which are largely independent of social variation) and its *representational* contents (which are, on the contrary, highly influenced by the surrounding culture), these results are not contradictory. Following Connell (1977), we might also remember that only some aspects of a culture are 'tied' to particular class positions in the society; a great deal of 'free-floating' information is available to any member of the society, especially through the mass media. Children whose knowledge about society heavily depends on television and who at the same time excluded from the main sources of 'tied information' (that is, jobs) live in such a homogeneous social environment that the similarity of their conceptions and judgements is not at all surprising. Connell's (1977) theory could help us to understand why clearer differences were found in adolescents (see the studies of Furnham, 1982; Roker, 1990; and the older subjects in the Leahy studies, 1981, 1983): only when subjects become capable of selecting information linked to their specific social environment do they become sensitive to different ideologies and accordingly elaborate their own convictions.

CHANGING PARADIGMS: THE PICTORIAL REPRESENTATION OF WEALTH AND POVERTY

The difficulty of research with young children in casting light on social differences could also be related to the way in which the data were obtained. The prevailing paradigm thus far encountered, including those studies which were critical towards the cognitive–developmental approach, was the semi-structured interview. This paradigm is derived from the Piagetian tradition and is very well suited to discovering the cognitive abilities underlying children's answers; it is less useful when the researcher's interests also include the image of, and the attitudes towards, particular aspects of the economic reality. What is pertinent is that some effort should be made to complete our investigation of children's economic world with a variety of methods. Thus the study presented in this section is an attempt at (provisionally!) abandoning the interview procedure, on which my own earlier research with A.E. Berti was based, and trying out an analysis of children's drawings, a technique which the present author is currently employing for the study of children's representations of interpersonal relationships (friendships, family and so on: Bombi and Pinto, 1993). Drawings are powerful, but limited, means of expression: they can transmit our descriptions of and feelings about a particular subject but not our explanations of it. Given a valid analysis of children's drawings,[1] only certain aspects of economic knowledge can be investigated; yet these aspects are precisely those representational contents of children's economic notions that, according to Emler's suggestion, should be less uniform through different social environments. If the pictorial approach proves useful, children's drawings would be good instruments for cross-cultural comparison, avoiding the not insignificant linguistic problems of translating and adapting interviews.

The representation of wealth and poverty is my subject here. The literature on this topic shows that, when differences related to social environment or social class were found, they appeared more often in children's explanations of social inequalities than in their descriptions of rich and poor people. This may be at least partly due to young children's difficulty in expressing verbally the entire complexity of their social representations. With the aid of children's drawings I hope to demonstrate that social factors can influence the representation of wealth and poverty (even in young children), especially when the social environment yields highly visible information about degrees of wealth.

A large number of elementary school children of similar economic condition (middle-class), living in four Italian cities, two north–central (Brescia and Florence), two southern (Naples and Potenza), were asked to communicate to us their ideas about wealth and poverty by drawing, on a single page, a rich person and a poor person.[2] In each city, about ten boys and ten girls were randomly selected from first to fifth grade, obtaining a sample of 390 children 6 to 10 years old, balanced with respect to age, sex and city. Age (6–8 v. 9–11 years old), sex and region (north–central v. southern cities) were compared (with chi-squares or variance analyses, according to the examined data); owing to the large quantity of data, results pertaining only to the regional factor will be discussed here. When compared with the north–central regions, Italian southern regions are considerably underdeveloped economically: factories are fewer, industrial support (roads, railways and so on) is insufficient, agriculture is less industrialized, unemployment rates are higher. These are the regions with marked emigration towards northern Europe, the Americas and Australia between the two world wars, with a continuing internal emigration towards Italian northern regions after the Second World War. The attempts of the Italian government to support the southern economy with special funds ('Cassa del Mezzogiorno') were largely neutralized by the lack of efficient regional administrations and the rival presence of organized delinquency, tragically encouraged by the failure of the population, whose history is one of recurrent foreigner domination and irresponsible government, to identify with public institutions (Mack Smith, 1977). This necessarily sketchy profile indicates that, even though the child might not be aware of all these economic factors, poverty in general should be much more visible in the southern cities, while wealth might be conceived in almost mythical terms.

Given the above considerations, the pictorial representation of wealth and poverty should be different between north–central and southern children: in particular, it was expected that the latter would emphasize the diversity between rich and poor people more than the former, mirroring the economic realities of their respective regions.

The request for a drawing of a rich and a poor person on the same page, with emphasis on the communicative aim of the task, gave rise to drawings in which the two figures are in sharp contrast. Children clearly made their drawing according to a unitary plan, often including the two figures in a single scene (64 per cent of the entire sample) or drawing opposing scenes for each of them (21.5 per cent); when only the two figures are drawn (14.5 per cent), they are different in such a way that it is obvious which one is the rich person, which one is poor. Looking at the drawings as a whole, an adult observer's identification corresponded without exception to that given by the child at the moment of handing in the drawing. Moreover, the neutral judge could easily recognize one or both characters in 86 per cent of the drawings, even when one of the figures was hidden (along with any qualifying objects or colours around it). Differences between the north–central and southern children are shown in Table 11.1. The biggest differences emerged with respect to the representation of the rich: subjects from Naples and Potenza characterize only the figure of the rich person more often than those from Florence and Brescia; the latter instead tend to make both figures distinctly recognizable. In other words, it seems that some southern children avoid putting in direct opposition the rich and poor person.

I then performed a more detailed examination of what precisely made the two figures recognizable, detecting several pictorial strategies, as follows.

Table 11.1   *Frequency of the various categories of figure recognizability in north–central and southern children's drawings*

	Neither	Rich person	Poor person	Both	Total
North–central	28	15	37	120	200
	(14)	(7.5)	(18.5)	(60)	(100)
Southern	25	37	31	97	190
	(13)	(19.5)	(16.5)	(51)	(100)
Total	53	52	68	217	390
	(13.5)	(13.5)	(17)	(56)	(100)

Notes:
1. Chi square = 12.19; df 3; $p = 0.007$.
2. Data in brackets are the percentages of the total for each row.

Similarity

The most basic way of contrasting the rich and poor person is to draw them with non coincident features. The degree of similarity between the two figures was measured by means of a similarity scale validated by Bombi and Pinto (1990, 1993) for the analysis of interpersonal relationships.[3] This scale compares the figures with respect to four distinct features:

1. *Dimensions* – in height and width: tall/short; thin/fat.
2. *Position* – posture and orientation: arms up/folded; sitting/standing; in profile/facing forward, and so on.
3. *Body* – form and colour of face and body: curly/straight hair; dark/blue eyes; large/small hands, and so on.

4. *Personal qualifiers* – form and colour of figure's clothes and objects: straight/pleated skirt; red/green trousers; holding a bag/a sack.

For each aspect, figures can be identical (score 2), slightly similar (1) or different (0); the mean of the four scores gives a global similarity score. In the entire sample, the similarity between rich and poor person resulted in 0.81, a score nearer to the 'difference' end of the scale than to the 'similarity' end. This low degree of similarity is about the same as that found when children of the same age were asked to draw two figures as different as they could (Cannoni, 1992; Bombi and Pinto, 1993). Children from the north–centre introduced less similarity between the two figures than those from the south (mean scores = 0.74 v. 0.89; $F = 21.04$; df 1382; $p < 0.001$). This result is due in particular to the older children from the north (younger/north–central = 0.86; southern/north–central = 0.92; older/north–central = 0.62; older/southern = 0.87; interaction between age and region: $F = 7.16$; df 1382; $p = 0.008$). Not all children, then, tend to increase their recognition of the differences between rich and poor people as they grow older: we find here that those children whose social environment presents the larger gap between wealth and poverty are less inclined to admit the existence of inequalities between people.

Value

The figural differences that limit, especially in older children from Florence and Brescia, the similarity between the rich and poor person do not necessarily express superiority of one person over the other: to take an example, having red hair is no better or no worse than having brown hair, and a green shirt is equivalent to a blue one. Yet examination of the drawings reveals that the figures of rich and poor are differently 'treated' from the pictorial point of view: for example, one may have more colours or more details than the other; he or she may be bigger or positioned higher. The completeness of the body, the number of added details and the colouring are an expression of the care with which the figure is realized, which in turn can be considered the expression of the value awarded by the young artist to the figure. The same can be said of the dimension and dominant position, both considered iconographic indices of the importance of a drawn character (as in the figure of Christ in Byzantine art, or of the Pharaoh in Egyptian paintings).

To test whether the two figures differed in the children's appreciation, a value scale (Bombi and Pinto, 1993) was then applied, in which five separate scores from 0 (= no difference) to 2 (marked superiority of value) are assigned to the figures for these features:

1. *Size* – higher and/or wider.
2. *Dominant position* – seeing the other figure from above or below.
3. *Body articulation* – presence of more parts.
4. *Attributes* – number of items of clothing, embellishments or accessories.
5. *Colours* – number of colours.

The figure with greater value was identified in each drawing by comparing the scores for each figure, and the frequency was calculated with which the rich person, the poor person or neither had greater value; moreover, the entity of the value inequality introduced by the young artist between the rich and poor person was measured by calculating, for each drawing, the difference between the two figures' scores.

It is important to note that, with this kind of measurement, the rich person does not necessarily come off best: the poor person, for instance, might be dressed in multicoloured rags, which are rich in details even though they might be patches and holes, while the rich person might be represented by a few monochrome details. In fact, the 'value' is treated here as independent of the meaning of the various elements (which will be discussed later); it expresses the importance and attention given to each figure from a graphic–pictorial perspective, reflecting the affective value which the child more or less consciously attributes to it.

Data analysis revealed that in both regions the great majority of children (75 per cent) privileged the figure of the rich person, while only 10 per cent drew more accurately and gave prominence to the poor person; the remaining 15 per cent balanced the two figures so that neither one had greater value. The degree of value inequality between rich and poor person is not large in absolute terms (2.17 on a range of 0–10), but it is close to that introduced by children of the same age when explicitly requested to differentiate the importance and value of two figures (Bombi and Delle Donne, 1993). The value inequality score tends to be affected by the subject's region in interaction with his or her sex ($F = 3.99$; df 1382; $p = 0.046$): north–central boys stressed the differences much more than those from the south (2.55 v. 1.9) while girls of the two regions obtained exactly the same score (2.15). This latter result complements that of the similarity scale: here too inequalities are more evident in north–central subjects, in this case the boys.

Status indicators

Here we examine those aspects of the drawings through which the social position of the figures is shown. Children introduced into their drawings many status indicators, such as a house and car, or material indicators, such as money and food, and distributed these indicators with either a presence/

absence strategy or a quality contrast strategy. The first strategy consists in endowing with one or more meaningful objects only one of the figures: the rich person with something desirable that the poor person does not have (house, food, car, a piece of jewellery); less frequently, the poor person is shown with something which is undesirable (ragged clothes) or indicative of his state (the money on a plate being used to ask for charity). The second strategy consists in giving both figures special clothes, houses or objects: smart clothes or evening dress for the rich person, more modest clothes or even rags for the poor person; a large house or a castle for the rich person, a hut or a shack for the poor person; a car for the first, a donkey for the second.

Almost all north–central children (99 per cent), and a large (yet significantly lower; chi-square 11.11; *df* 1; $p = 0.001$) proportion of southern children (92 per cent) had included one or more of these rich/poor indicators in their drawings. Very often several indicators appeared in a single drawing; these are used both with the presence/absence and the quality contrast strategy, in a large number of different combinations. It was not therefore possible to organize a typology of objects possessed by the two figures which could enable drawings to be individually categorized; instead a calculation was made of the absolute individual frequency of each of the following indicators:

1. *House* – large/small; house/hut; house/no house.
2. *Vehicle* – car/bicycle or donkey; car/no car.
3. *Clothes* – beautiful/ugly; intact/torn; top hat/beret; shoes/barefoot.
4. *Objects* – jewellery/no jewellery; dog as pet/dog as co-worker; sceptre/ walking stick.
5. *Money* – bags or pockets full of money/no money; money received/given to charity.
6. *Food* – rich person eating/poor person watching; poor person dreaming of food.

The frequencies of these six types of indicators are ordered by rank in Table 11.2. The mean number of indicators included by children from the two regions is similar (south = 2.24; north = 2.03), as well as the rank order of frequency with which any single indicator appears, with the exception of the house and money, where ranks are reversed in the southern children as compared to the entire sample. This particular result could reflect the widespread concern about housing in southern cities; but it is more interesting to note that, once again, there are more children in the southern group that present a 'neutral' drawing, in this case a drawing in which status indicators are lacking.

Table 11.2   Frequency of the various indicators of social condition in north–central and southern children

	Clothes	Objects	Money	House	Vehicle	Food	Total
North–central	153	112	77	48	13	3	406
	(38)	(27)	(19)	(12)	(3)	(1)	(100)
Southern	142	98	66	71	30	5	12
	(34)	(24)	(18)	(17)	(7)	(1)	(100)
Total	295	210	143	119	43	8	813
	(36)	(26)	(17)	(15)	(5)	(1)	(100)

Notes: Numbers in parentheses are the percentages of the total for each row.

Social Categories

The representation of rich and poor as having different personal possessions does not necessarily match their belonging to specific social categories: for example, the rich person might be dressed better than the poor person without it being possible to infer anything as to his or her occupation or role. However, in many drawings the kind of objects belonging to the figures allowed them to be classified as particular categories of person: for example, the money being received by the poor person as charity, he thereby appearing as a beggar. Actions carried out by figures and the words they use (in cartoon bubbles) helped to recognize them as servant or master, robber or robbed, orphan or benefactor.

Children characterized the poor person as belonging to a particular group far more often ($n = 234$) than the rich person ($n = 44$); in 22 of these drawings both figures were identifiable in opposite social roles. The three social roles most frequently attributed to the poor person in the entire sample were beggar (24 per cent), tramp or ragamuffin (23 per cent) and weak person, such as child, orphan, old, sick or mutilated person (8 per cent). In a few cases (3 per cent) the poor person was working (compared to somebody who does not need to work); two children drew a thief (0.5 per cent). The typical social categorization of the rich person is as a king or queen (10 per cent), generally indicated by a crown and sometimes a cloak, sceptre or throne. When both figures had a definite social role, the opposition was between a king or queen and one of the described characterizations of the poor above (5 per cent); rarely (1 per cent) are rich and poor differentiated by their status in work (employer–employee). Overall, a social role can be attributed to one or both figures in 65 per cent of the drawings; but since two of the categories described above were much less frequent in southern children (tramp: south =

19 per cent; centre–north = 27.5 per cent; king/queen: south = 6 per cent; centre–north = 13.5 per cent) a significant difference emerged between centre–north and south in the total frequency of drawings where a social role is detectable (59 per cent v. 71 per cent) (chi-square = 6.232; df 1; p = 0.012). Southern children avoided referring to extremes in both categories – the most humiliating sort of poverty and the enormously wealthy – once again softening the contrast between these social roles.

Figures' Gender

An aspect which is relevant both to social categorization and to personal definition of the rich and poor person is the gender attributed to the two figures: they can both be male or female, or each can be of a different gender.[4] The great majority of children represented the figures as being of the same gender (both male = 52 per cent; both female = 23.5 per cent); when figures' genders were different, we found only rarely a rich man with a poor woman (3 per cent of the entire sample), while the most common case is that of a rich woman with a poor man (21.5 per cent). A larger percentage of the southern children (29.5 per cent v. 19.5 per cent; chi-square = 5.26; df = 1; p = 0.02) juxtaposed male–female figures to stress the difference between rich and poor; closer inspection of the data shows that it is southern girls above all (n = 45) who represented rich and poor as being of different gender, especially depicting the rich woman with the poor man (n = 43).

For the first time, we found in the southern group a larger number of drawings where the opposition between rich and poor is emphasized (in this case, by their different gender). This opposition characterizes only the girls, whose future economic responsibilities in a traditional society like the Italian south were significantly less than those of boys; being less personally involved in the risk of poverty; these girls made use of the gender contrast to identify themselves with the more favoured person.

Emotional Indicators

In many drawings the emotional state of the characters could be detected either directly from their facial or verbal expressions or metaphorically from certain features of the background. There are five indicators that allowed us to evaluate the rich and poor person's emotional state separately:

1. *Facial expression* – happy (smiling); sad (as shown by mouth shape, frown, tears).
2. *Verbal statements* – of happiness, satisfaction; of sadness, discomfort.

3. *Background* – coloured/not coloured; if outside; green/bare; if inside: decorated/bare.
4. *Weather* – good/bad.
5. *Company* – with others/alone.

Positive and negative emotional states could be indicated in the same figure by combining one or more of these drawing features. Each figure was then scored +1, 0, –1 for each indicator according to whether it was used in a positive, neutral or negative way. The positive and negative scores obtained for each indicator were added up to obtain an overall well-being score for each figure.

As could easily be anticipated, analysis of variance with repeated measures on the rich/poor scores showed a significant difference in favour of the rich person's emotional well-being (rich = 1.13; poor = 0.28; $F = 141.72$; df 1382; $p < 0.001$). Not only was the rich person viewed as happier, he or she was also viewed more constantly so; in fact variance in the subject's score is higher for the poor person, indicating that the poor person's emotional situation was more 'controversial'. The higher complexity of this figure was confirmed when we analysed children's pictorial strategy in detail; for the rich person, 95 per cent of the subjects chose a single-dimensional characterization, either positive or (less frequently) negative; for the poor person, the percentage decreased to 87 per cent, due to a larger number of children attributing to this figure both positive and negative indicators (McNemar test < 0.001). It is interesting to note that the few children who presented the rich person with signs of both positive and negative emotions were mostly from the southern group (7 per cent v. 2.5 per cent; chi-square = 3.98 $df = 1$; $p = 0.04$).

Another effect of the region emerged in the absolute scores (centre–north = 0.61; south = 0.81; $F = 6.91$; df 1382; p 0.009), without interaction with the drawn figure. In sum, the emotional characterization of both rich and poor person is more marked and more complex in southern children.

CONCLUSIONS

The opposition of wealth and poverty is very sharply distinguished in children's drawings, with figures not only distinct and recognizable for an adult observer, but also vividly characterized. The rich person is subjectively the more appreciated: his or her figure is pictorially more detailed and/or bigger, and it has preferentially the same sex as the young artist. The situation of the rich person is generally depicted as favourable, both through the direct or metaphorical representation of his or her well-being and through the attribution of desirable possessions that act as status indicators. The figure of the poor, by contrast, is pictorially less refined and/or smaller; often subjects 'maintain a distance' from this figure, drawing it as of the opposite sex from their own. The poor person enjoys a lesser degree of well-being and his or her belongings are clearly worse than those of the rich person, or are totally lacking. From a conceptual point of view, however, the poor person is more often clearly identified in individuals from specific social groups (beggars, tramps, weak people), while the rich person seems to be defined mostly 'by default': his or her only recurrent role, that of king or queen, is totally unrealistic. All together, these data show that children in the age range examined here are able to use drawings to communicate their ideas about this aspect of economic and social life in a very effective way. It seems that our subjects did not limit themselves to describing wealth and poverty in the austere fashion found in those studies conducted with interviews; here, instead, children were able to express via drawings their attitudes towards the social conditions they were asked to illustrate.

The drawings also allowed us to find differences between specific groups of subjects, in our case north–central and southern Italian children, but these differences were more subtle than those hypothesized. Southern children, whose opportunities to encounter poor people and observe social gaps between wealth and poverty are more numerous, did not emphasize differences. These children continued to represent rich and poor persons as relatively similar, while their north–central peers introduced sharper distinctions. Southern children more often omitted status and role indicators, especially the more 'extreme' ones such as the rich person as a king or queen and the poor person as a tramp; they attributed to both rich and poor person a higher degree of well-being, and they sometimes also presented the rich person as someone who can experience both positive and negative emotions; finally, the boys in their group introduced less inequality of value between the two figures: in short, they seemed to be trying to mitigate the representation of a problematic reality. Another interpretation might be that, in the highly personalized southern Italian culture, children focus on the individual's common human attributes rather than on the societal characteristics. The only case in which a differing tendency was found was the preference of southern girls for depicting a rich female and a poor male. This could be either a way of asserting (with a vengeance) their sense of superiority in a society where the woman's role is still subdued (when they draw a queen with a beggar) or a more traditional assuming of maternal functions (when the poor is an orphan or a sick person assisted by a benevolent rich lady); in any case it is a way of stressing the difference between rich and poor which is perhaps influenced by the lesser economic responsibilities that southern girls expect in their future.

NOTES

1. This is not the place to discuss in detail the merits and shortcomings of pictorial analysis; the interpretation of children's drawings has been a tradition in developmental psychology and is gaining new strength in the light of recent research (see Goodnow, 1977; Thomas and Silk, 1990; Cox, 1993, for an overview; see Freeman and Cox, 1985, for a more detailed discussion).
2. Each child made his own drawing while working in the classroom. There was no time limit; on average about one hour was necessary to complete the task. No child refused to do the drawing or omitted either figure; only two children copied their drawing from a nearby classmate and were then dropped from the sample. Data were collected by P. Morelli (Florence and Naples), F. Ferrari (Brescia) and F. Dall'Asta (Potenza); dr. E. Cannoni scored the drawings. I also scored 30 per cent of the drawings, with agreement levels ranging from 76 per cent to 94 per cent. This research was partially supported by funds from CNR (T. Consiglio Nazionale delle Ricerche).
3. It is not possible to summarize here the validation of the similarity scale, which procedure is described in a volume in Italian (Bombi and Pinto, 1993). The validation included an empirical study of the children's ability intentionally to draw similar and different figures, theoretical examination of the items to be included for the drawings scoring, correlational analyses of the scale structure, and a between-subject comparison of drawings of two friends and two enemies, which showed the discriminant power of the scale. The scoring manual is available in English and can be obtained on request. The validation of the value scale, also published in Bombi and Pinto (1993), was conducted through the same steps of the similarity scale validation.
4. In this sample there were no cases of sexually untyped figures.

REFERENCES

Bellelli, G., Morelli, M., Petrillo, G. and Serino, C. (1984), 'La rappresentazione dei rapporti economici e lo sviluppo degli orientamenti d'azione: una ricerca a partire dal lavoro minorile', *Psicologia e Società*.
Berti, A.E. and Bombi, A.S. (1988), *The Child's Construction of Economics*, Cambridge: Cambridge University Press.
Berti, A.E. and Bombi, A.S. (1990), 'Environmental differences in understanding production and distribution', in J. Vaalsiner (ed.), *Child Development in Cultural Context*, Toronto: Hogrefe and Huber.
Berti, A.E., Bombi, A.S. and Lis, A. (1982), 'The child's conceptions about means of production and their owners', *European Journal of Social Psychology*, **12**, 221–39.
Bombi, A.S. and Delle Donne, E. (1993), 'Experimental contribution to the study of value indicators in children's drawings' (unpublished manuscript).
Bombi, A.S. and Pinto, G. (1990), 'Drawings as a tool for investigating children's social cognition', poster presented at the IVth European Conference on Developmental Psychology, Stirling.
Bombi, A.S. and Pinto, G. (1993), *I colori dell'amicizia. Studi sulle rappresentazioni pittoriche dell'amicizia tra bambini*, Bologna: Il Mulino.
Burris, V.L. (1983), 'Stages in the development of economic concepts', *Human Relations*, **36** (9), 791–812.
Cannoni, E. (1992), 'La rappresentazione di somiglianze and differenze nei disegni infantili di figure umane', VII Congresso Nazionale della Divisione SIPS di Psicologia dello Sviluppo, Cagliari.

Connell, R.W. (1977), *Ruling Class, Ruling Culture*, Melbourne: Cambridge University Press.

Cox, M. (1993), *Children's Drawings of the Human Figure*, Hove: Erlbaum.

Danziger, K. (1958), 'Children's earliest conceptions of economic relationships', *Journal of Genetic Psychology*, **91**, 231–40.

Duveen, G. and Shields, M. (1984), 'The influence of gender on the development of young children's representations of work roles', paper presented to the First European Conference on Developmental Psychology, Groningen, Netherlands.

Duveen, G. and Shields, M. (1986), 'The social transmission of economic concept', symposium on 'Economic socialization in developmental context', 2nd European Congress of ISSBD, Rome.

Emler, N. (1986), 'Perception of occupation-related income differences in middle childhood: a cross-national comparison of class differences', symposium on 'Economic socialization in developmental context', 2nd European Congress of ISSBD, Rome.

Emler, N. and Dickinson, J. (1985), 'Children's representation of economic inequalities: The effect of social class', *British Journal of Developmental Psychology*, **3**, 191–8.

Fabbri, D. and Panier Bagat, M. (1989), 'Ricchi banchieri, vecchi contadini. Qualitá scelte da ragazzi di varie etá per differenziare le persone che svolgono determinate attivitá lavorative', *Studi di Psicologia dell'Educazione*, **8** (2), 35–50.

Freeman, N.H. and Cox, M.V. (eds) (1985), *Visual Order: The nature and development of pictorial representation*, Cambridge: Cambridge University Press.

Furby, L. (1979), 'Inequalities in personal possession: explanations for and judgements about unequal distribution', *Human Development*, **22**, 180–202.

Furnham, A. (1982), 'The perception of poverty among adolescents', *Journal of Adolescence*, **5**, 135–47.

Furnham, A. (1986), 'Children's understanding of the economic world', *Australian Journal of Education*, **30** (3), 219–40.

Furth, H.G. (1980), *The World of Grown-ups*, New York. Elsevier.

Goldstein, B. and Oldham, J. (1979), *Children and Work. A study of socialization*, New Brunswick, NJ: Transaction Books.

Goodnow, J.J. (1977), *Children's Drawings*, Cambridge, Mass.: Harvard University Press.

Hong Kwan, T. and Stacey, B. (1981), 'The understanding of socio-economic concepts in Malaysian Chinese school children', *Child Study Journal*, **11**, 33–49.

Jahoda, G. (1959), 'Development of the perception of social differences in children from six to ten', *British Journal of Psychology*, **50**, 158–96.

Jahoda, G. (1979), 'The construction of economic reality by some Glaswegian children', *European Journal of Social Psychology*, **9**, 115–27.

Jahoda, G. (1981), 'The development of thinking about economic institutions: The bank', *Cahiers de Psychologie Cognitive*, **1**, 55–73.

Jahoda, G. (1983), 'European "lag" in the development of an economic concept: A study in Zimbabwe', *British Journal of Developmental Psychology*, **1**, 113–20.

Jahoda, G. and Woerdenbagch, A. (1982), 'The development of ideas about an economic institution: A cross-national replication', *British Journal of Social Psychology*, **21**, 337–8.

Leahy, R.L. (1981), 'The development of the conception of economic inequality: Descriptions and comparisons of rich and poor people', *Child Development*, **52**, 523–32.

Leahy, R.L. (1983), 'Development of the conception of economic inequality: II. Explanations, Justifications, and concepts of social mobility and change', *Developmental Psychology*, **19**, 111–25.

Mack Smith, D. (1977), *Storia D'italia*. Milan: Feltrinelli.

Mookherjee, H.N. and Hogan, H.W. (1981), 'Class consciousness among young rural children', *The Journal of Social Psychology*, **114**, 91–8.

Moscovici, S. (1984), 'On social representations', in R. Farr and S. Moscovici (eds), *Social Representations*, Cambridge: Cambridge University Press.

Ng, S.H. (1983), 'Children's ideas about the bank and shops' profit: developmental stages and the influences of cognitive contrasts and conflict', *Journal of Economic Psychology*, **4**, 209–21.

Ng, S.H. and Cram, F. (1990), 'Effects of cognitive conflict on children's understanding of public ownership', paper presented at the 22nd International Congress of Applied Psychology, Kyoto, Japan.

Ng, S.H. and Jhaveri, N. (1988), 'Young people's understanding of economic inequality: an Indian–New Zealand Comparison', paper presented at the XXIV International Congress of Psychology, Sydney, Australia.

Roker, D. (1990), 'The economic socialization of British youth: the impact of different school types', paper presented at the 22nd International Congress of Applied Psychology, Kyoto, Japan.

Siegal, M. (1981), 'Children's perceptions of adult economic needs', *Child Development*, **52**, 379–82.

Thomas, G.V. and Silk, A.M.J. (1990), *An Introduction to the Psychology of Children's Drawings*, New York: Harvester Wheatsheaf.

Turiel, E. (1983), *The Development of Social Knowledge*, Cambridge: Cambridge University Press.

Index

Abercrombie, N. 81
Abramovitch, R. 7, 17, 45, 94, 95–6, 134
Abt, V. 149
achievement tests 30, 175, 176, 177
'A' level economics courses 27
alienation, economic 99, 101–5 *passim*, 107–8, 178
allowances *see* pocket money
Alston, R.M. 174
American National Election Survey 77
Aries, Ph. 93
Askegaard, S. 79
ATE 172–3, 175, 176
attitudes and opinions, economic 162
  attitudes
    components of 165–6
    measurement of 164, 171–5, 176, 177
    research on attitudes towards economic issues 177–9
    research on attitudes towards economics 175–6
  economic knowledge and 25, 26, 27–8, 98, 105–6, 163, 164–6, 167–71, 175–80
  interest in 163–5
  opinions 166–7
    public opinion surveys 7, 164, 167–71
  see also values, economic
attribution theory 76

Bach, G.L. 164
Bakeman, R. 112
Baldus, B. 61, 79, 81
banking
  savings accounts 136
  understanding of 19, 78, 121, 184
Bardill, J. 152
Barlow, W. 178

barter systems *see* swopping
Basic Economic Test 30, 175
Baudrillard, J. 5
Bayless, J.K. 73
Becker, W.E. 171
Belk, R.W. 70, 72, 75, 76, 84
Bellelli, G. 185
Berkowitz, M.W. 123, 124
Beron, K.J. 176
Berti, A.E. 2, 11, 15, 16–17, 18, 20, 47–8, 49, 57, 98, 105, 118–19, 149, 156, 184, 185, 186, 187, 189
betting 15, 32, 149
Billig, M. 64, 82
Birkey, C. 13
Blatchford, P. 150
Bombi, A.S. 1, 2, 7, 8, 9, 11, 15, 16–17, 47–8, 49, 98, 105, 119, 149, 156, 185, 186, 187, 189, 191, 192, 193, 199
'boss', concept of 20, 119, 120, 122, 126
Bourdieu, P. 3, 70, 137
Bourdy, M.C. 135
Brennan, J. 177
Briggs, M. 36
Brinkerhoff, D.B. 95
Britain *see* United Kingdom
Brook, J.S. 62
Brossard, A. 126
Brownlee, J.R. 112
Buchanan, L. 72
Buckley, H.M. 73
Burgard, P. 25
Burris, V. 13, 14, 113, 149, 156, 187
Burroughs, W.J. 69, 72
buses, ownership of 20, 118–20, 122–4, 125–6
Bush, George Herbert Walker 163
business, attitudes towards 99, 101, 102, 105, 164, 177, 178

Printed and bound by CPI Group (UK) Ltd, Croydon, CR0 4YY

23/04/2025

14660956-0005